Concurrent Urbanities

Design has been employed as an agent of social and political change and a catalyst for spatial and urban transformations in cities across the world. *Concurrent Urbanities* argues for the centrality of designing in the conceptualization and production of inclusive and participatory urban space, by bringing together civic and urban activists, urbanists, designers, and architects committed to exploring designing as a socio-spatial praxis concerned with the reorganization of urban socio-economic systems and relations of power.

The blend of first-hand experiences and reflections of the urban practitioners featured reframes design practice beyond the design of physical objects and public amenities, to the design of social protocols, processes, and infrastructures for radically reframing practices of socio-spatial inclusion "on the ground." Through illustrated examples, this book features the work of Stalker and Stealth who employ design to negotiate new social contracts; Teddy Cruz's design of urban political and economic processes; models of urban pedagogy by the Center for Urban Pedagogy; Cohabitation Strategies' work on designing urban social cooperatives; and others.

Concurrent Urbanities presents a compendium of the emerging models of design-driven urban practice that offers important new insights to professional urban practitioners as well as to students of urbanism, architecture, urban design, and urban and spatial planning.

Miodrag Mitrašinović is an architect, urbanist, and author. Miodrag is an Associate Professor of Urbanism and Architecture at Parsons School of Design, The New School, USA, where he has served as Dean of The School of Design Strategies (2009–12), and Chair of Urban and Transdisciplinary Design (2007–09). He is the author of *Total Landscape, Theme Parks, Public Space* (Ashgate 2006), co-editor of *Travel, Space, Architecture* (with Jilly Traganou, Ashgate 2009), and editor of *Concurrent Urbanities* (Routledge 2015). His first two books received Graham Foundation Grants in 2004 and 2006 respectively. His professional and scholarly works have been published internationally.

Concurrent Urbanities
Designing Infrastructures of Inclusion

Edited by Miodrag Mitrašinović

Routledge
Taylor & Francis Group
NEW YORK AND LONDON

First published 2016
by Routledge
711 Third Avenue, New York, NY 10017

and by Routledge
2 Park Square, Milton Park, Abingdon, Oxon OX14 4RN

Routledge is an imprint of the Taylor & Francis Group, an informa business

© 2016 Taylor & Francis

The right of the editor to be identified as the author of the editorial material, and of the authors for their individual chapters, has been asserted in accordance with sections 77 and 78 of the Copyright, Designs and Patents Act 1988.

All rights reserved. No part of this book may be reprinted or reproduced or utilised in any form or by any electronic, mechanical, or other means, now known or hereafter invented, including photocopying and recording, or in any information storage or retrieval system, without permission in writing from the publishers.

Trademark notice: Product or corporate names may be trademarks or registered trademarks, and are used only for identification and explanation without intent to infringe.

Library of Congress Cataloging in Publication Data
Concurrent urbanities: designing infrastructures of inclusion/
edited by Miodrag Mitrašinović.
  pages cm
  Includes index. 1. City planning. 2. Architectural design.
  3. Public spaces—Design. 4. Public art. 5. Community
  development. I. Mitrašinović, Miodrag, 1965–
  NA9031.C65 2015
  729—dc23   2015016696

ISBN: 978-1-138-81022-8 (hbk)
ISBN: 978-1-138-81023-5 (pbk)
ISBN: 978-1-315-74965-5 (ebk)

Typeset in Avenir
by Florence Production Ltd, Stoodleigh, Devon, UK
Printed by Bell & Bain Ltd, Glasgow

Contents

	List of Contributors	vii
	Acknowledgments	x
1.	Preface: We Are Here	1
2.	Where is Our Civic Imagination?	9
	Teddy Cruz	
3.	Walking Out of the Contemporary	24
	Lorenzo Romito	
4.	Walks On the Wild Side	37
	Ana Džokić and Marc Neelen	
5.	Hester Street Collaborative: Developing a Model for Community-Led Design	61
	Anne Frederick	
6.	Images of the City: The Work of the Center for Urban Pedagogy	76
	Christine Gaspar	
7.	Citizen Collectives, Co-Design and the Unforeseen Future(s) of the Post-Socialist City	87
	Ivan Kucina	
8.	Cohabitation Strategies: Socio-Spatial Approaches, Practices, and Pedagogies with a Dialectical Perspective	99
	Gabriela Rendón	
9.	Citizenship by Design	114
	Kadambari Baxi and Irene Cheng	
10.	Urban Method Acting	124
	Tobias Armborst	

11. **Building Community Capacities through Design: Amplify New York** — 140
   Lara Penin and Eduardo Stasowski

12. **Design Action** — 155
   Deborah Gans

13. **Handball Stadium: The Center for Recreation and New Media in Novi Sad** — 168
   Srdjan Jovanović Weiss

14. **Concurrent Urbanities: Design, Civil Society, and Infrastructures of Inclusion** — 179
   Miodrag Mitrašinović

   Index — 204

Contributors

Tobias Armborst is Assistant Professor of Art and Urban Studies at Vassar College and Principal and cofounder (with Georgeen Theodore and Daniel D'Oca) of Interboro Partners. The Brooklyn-based architecture, planning, and research firm has won many awards for its innovative projects, including the MoMA PS1 Young Architects Program, the Architectural League's Emerging Voices, Young Architects Awards, and the New Practices Award from the AIA.

Kadambari Baxi is Professor of Practice in Architecture at Barnard College, Columbia University, New York City. Her design, media, and research projects explore globalization and visual culture. Recent work includes Two Cities/Three Futures, Triptych-Apps, as well as co-authorship of *Multi-National Cities: Architectural Itineraries* (Actar 2007) and *Entropia* (Black Dog Publishing 2001).

Irene Cheng is Assistant Professor of Architecture at the California College of the Arts and principal of Cheng+Snyder. Her research focuses on the politics of space and architecture. Her work appeared in *Frieze*, *Cabinet*, *2BNY* and *Surface*, and she is coeditor of *The State of Architecture at the Beginning of the 21st Century* (Monacelli Press 2004).

Teddy Cruz is Professor of Public Culture and Urbanism at the University of California, San Diego, and also the founder and principal of Estudio Teddy Cruz, an architectural practice recognized internationally for the urban research of the Tijuana–San Diego border. He received numerous prestigious awards and recognitions, among them the Rome Prize in Architecture, the James Stirling Memorial Lecture on The City Prize, and the participation in the United States Pavilion at the Venice Architecture Biennale in 2008.

Anne Frederick is the founding director of Hester Street Collaborative. She has developed a community design practice that responds to the needs of local neighborhoods in New York City. Her unique approach to community design integrates education and youth development programming with participatory art, architecture, and planning strategies, in partnerships with community-based organizations, schools, and local residents.

Deborah Gans is the Principal of Gans Studio and Professor of Architecture at the Pratt Institute. Her publications include *Bridging the Gap: Rethinking the Relation of Architecture and Engineering* (Coeditor, Van Nostrand Reinhold 1991), *Extreme Sites: Greening the Brownfield* (with Claire Weisz, Academy Press 2004), and *The Organic Approach* (with Zehra Kuz, Academy Press 2003).

Christine Gaspar is Executive Director of the Center for Urban Pedagogy, a nonprofit organization whose mission is to use art and design to increase meaningful civic engagement, particularly among historically underrepresented communities. Christine has over ten years of experience in community design. In 2012, she was identified as one of the "Public Interest Design 100."

Ivan Kucina has worked as Assistant Professor of Architecture at the University of Belgrade since 2002. Since 2013, he has been Guest Professor at the Dessau International Graduate School of Architecture (DIA), Anhalt University in Germany. In 2006, he cofounded the Belgrade International Architecture Week (BINA) and currently serves as its Program Director.

Miodrag Mitrašinović is Associate Professor of Urbanism and Architecture at Parsons School of Design, The New School University. He is the author of *Total Landscape, Theme Parks, Public Space* (Ashgate 2006), and coeditor of *Travel, Space, Architecture* (with Jilly Traganou, Ashgate 2009). His professional and scholarly works have been published internationally.

Lara Penin is Associate Professor of Transdisciplinary Design at Parsons School of Design, The New School University. She is cofounder of Parsons DESIS Lab. Penin works at the intersection of service design and design for social innovation. She was the Principal Investigator of Amplifying Creative Communities, which was awarded the Rockefeller Foundation Cultural Innovation Funds.

Gabriela Rendón is cofounder of Cohabitation Strategies, an international cooperative for socio-spatial research, design, and development based in Rotterdam and New York City. She is Assistant Professor of Urban Planning at Parsons School of Design, The New School University. Her current work centers on politics, practices, and constraints of socio-spatial restructuring through citizen participation.

Lorenzo Romito is an architect, independent researcher, curator, artist, activist, and cofounder of Stalker. He works at the intersections of art, architecture, and cultural/environmental/social/urban studies. Romito has developed projects and published across the world, and is also the recipient of numerous international awards and recognitions, among them Prix de Rome, Venice Architectural Biennale, and Manifesta.

Eduardo Staszowski is an Assistant Professor of Design Strategies at Parsons School of Design, The New School University, as well as co-founder and Director of the Parsons DESIS Lab. Eduardo's research interests center on the intersection of design, social innovation, and public policy, which has at its core the development of experimental yet practical approaches to enhancing public and private participation in policy development, research for public interest, and public service design.

STEALTH.unlimited (Ana Džokić and Marc Neelen) is a practice that spans urban research, spatial intervention, curation, and cultural activism. STEALTH is part of a group of protagonist-practices pointing to the responsibilities and capacities of architecture in contemporary societies. STEALTH co-curated the Dutch Pavilion at the Venice Architecture Biennial, the International Contemporary Art Biannual in Tirana, Albania, and Bordeaux's Evento.

Srdjan Jovanović Weiss is founding principal of Normal Architecture Office and cofounder of School of Missing Studies. His books include *Socialist Architecture: The Vanishing Act* (with Armin Linke, 2012), *Almost Architecture* (2006), *Lost Highway Expedition Photobook* (Coeditor, 2007), *Evasions of Power: On the Architecture of Adjustment* (Coeditor, 2011), and *Architecture of Balkanization* (2015).

Acknowledgments

This book emerges out of three *Concurrent Urbanities* public events that took place at Parsons School of Design in New York City. The first idea to bring together a group of like-minded scholar-practitioners emerged in February 2009, when my colleague Ivan Kucina and I put together a proposal for the first *Concurrent Urbanities* conference. We worked together with Laetitia Wolff to organize a day-long event to take place alongside the "Into the Open" exhibition curated by William Menking, Aaron Levy, and Andrew Sturm. The exhibition brought the 2008 United States Pavilion designed for Venice Architecture Biennale to Parsons, and showcased "a new wave of architect-activists." Teddy Cruz, Deborah Gans, and the Center for Urban Pedagogy had their work exhibited as part of this event, and we invited them—together with other colleagues—to take part in *Concurrent Urbanities 1*. In fact, we were able to schedule the event to coincide not only with the "Into the Open" exhibit, but also with the inaugural Urban Festival at The New School.

Ivan and I spent a considerable amount of time debating the concept for the event, and once we were set on the concept we were happily uncertain how to capture it by a title that would resonate with intended audiences. The term "concurrent urbanities" indeed resonated with us, and seemed to both of us most appropriate although not ideal. Ivan subsequently employed the term "urban concurrencies" in different publications and defined it briefly as the "spatial implications of the various simultaneous states of existence." In Chapter 14, I will elaborate on "concurrencies" in more detail.

In 2011, I co-organized *Concurrent Urbanities 2* with my colleague Vyjayanthi Rao, and finally *Concurrent Urbanities 3* took place in May 2013. All of the lectures and panel conversations were video-recorded and subsequently transcribed. The transcribed talks were sent to the contributors, who then used them as the basis for writing the chapters that appear in this publication. In all the cases, there are significant differences between the public talks and the chapters published herein. The only individuals who took part in *Concurrent Urbanities 1* and do not appear in this book are Rosten Woo and Marc Turkel. Woo served as the director of the Center for Urban Pedagogy in 2009, and is no longer with the Center. Instead, I asked Christine Gaspar, the current director, to contribute a chapter loosely based on the initial premises established by Woo's talk. Turkel and Anne Frederick, who delivered the talk together in 2009, decided that Frederick alone would write a chapter for this volume. A few additional colleagues could not contribute to this publication for a variety of reasons. Early in the process of putting this book together, I made a choice to include only authors who took part in the three events.

This book would not have been possible without the support of many individuals who generously offered assistance in the process. I would like to thank Joel Towers for his generous support for Concurrent Urbanities 1: Joel not only offered financial support for the event, as then Dean of the School of Design Strategies but, even more importantly, provided constructive criticism, deeply thoughtful commentary, and kind reassurance. Robin Campbell and her team always went beyond the call of duty to organize the events and orchestrate all backstage activities smoothly and efficiently. I am grateful to Robin for all her help along the way. My colleagues Joseph Heathcott and Vyjayanthi Rao both exhibited generosity and vigorous intellectual insight as they helped me prepare the first two events, and also served as moderators for the panels. Carol Overby, Jesse Metts, and Savitri Lopez-Negrette helped with the organization of the events in numerous ways. Caitlin Charlet was particularly supportive and made *Concurrent Urbanities 3* logistically possible. Dan Winckler of Really Useful Media recorded all of the events and was an excellent collaborator in this project. I would also like to thank the School of Design Strategies at Parsons (particularly its current Dean Alison Mears), The New School Urban Festival fund, and the New School's Provost Office for the financial support that made the events and this book possible.

I am most sincerely thankful to Ivan Kucina for his friendship, intellectual camaraderie, and the contributions he has made to this project. I also wish to thank Brian DeGrazia for his excellent work on translating Lorenzo Romito's chapter from Italian to English. I am indebted to my copyeditor Anna Fridlis for her outstanding work, persistence, and kindness. I would also like to thank Anze Zadel for providing tremendous help in creating the index and helping in the last preparations of this manuscript for print. Finally, I would like to express my gratitude and sincere appreciation to my editors at Routledge, Nicole Solano and Judith Newlin, for their kind support and considerable patience in the two years it took to put this book together, and also to Kelly Derrick at Florence Production, for guiding the production process with conviction and elegance.

Chapter 1

Preface: We Are Here

The 2014 NYC mayoral transition from the era of Michael Bloomberg's administration to the new one headed by Bill de Blasio took place in the midst of an ongoing economic, cultural, ecological, and political crisis. At the same time, the NYC Department of Planning released *The Newest New Yorkers, 2013 Edition*, which prompted wide media coverage reporting that more foreign-born legal immigrants "live in NYC than there are people in Chicago,"[1] some three million individuals, or thirty-seven percent of NYC residents. The largest groups of these new urban citizens are from the Dominican Republic, China, and Mexico, and a great majority has immigrated since early 1990s. Most have limited English language proficiency and make between thirty-five and seventy percent of the city's median family income. Two thirds live in Brooklyn and Queens, and along B, Q, N, and 7 subway lines in urban territories predominantly populated by immigrant groups, situated outside of the main corridors of commodity and capital flow, and at the receiving end of little to no improvement in municipal services and capital investments under the Bloomberg administration.

In large part, Mayor de Blasio won the election by forcefully and rightfully criticizing Michael Bloomberg's neoliberal policies, particularly in relation to urban development. His political campaign was centered on fighting urban inequality as exemplified by "the tale of two cities" slogan.[2] After all, Bloomberg's rezoning of nearly forty percent of the city's most commercially promising land is an act of historic proportions (Figure 1.1).[3] Rezoning it for the purposes of further commodifying urban space without significant public participation in the process is an act of wicked proportions. Even though some progress was made in areas such as public health, civic architecture, and environmental protection,[4] the Bloomberg administration's vision of urban development was firmly based on the synergies between neoliberal land-zoning policies, private ownership, and hyperinflated real estate values. As such, it encouraged foreign investments, induced wholesale gentrification, naturalized mass displacement and deterritorialization of low-income residents,[5] and established stop-and-frisk policing as a way of managing social, racial, and class conflict in the city.[6] As expected, *The New York Times* poll, conducted four months before the end of his last term as mayor, revealed that New Yorkers were deeply conflicted over Michael Bloomberg's legacy.[7]

When Mayor Bloomberg took office on January 1, 2002, he inherited an enormous budget deficit of over US$3 billion. In January 2014, he left office with

◀ **Figure 1.1**

New York City Department of City Planning Rezonings 2002–2013. Used with permission of the New York City Department of City Planning. All rights reserved.

an astounding US$2.4 billion budget surplus.[8] However, during his twelve years as mayor, NYC became one of the most inequitable cities in the United States: the top 1 percent of the city's residents made over 30 percent of its total personal annual income as the number of billionaires residing in NYC rose to 103, more than in any other city in the world.[9] When Bloomberg became mayor, 1.6 million New Yorkers lived below the poverty line (20.1 percent),[10] while in his last year in office 1.7 million New Yorkers fell below the official federal poverty threshold (21.2 percent).[11] Between 2002 and 2013, the number of homeless New Yorkers registered for overnight stays in shelters rose from 25,000 to nearly 68,000, with more than half of the homeless population being entire families.[12] "What a shameful record," observed Brian Lehrer, host of the WNYC/NPR *The Brian Lehrer Show*, "that we have a record number of homeless people living in shelters today, of all times in the city's history, when there is so much wealth, so much prosperity, when neighborhood after neighborhood is gentrifying."[13] John C. Liu, a democratic NYC comptroller during the Bloomberg administration, argued in 2012 that New York City's economy "would be healthier and more dynamic if the benefits of growth were more fairly distributed."[14]

The Bloomberg administration's *modus operandi* of economic development is best described by the principle of "accumulation by dispossession"

(Harvey 2003, 2007).[15] Julian Brash called it "The Bloomberg Way," the epitome of neoliberal urban governance in which the mayor is cast as CEO, the city government as a corporation, businesses as clients, residents as customers, and the city itself as a product (Brash 2011). As *The New York Times* reported, Bloomberg's own observations on the effects of his policies on poor and the underprivileged New Yorkers ranged "from thoughtless to heartless."[16] His administration's view of urban development was formulaic at best. Its political imagination was bound by economic confidence in the idea that city building is the *tour de force* of capital accumulation and of production of supreme surplus values (Smith 2008). In Manhattan, luxury buildings by starchitects, such as Daniel Libeskind, Frank Gehry, David Adjaye, Herzog and De Meuron, Jean Nouvel, and Renzo Piano, decorated the skyline of the ambitious global city. Ultra-expensive public projects showcased two important beliefs of Bloomberg's administration: first, the superiority of public–private partnership as the model for private management of public resources and second, the belief in the efficacy of strictly managing public space for the purpose of attracting continued investment in real estate and driving up its value. For both to work, public spaces had to be disabled as sites of collectivization for building citizen alliances and for the politicization of everyday life; instead, a spectacularization of the commodified public encounter that has been carefully choreographed with Jan Gehl as the chief consultant for the "pedestrianization of Manhattan."[17] Similarly, "urban beautification" projects were encouraged and supported, such as the one launched by The Fund for Park Avenue and the Department of Transportation with sculptures by Albert Paley, Alice Aycock, and others installed along the Fifth Avenue median.

In the other boroughs, Department of City Planning practiced both "downzoning" and "upzoning." In neighborhoods where real estate and land values had skyrocketed, downzoning was meant to reinforce and preserve "neighborhood character" by limiting new construction and codifying the existing urban fabric, all in order to empower building owners to keep the neighborhood from changing. Through the practice *The New York Times* called "downzoning uprising," communities practiced downzoning to preserve "moderate density," avoid crowding local schools, and, in many cases, to avoid immigrant influx.[18] In parallel, the upzoning and "revitalization" of the Brooklyn–Queens waterfront had facilitated developments like the Industry City in Sunset Park,[19] the Navy Yard Industrial Park in Brooklyn,[20] and Long Island City in Queens,[21] all reusing the dilapidated industrial facilities to boost the birth of creative industries and the technology sector. It has also scaled up the construction of luxury residential properties along the waterfront, often mixed with creative industry, such as Richard Rogers-designed Silvercup West, a US$1 billion development south of the Queensboro Bridge in Queens. Since all of the new waterfront developments are, in part, financing the development of publicly-accessible promenades and linear parks, it remains to be seen how degrees of public access will be designed and managed on the ground.

Most importantly for this book, the Bloomberg administration had also naturalized the role of "design"—including architecture, urban design, spatial planning, product and interior design as well as public art and much of the crafts under one umbrella—as "disciplinary technology" (Deutsche 1998; Foucault 1975) whose purpose is to enable economic power to be exercised strategically and differentially, and to subject urban citizens to a view of citizenship and civility framed by consumption (Zukin 1995). As such, design is mandated as a form-giving practice in which form follows fiction, finance, fear (Ellin 1996: 133–181), and the logic of profit and capital accumulation (Harvey 1991). The role of design (and public art) so construed within neoliberal practice is taken to be self-evident, universal, and necessary as a central mechanism of capital valorization (Mouffe 2000, 2007). As Rosalind Deutche argued, viewed in this way, urban planning and design, architecture, and public art are employed to bring coherence, order, and rationality to the production of capitalist urban space.

An excellent example of this principle is the High Line Park,[22] a 1.5 mile-long linear park built on the derelict elevated New York Central Railway line between 2006 and 2015. The High Line showcases "an architectural theme park"[23] extending south–north between Gansevoort Street and 34th Street, and blending into the Hudson Yards Redevelopment Project. Together, they form the largest private real estate development in United States history,[24] and the single largest development in New York City since the Rockefeller Center was completed in 1939.[25] It is undeniable that the Bloomberg administration intentionally framed (spatial) design as an instrument of capitalist organization of urban space, instrumentalized it as a tool of social control, and mobilized it as consumerist ideology. In the context of current transnational neoliberal urban developments across the globe, the practice of transfiguring projected socioeconomic realities into design has been emblematic. The role of architecture has been ultimately reduced to decoration, a Harlequin dress designed to spectacularize the scenographic effects of pseudo-urban settings and to fabricate social consensus via consumption; a consensus that, no doubt, also needs heavy policing to be sustained (Mitrašinović 2006: 271).

At the very least, these developments ask for the revaluation of the principles of representative democracy, particularly at the metropolitan and municipal levels, and above all for scrutinizing the role urban citizens play in important decision-making processes in their cities. It would be fair to suggest that concepts and practices of democracy, citizenship, participation, and design have never been more necessary or more ambiguous than today. Simultaneously, the term urban has never before represented such a rich spectrum of practices, relations, processes, meanings, and human experiences, nor has it ever before indicated such an incredible multiplicity, variety, and diversity.

In January 2015, in a somewhat delayed epilogue to Bloomberg's plan to develop the Brooklyn–Queens waterfront, the Sunset Park City Council Member Carlos Menchaca stopped the South Brooklyn Marine Terminal project after the Bloomberg administration invested nearly US$100 million to renovate the dilapidated pier in Sunset Park, and the NYC Economic Development Corporation (EDC)[26] was just about to begin leasing out spaces to future tenants.[27] Namely, New York City law mandates that a city-district councilman approve a project in order for it to move forward. The terminal was supposed to create 350 jobs, but as in the nearby and already revitalized Industry City, most are low-paid jobs and may require skill sets that the local Sunset Park residents do not possess. In fact, there is no evidence to suggest Sunset Park would see any benefit from the proposed development of the waterfront until, and unless, local communities and community-based organizations get involved.

Menchaca, a Democrat, rose to prominence as a community organizer in Sunset Park after Hurricane Sandy ravaged the city in 2012. In 2013, he was the first Mexican–American Council Member ever to be elected in New York City.[28] The same year, he introduced the participatory budgeting process[29] in district 38 and encouraged his constituents to take part in establishing funding priorities. In 2014, he asked the city to develop the Marine Terminal by first creating a special development corporation in order to design and enable the process of community involvement in the waterfront development, create educational and job-training programs tailored to his immigrant constituents, and set aside a budget to construct publicly accessible green spaces along the waterfront.[30] All these projects were rejected outright by the EDC, and as a result the project is on hold at the time of this writing. Even though Menchaca's intervention may seem insignificant in the context of larger developments in NYC, it is exemplary because it scrutinizes the antagonistic conditions of urban conflict, and proposes critical connective possibilities; it represents an attempt to organize the political power needed to overcome socio-spatial exclusion, fear, and obliteration of urban communities. Menchaca, in fact, put forward the idea that rezoning—and the consequential macroeconomic development—should be seen as generative of the context-dependent hybrids of social and economic activity, of macro- and microeconomic benefits, and of both collective and individual prosperity.

In sharp contrast to the ideology and practice of the Bloomberg Administration, *Concurrent Urbanities* emerged in a search for a different approach to cities and urban transformation, and out of the need to operationalize design-driven strategic approaches to the production of inclusive, participatory, and resilient urban space. It explores how design can be employed as an agent of progressive social and political change, and as a catalyst for spatial and urban transformations. The book likewise argues for the centrality of *designing* in the conceptualization, production, and representation of the democratic public realm, and explores new roles that design and designers play—and the design theories, methods, processes, and techniques they employ—to encourage radical democratization, socio-spatial justice, social resistance and conviviality, economic equity as well as environmental sustainability. It also suggests ways in which design can challenge the conventional practice of neoliberal urbanization, highlight masked contradictions of capitalist spatial politics, and facilitate the self-expression of excluded social and civic groups.[31] As such, design has the capacity to transform itself into a practice of reappropriation, protection, and enhancement of public resources (Harvey 2012: 73) and into the socio-spatial praxis of commoning (Deutsche 1998: 78; Hardt and Negri 2011: 175; Harvey 2012: 73). In order to understand the role of design beyond its conformist professional applications, the book explores expanded definitions, scopes, and fields of design: the expanded field of design as a socio-spatial praxis concerned with a realm much broader than that of material form and practice, a realm concerned with an urbanism that seeks a fundamental reorganization of urban socio-spatial systems and relations of economic and political power.

Notes

1. "More foreign-born immigrants live in NYC than there are people in Chicago," *Huffington Post*, December 19, 2013. (www.huffingtonpost.com/2013/12/19/new-york-city-immigrants_n_4475197.html). See also: "Immigrant population highest in a century," *New York Post*, December 19, 2013. (www.nypost.com/2013/12/19/immigrant-population-highest-in-a-century/); and the NYC Department of Planning Press Release of 18 December 2013. At: www.nyc.gov/html/dcp/html/census/nny.shtml (Last accessed on February 15, 2015).
2. For the full text of De Blasio's inauguration speech, see: www.nytimes.com/2014/01/02/nyregion/complete-text-of-bill-de-blasios-inauguration-speech.html (last accessed on February 15, 2015).
3. For an excellent visualization of the rezoning, see *The New York Times*' special on "The Bloomberg Years:" www.nytimes.com/indexes/2013/08/17/nyregion/nyregionspecial/index.html (Last accessed on February 15, 2015).
4. Particularly impressive is the work done by Pratt Institute professor David Burney who served as Commissioner of the New York City Department of Design and Construction (2004–2014) where he initiated the "Design and Construction Excellence Initiative." The initiative was intended to address the quality of design and construction of civic architecture across New York City, and resulted in a number of high-quality public buildings, featured in *We Build the City* (Bloomberg et al. 2014).
5. Because gentrification often masks displacement, it is very difficult to track the number of displaced individuals and therefore, the scale of socio-spatial disaster that such urban development policies generate. For example, the New York City Housing and Vacancy Survey (NYCHVS) aims at getting the reasons for moving from displaced individuals but doesn't offer "displacement" as a category.
6. For reference see: www.nydailynews.com/new-york/mayor-bloomberg-stop-and-frisk-disproportionately-stop-whites-minorities-article-1.1385410 (Last accessed on February 15, 2015).
7. For reference see: www.nytimes.com/2013/08/18/nyregion/what-new-yorkers-think-of-mayor-bloomberg.html?ref=nyregionspecial (Last accessed on February 15, 2015).
8. For reference see: www.nytimes.com/2013/12/29/opinion/sunday/12-years-of-mayor-bloomberg.html (Last accessed on February 15, 2015).
9. For reference see: www.huffingtonpost.com/2014/10/08/new-york-homelessness-billionaires_n_5953464.html (Last accessed on February 15, 2015).
10. For reference see: www.nytimes.com/2011/09/22/nyregion/one-in-five-new-york-city-residents-living-in-poverty.html (Last accessed on February 15, 2015).
11. For reference see: www.nytimes.com/2013/09/19/nyregion/poverty-rate-in-city-rises-to-21-2.html (Last accessed on February 15, 2015).
12. www.nytimes.com/2001/02/07/nyregion/08HOME.html (Last accessed on February 15, 2015).
13. For reference see: www.wnyc.org/story/bad-new-record-high-homelessness (Last accessed on February 15, 2015).
14. Liu said: "New York City's economy would be healthier and more dynamic if the benefits of growth were more fairly distributed. We need to promote a shared prosperity through policies that narrow the income gap, like strengthening investments in education and implementing a more progressive income-tax structure." For reference see: www.nytimes.com/2012/05/21/nyregion/middle-class-smaller-in-new-york-city-than-nationally-study-finds.html (Last accessed on February 15, 2015).
15. Harvey's concept of "accumulation by dispossession" describes predatory neoliberal urbanization practices of privatization, financialization, fabrication of urban crises, and state redistributions. Cumulatively—and that's the way in which I employ it here—they result in the appropriation and centralization of wealth and power in the hands of the

urban elites by dispossessing the public of the commons, public land, and public resources (Harvey 2003).

16. For reference see: www.nytimes.com/2013/12/29/opinion/sunday/12-years-of-mayor-bloomberg.html (Last accessed on February 15, 2015).
17. For reference see: www.nytimes.com/2008/07/11/nyregion/11broadway.html?_r=2&oref=slogin&. For the Department of Transportation's *World Class Streets: Remaking New York City's Public Realm* manual developed with Jan Gehl Architects, see: www.nyc.gov/html/dot/downloads/pdf/World_Class_Streets_Gehl_08.pdf (Last accessed on February 15, 2015).
18. For reference see: www.nytimes.com/2005/10/10/nyregion/10density.html?pagewanted=all (Last accessed on February 15, 2015).
19. For reference see: www.industrycity.com/ (Last accessed on February 15, 2015).
20. For reference see: www.brooklynnavyyard.org/ (Last accessed on February 15, 2015).
21. For reference see: www.licpartnership.org/ (Last accessed on February 15, 2015).
22. I do not deny the intricate and inspiring contributions of Joshua David and Robert Hammond (David and Hammond 2011); the efforts of hundreds of enthusiastic citizens, city administrators, and politicians; nor the high professional accomplishments of Diller, Scofidio & Renfro and James Corner and his Field Operations. I simply refer here to the High Line as an instrument framed by the larger, strategic interests of Bloomberg's administration, the banks as well as the developers involved in the Hudson Yards project.
23. For reference see: Davidson, J. (2009) "The Twin Pleasures of the High Line: A Petite New Park, and a District of Lively Architecture." *New York Magazine*, June 8, 2009. At: www.nymag.com/arts/architecture/features/57176/ (Last accessed on February 15, 2015).
24. Hudson Yards Redevelopment project is the single largest private development project during the Bloomberg's administration, a US$20 billion investment in the 28-acre site designed by Kohn Pederson Fox and Skidmore, Owings & Merrill, and developed by Stephen Ross. This "biggest real estate development in U.S. history," as Fortune called it, was preceded by the rezoning of the Far West Side of Manhattan. For reference see: Tully, S. (2014) "NYC's Hudson Yards Project Will Be an Entire City—On Stilts." In: *Fortune*, 14 September 2014. At: www.fortune.com/2014/09/04/hudson-yards-city-on-stilts/ (Last accessed on February 15, 2015).
25. For reference see: Taylor-Foster, J. (2014) "Construction Begins on the Vast Platform for New York's Hudson Yards." In: *ArchDaily*, March 22, 2014. At: www.archdaily.com/488903/construction-begins-on-the-vast-platform-for-new-york-s-hudson-yards/ (Last accessed on February 15, 2015).
26. For mission and history of the EDC see: www.nycedc.com/about-nycedc/history (Last accessed on February 15, 2015).
27. For reference see: www.nydailynews.com/new-york/sunset-park-city-councilman-sunk-plan-convert-pier-article-1.2069528 (Last accessed on February 15, 2015).
28. Manchaca represents Brooklyn District 38, which includes Red Hook and Sunset Park. For reference see: www.theepochtimes.com/n3/360513-city-gets-first-mexican-american-council-member/ (Last accessed on February 15, 2015).
29. For reference see: www.menchaca.org/participatory-budgeting/ (Last accessed on February 15, 2015).
30. For reference see: www.nytimes.com/services/xml/rss/yahoo/myyahoo/aponline/2013/11/14/us/ap-us-mexican-american-councilman.xml (Last accessed on February 15, 2015).
31. I develop this line of argument following Rosalyn Deutsche's reasoning in Evictions, where she argues that public art, urban design, and architecture should move away from being disciplinary technologies involved in confirming the current dominant organization of the city and instead illuminate the contradictions and repressions, and help appropriate the city (Deutsche 1998).

Bibliography

Bloomberg, M., Merkel, J. and Burney, D. (2014) *We Build the City: New York City's Design + Construction Excellence Program*. ORO Editions.

Brash, J. (2011) *Bloomberg's New York: Class and Governance in the Luxury City*. University of Georgia Press.

David, J. and Hammond, R. (2011) *High Line: The Inside Story of New York City's Park in the Sky*. FSG Originals.

Davidson, J. (June 8, 2009) "The Twin Pleasures of the High Line: A Petite New Park, and a District of Lively Architecture." In: *New York Magazine* www.nymag.com/arts/architecture/features/57176/.

Deutsche, R. (1998) *Evictions: Art and Spatial Politics*. MIT Press.

Ellin, N. (1996) *Postmodern Urbanism*. Blackwell.

Foucault, M. (1975) *Discipline and Punish: The Birth of the Prison*. Random House.

Hardt, M. and Negri, A. (2011) *Commonwealth*. Belknap Press.

Harvey, D. (1991) *The Condition of Postmodernity: An Enquiry into the Origins of Cultural Change*. Wiley–Blackwell.

Harvey, D. (2003) *The New Imperialism*. Oxford University Press.

Harvey, D. (2007) *A Brief History of Neoliberalism*. Oxford University Press.

Harvey, D. (2012) *Rebel Cities: From the Right to the City to the Urban Revolution*. Verso.

Mitrašinović, M. (2006) *Total Landscape, Theme Parks, Public Space*. Ashgate.

Mouffe, C. (2000) *The Democratic Paradox*. Verso.

Mouffe, C. (Summer 2007) "Artistic Activism and Agonistic Spaces." In: *Art & Research*, Vol. 1, No. 2.

Smith, N. (2008) *Uneven Development: Nature, Capital, and the Production of Space*. University of Georgia Press.

Taylor-Foster, J. (March 22, 2014) "Construction Begins on the Vast Platform for New York's Hudson Yards." In: *ArchDaily*.

Tully, S. (September 14, 2014) "NYC's Hudson Yards Project Will Be an Entire City—On Stilts." In: *Fortune*.

Zukin, S. (1995) *The Cultures of Cities*. Blackwell.

Chapter 2

Where is Our Civic Imagination?

Teddy Cruz

I will focus on three particular topics in order to propose three provocations in the context of my ongoing research and work at the Tijuana/San Diego border. The first has to do with the proposition that the informal is not an image. Even though "informality" has come back to the public debate in recent years, it has often been trivialized as an aesthetic category. I propose to amplify it primarily as a praxis. The second provocation has to do with the fact that surplus value, the profits of urbanization, is not a bad thing: the problem is the way in which these profits have been only benefitting private interests. Surplus value today needs to be redistributed and redirected to the public, and such redistribution, countering current austerity measures from Germany to the United States, would open new forms of economic vitality, from large public infrastructural projects to urban economic production at localized scales. The third provocation is that government is not evil. One particular contradiction in the ongoing polarization of the political spectrum between the right and the left is that, today, the extreme right and the extreme left are united in their mistrust of civic institutions. They are antigovernment. The polarization of government today should not close the potentialities of progressive forms of governance—a political leadership that is inclusive of localized modes of production and community dynamics—both at top-down and bottom-up scales. In that sense, my most recent research has focused not on the urban explosion of new cities in China and the Arab Emirates, but on the emerging urban practices and forms of governance that have been unfolding in Latin America, from Curitiba, Brazil to Medellin, Colombia. The urban transformations that occurred in those cities in recent years reflect dramatic institutional transformations and new collaborative forms of governance.

Obviously, I am addressing what has become apparent in the last two decades: the fact that the celebrated urban explosions in the so called global capitals, from Shanghai to Dubai, during the glamorous years of economic boom also produced, in tandem, a dramatic project of marginalization. I am referring to the bad sisters of the global city, the many slums that have also exploded around the world as a bi-product of the uneven growth that neoliberalism has perpetuated. Such urban asymmetry is at the center of the ongoing urban crisis, in the polarization between the enclaves of mega wealth and the sectors of marginalization, precariousness, and poverty that surround them. What are the conditions that produced this crisis in the first place? Can we, as architects, open them up? Can they be the material employed to reorganize our ways of thinking?

These have been my questions. Moreover, we are very seldom aware of the conditions that produce such a crisis in the first place: What are the institutional mechanisms that have produced these urban conflicts? And how can they be reorganized?

Whereas we concentrate our attention on today's urban crisis as merely environmental or economic, I want to amplify it primarily as a cultural crisis, pertaining to the inability of institutions to reorganize their own protocols and their ways of thinking and making. This refers to the inability of public and private institutions to reexamine the thoughtless ways by which we have grown, unable to reconceptualize the oil-driven urban sprawl and the faulty politics of economic development that have endorsed this urban growth. This is not to diminish the fact that the crisis today is also environmental. But this emphasis on the environmental dimension, often framed through global warming debates, has hijacked the issue of socioeconomic sustainability, and the fact that the current crisis has been prompted by institutions of exclusion. In other words, I think that any debate today about the contemporary city must begin by reflecting on the issue of inequality. In such a context, and in order to discover new modalities of urban work, emerging urban practices are trying to enter into other procedural conditions beyond the production of singular artifacts: buildings as isolated objects of beautification in the city. These emergent architectural and artistic practices are beginning to challenge the very political and economic conditions of exclusionary urban growth that induces marginalization, displacement, and impoverishment of many communities across the world. They are doing this by expanding notions of design beyond aesthetics for aesthetics' sake and toward the design of political and civic processes.

Radical polarization of wealth and poverty in many ways characterizes the border region where my practice is located: Barely thirty minutes away from some of the poorest Latin American settlements found in Tijuana, Mexico, one finds some of the wealthiest North American real estate developments on the edges of San Diego, California (Figure 2.1). One could argue similar polarization of wealth and poverty happens in many cities across the world, particularly large cities such as New York, but it is nowhere more evident, alarming, and dramatized than in the border territories (Figure 2.2). In that sense, my practice has been focused on the investigation of the social practices of adaptation: the social processes which can play a role in reimagining spatial configurations that embody alternative forms of urban practice (Figure 2.3). At this very juncture—between

▼ Figure 2.1

Border urbanism © estudio teddy cruz.

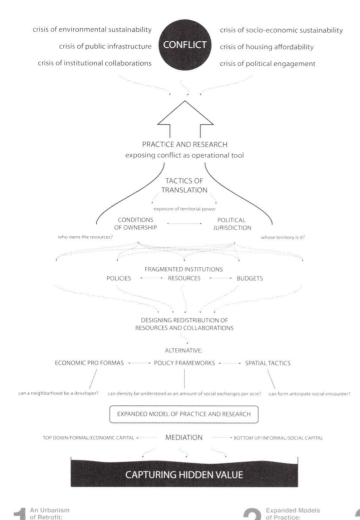

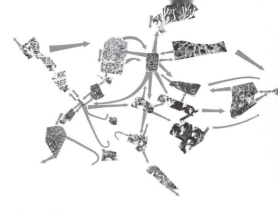

▲ Figure 2.2

Border urbanism © estudio teddy cruz.

◄ Figure 2.3

New protocols for urban practice © estudio teddy cruz.

▼ Figure 2.4

Expanded model of design practice © estudio teddy cruz.

two cities that collide, two very different systems of producing the urban environment—we can reimagine the political in the midst of the conflict between top-down and bottom-up urbanization. Even though one is aware that these categories tend to be binary and thus at times problematic, we are interested in recuperating their difference and have argued that when the top-down and the bottom-up collide, the political emerges (Figure 2.4). By visualizing the procedures that these collisions engender, we expose other ways of constructing the city as well as citizenship. In our work, we embrace the construction of citizenship as a creative act, as an enabling process that reorganizes institutional protocols as well as the urban space where it is inscribed. We are interested in visualizing these creative acts of citizenship. Antanas Mockus, the former mayor of Bogota, recently argued that the erasure of the anecdotal in the urban milieu is a form of social injustice. In our work, the anecdotal emerges from the analysis of the bottom-up dynamics. In that respect, the informal is a set of practices, procedures, and protocols that we carefully visualize, translate, and interpret, ultimately representing what we call "chronologies of invasion," a process of constructing citizenship that builds on the anecdotal dimension of urban transformation.

▼ **Figure 2.5**

Archipelago of empty spaces in San Diego © estudio teddy cruz.

We capture the anecdotal dimensions of cross-border urbanization through stories, sometimes trivial and simplistic, but for us, nevertheless, containing incredible lessons from which to harvest new ways of practicing. Take for example a simple image such as the one depicting an archipelago of empty spaces in San Diego (Figure 2.5). When we remove traces of the city from the map of San Diego, and leave the islands of abandoned brownfields, setbacks, easements, and watershed systems intact, we recognize that these spaces are spaces of contestation, political remnants of the deliberate fragmentation of the city. While artists and architects have helped perpetuate the "reading" of such spaces solely through poetic and metaphorical tropes by idealizing their vacant state, this "archipelago of voids" is the result of a planning policy aimed explicitly at the separation of jurisdictions and communities. As we descend into one of these spaces, we begin to discover particular stories of encroachment and alteration.

In 1999, a group of San Diego teenagers decided to organize themselves in response to the lack of a skateboard park in the city. One night, armed with shovels, they invaded an underpass under the interstate highway I-5, the typical site of collision between freeway and neighborhood. The teenagers began to dig with the aim of building their own skateboard park, and after two weeks of digging the police stopped them, and subsequently barricaded the place and expelled the group from it. The teenagers decided to organize themselves more adequately and begin a process of confronting the City to demand a park. The first task they engaged in is something we very seldom do as designers: they were curious to map out the political jurisdictions that defined the seemingly neutral territory: What was the specificity of political jurisdiction embedded in that juncture? They realized that they had been lucky, because they had not dug under Caltrans[1] territory but under an arm of the freeway that belonged to the local municipality (Figure 2.6a). They also discovered that their location was in a Bermuda Triangle of jurisdiction, between Port Authority, Airport Authority, two city districts, and the Pacific Coast Highway Review Board. All the red jurisdictional lines traced by the teens on the map ultimately represented the visualization of the hidden political jurisdictional power inscribed in that otherwise abstract space (Figure 2.6b). By working in the municipal territory—and not the territory of the state—they had acquired a point of access for local negotiations as Caltrans would have made it impossible to negotiate. They decided to organize themselves as skaters and begin seeking the political actors behind each of the identified jurisdictional powers to engage and negotiate with city officials, the city attorney, and the city council. Once at the municipality, they were advised that in order to continue the process of negotiations, they had to form an NGO. They did not know what an NGO was, so they sought help from a group of skateboarders in Northern California who had gone through the same experience.

From our perspective, this marks an interesting learning moment, because the transference of procedural knowledge across urban activist practices is crucial to this story. The teenagers realized that they had to get their act together in more concrete ways: to fundraise, to hire a lawyer, to get construction insurance, to organize their budgets, and ultimately to find "evidence" for the need for reform by familiarizing themselves with the countless permits and faulty definitions that only served to block community action. The right of entry permit, land use

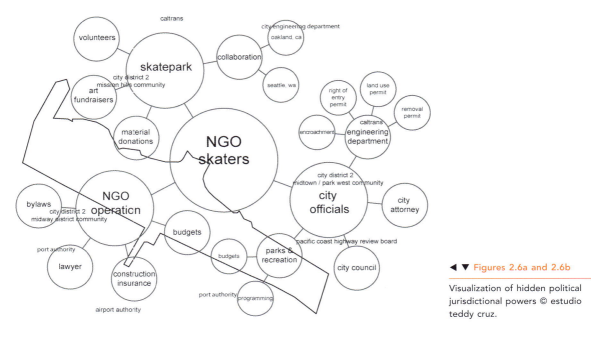

▲▼ Figures 2.6a and 2.6b

Visualization of hidden political jurisdictional powers © estudio teddy cruz.

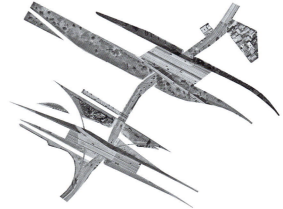

permits, removal permit, and temporary encroachment permit can all be recognised as devices to make the case for a new definition of land use category at that location. In other words, they began to realize that they needed to argue for opening up new definitions of zoning that enabled temporary uses, and different types of activities and programs, beyond the generic undifferentiated "green space" usually drafted by city officials. After researching these disparate pieces of legislation, the teenagers organized themselves as an activist practice by reconstructing the political itself, and by consolidating the fragmented resources and knowledge inside the municipal system, ultimately making such a compelling case that in 2002 they won the rights to the space. By transferring liability from the public to the newly founded semiprivate agency, the City allowed them use of the site for one cent a year, entering into a social and political agreement with the municipal government in order to manage a piece of vacant public land through self-initiated programming and economy. Subsequently, they constructed what they called the "Washington Street Skate Park" (Figure 2.7).

This story helped me to clarify something essential to my urban research: An informal act of encroachment like this one did not stop at the small and symbolic gestural scale, but it began to trickle upwards with self-assurance, constructing a political process that ultimately transformed top-down policy. This journey from a bottom-up act of jurisdictional transgression into a complex

▶ Figure 2.7

Washington Skate Park ©
estudio teddy cruz.

process that enabled top-down institutional transformation is what is urgently required today. However, these processes of urban transformation need translation and facilitation, and that is a space of operation that I have been interested in pursuing in my practice, through what we call "tactics of translation": A deliberate effort to expose and visualize urban conflict as an operational and creative tool capable of reappropriating these broken pieces of urbanization that have been manifested in the space of the metropolis, the by-products of imposed, exclusionary political and economic urban recipes of privatization.

This story contains the DNA for rethinking different paradigms. One of them is the meaning of "community." The question of "what constructs a community" is a fundamental question. More often than not, the notions of community are deployed too gratuitously. This particular community constructed itself out of urgency. It became a "community of practice," committed to enabling the production of new systems of signification and of new spatial possibilities. Another fundamental provocation the teenagers opened up is the fact that we need to rethink public space beyond the low-cost formulas of beautification—the generic recipes driven by form and style that new urbanism and smart growth paradigms have endorsed to support developers—and instead elevate the contingency of community-based social economy as the main element to sustain civic space in the long-term.

As architects, we generally never ask questions such as: Who will maintain the civic space, and who will assure inclusion and programmatic sustainability? The foundational questions that these teenagers asked should be the essential questions that any of us, design professionals, should ask when intervening in the city: "Whose territory is this?" "Who owns the resources?" By exposing and visualizing the conditions they encountered, the teenagers began to reorganize public resources as well as the jurisdictional conditions that had, in such hermetic ways, disabled these spatial assets as public availabilities. Thus, the teenagers were not only designing and constructing physical space, but simultaneously,

◀ Figure 2.8

Informal border urbanism © estudio teddy cruz archives.

they were also designing the protocols as well as the systems of shared management that would assure economic and social sustainability. This is the ultimate lesson behind this story of adaptation: Certain public spaces must be designed not only as physical commodities, or ambiguous environments where people somehow come together, but as spaces that anticipate social encounter, more deliberate in the choreography of the programmatic conditions, the forms of governance, the economic composition and the strategies of social organization that can assure their longevity and inclusion.

A recurring theme in our work at the United States–Mexico border has been imagining other modalities of economy, other frameworks that would move us away from urbanisms of consumption to urbanizations of social production (Figure 2.8). The key issues here are how are we to recalibrate the relationships between individuals, collectives, and institutions? How are we to enable the redistribution of resources, mediating top-down and bottom-up dynamics? How are we to enable local communities to benefit from their own modes of production? And, how are we to imagine new models of public housing and infrastructure in order to rethink urban development today? In that respect, we have argued that the surplus value is not necessarily evil; what is appalling is the fact that it has been amassed by the very few at the expense of the many. I believe that the task of any activist urban practice today is to reorganize, redistribute, and redirect that surplus, so that it acquires a social mandate. For instance, can the developer's spreadsheet be used as an instrument to construct community? Can we, as communities of practice, appropriate the knowledge of the developer's *pro forma* in terms of managing time and resources to maximize profit? Can such profit actually sustain a community instead of exclusively benefitting individual economic expansion? Can the developer's pro forma be framed as a site of intervention and experimentation today, where we can begin to insert the hidden value of informal economy, of sweat equity, of collaboration, and of new political representation? In that respect, our research in San Diego has focused on immigrant communities where one finds many examples of social and economic entrepreneurship embedded in neighborhoods. For example, two women rented a three-bedroom apartment and transformed it into an informal nursery. The nursery is represented by a community-based social organization that camouflages the economic activity, while supporting it with knowledge and economic resources, channeling and redirecting subsidies and other cash flows. Such social and economic agency embedded in communities needs to be framed as an operative tool to rethink economic development, and ultimately help us to also reimagine typologies of housing and public space. For instance, how many informal, neighborhood-based practices can be translated, evaluated, and represented? By enabling the operational dimension of this stealth knowledge to alter the developer's spreadsheet—transforming it into a social engine and incorporating the hidden value of such activities and dynamics—communities can lead their own modes of production and become the developers of their own housing, while redefining the social economy of public space.

For these reasons, another crisis we face today is *the crisis of knowledge transfer*, from communities to institutions and from institutions to communities. As academics and practitioners we have fallen victim to an emergent polarization of institutions and we have been fearful of interfering in certain aspects of institutional thinking. To intervene into the bureaucratic structures would be anathema for many artists working today. While we in academia enabled the most emancipatory cultural concepts that had emerged in the 1980s—such as hybridization, self-organization, nonhierarchical procedures—and then remained mere metaphorical tropes to decorate art galleries or enclosed in the classroom, all that amazing theory was hijacked and made operational by neoliberal digital capitalism. We need to recuperate, reenact, and reapply those concepts as operational practices. By that, I mean that we need to reclaim that knowledge while also appropriating the knowledge of economic development. We should not be afraid to enact, for our collective ends, the developer's profitable economic equation or the capitalist's entrepreneurial drive. We can aspire to other ways of thinking and making by engaging strategies for knowledge transfer and by opening other modalities of co-producing the city. This is not a time to retreat from the institutions or simply criticize them from afar; this is the time to infiltrate them and retrofit their own mechanisms toward social ends.

The democratization of urban development today is an urgent matter, mainly when it has been controlled and monopolized by a few urban actors working together—such is the alliance of private developers, housing authorities, and municipal governments. The question for us ought to be: How can we open alternative points of access into urbanization and expand the horizon of opportunity for artists, architects, and communities to act as developers so that other forms of economic development can begin to appear, supported by more inclusive and collaborative forms of governance? This might seem unattainable today, but such opening toward more democratizing forms of urbanization and social justice has already happened in Latin America. It is here that many cities across the continent have begun to rethink public infrastructure by enabling very innovative political and civic processes that negotiate the interface between the top-down and bottom-up, tapping into social networks, informal economies, and other forms of public participation. The traces of such developments are found across Latin America, from the legendary participatory budgets in Porto Alegre, Brazil, where this city's mayor opened the municipal budget so that communities could have a say in the redistribution of resources; to the innovative public transportation infrastructure through an urbanization of retrofit in Curitiba, Brazil; and to the amazing transformations of Medellin, Colombia, made possible by rethinking municipal bureaucracy and public management, and reorienting surplus value to the poorest zones in the city. All these examples are characterized by a belief in public imagination, something we have lost in the United States.

In the case of Medellin, as its former mayor Sergio Fajardo frequently points out, what transformed this city was not an architectural or urban project; it was first a political project. In other words, the foundational project was to

▼ Figure 2.9

Notes and diagrams from the Medellin interviews © estudio teddy cruz.

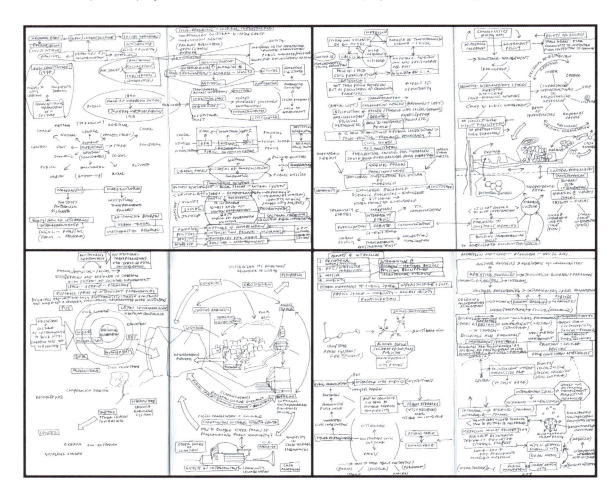

▶ Figure 2.10

Lineage of progressive institutional transformations in Medellin and across Latin America © estudio teddy cruz.

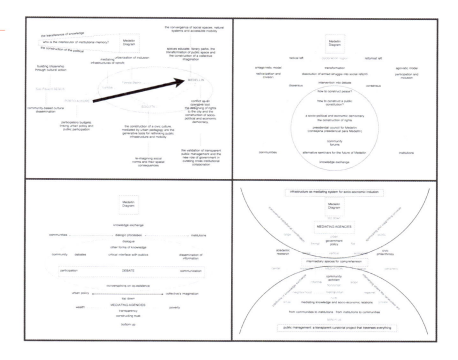

rethink the role of government, to open it up, enabling cross-sector collaboration, to reorganize its protocols, and negotiate other types of relationships by curating cross-institutional relations spanning the top-down and bottom-up. Ultimately, the objective was to confront inequality. Medellin has taught me that progressive forms of government still exist, and that the question today is not about getting rid of government but reinventing it, reorganizing it in more efficient and aspirational ways. This is only to say that our disillusionment with government in the United States should not prevent us from reimagining other forms of governance. It is in Latin America today where we can learn from local municipal processes in order to regain faith in a political leadership that can guarantee social equity and economic inclusion.

For my current research project, I went to Medellin to interview some thirty people involved in the political processes of this city's urban transformation, from the mayor to social workers, from artists to civic philanthropists (Figure 2.9). My idea was to piece together the political and civic processes that made these transformations possible. This was essential since the media had been focusing on the final architectural and urban products but very seldom on the institutional project that took place before building. What happened there pertains to a complex process of negotiation and collaboration across institutions and communities, and the visualization of such a process is an urgent project: I believe that the anecdotal exchanges contain the knowledge and experience of the process, rich with lessons, tactics, and strategies that can be reproduced in other cities. I began to translate many of my interviews into diagrams (Figure 2.10). From this exercise emerged a new political language structured by a complex palimpsest of institutional relationships and dialogical processes with communities. I have translated stories and anecdotes, mapped them out, and looked for connections, tracing the ideas and tendencies across time and geographies. I discovered, for example, that some of the ideas that transformed Medellin emerged a while back, and that they were part of a lineage of progressive institutional transformations across the continent.

Progressive institutional reform in Latin America may date back to São Paulo's Social Service of Commerce (Serviço Social do Comércio, SESC),[2] a privately run, nonprofit institution with the purpose of promoting culture and healthy living in urban communities. Founded in 1946, these engines for rethinking citizenship through cultural action spread throughout Brazil, and the city of São Paulo alone has fifteen operating today. They are organized and run by social and cultural entrepreneurs, and focus on education, health, culture, and leisure. In the 1970s, Curitiba's mayor Jamie Lerner began to re-imagine the notion of infrastructure as a mediating system to manage urban complexity, through low-tech and economic strategies of adaptation of existing spaces in the city. Also significant was the idea of community-based cultural dissemination from Porto Alegre, Brazil, where participatory budgeting began to link urban policy and public participation in 1989. The transformations of Favela-Bairro in Rio de Janeiro, Brazil, that began to take place in 1993 under the leadership of Sérgio Magalhães offer lessons toward an urbanization of inclusion, by engaging slums as new laboratories to rethink community-based anti-gentrification urban development. In Bogota, Colombia the election of Antanas Mockus as mayor in 1995 marked the beginning of the project of constructing a civic culture mediated by urban pedagogy, namely the creation of an urban educational model as a generative tool for rethinking public infrastructure and urban mobility. Mockus' belief that the transformation of social behavior ought to precede the transformation of the physical city is fundamental to these stories. The ideas, tendencies, and actions aimed at reimagining the relationship of social norms and the city all led to Medellin, the most violent city in the world in the late 1980s. In Medellin, urban conflict truly became an operational tool to design new rights to the city and the construction of a more radical urban democratization. Among the most salient ideas behind the Medellin project were the rethinking and validation of transparent public management and a new role of government in curating cross-institutional collaborations to transform public space as a place of education. This project is emblematized by the well-known Library Parks, which were built in the most disenfranchised parts of the city as a way to fight poverty as the root of violence through education and public investment (Figure 2.11).

As amazing as the above projects are, some of the urban actors involved do not necessarily tend to articulate what really happened—either conceptually or operationally. So, the role of our practice is to act as translators of the process, by stitching and visualizing such complexity. My current work attempts to establish the linkage of these practices and to suggest a complex transfer of knowledge towards institutional transformation. The question remains: Who is the interlocutor of institutional memory? Who will recuperate and manage the transfer of this urban knowledge and civic imagination, so that it can be instrumentalized in the construction of the new political today? I think that architects and artists can lead this effort.

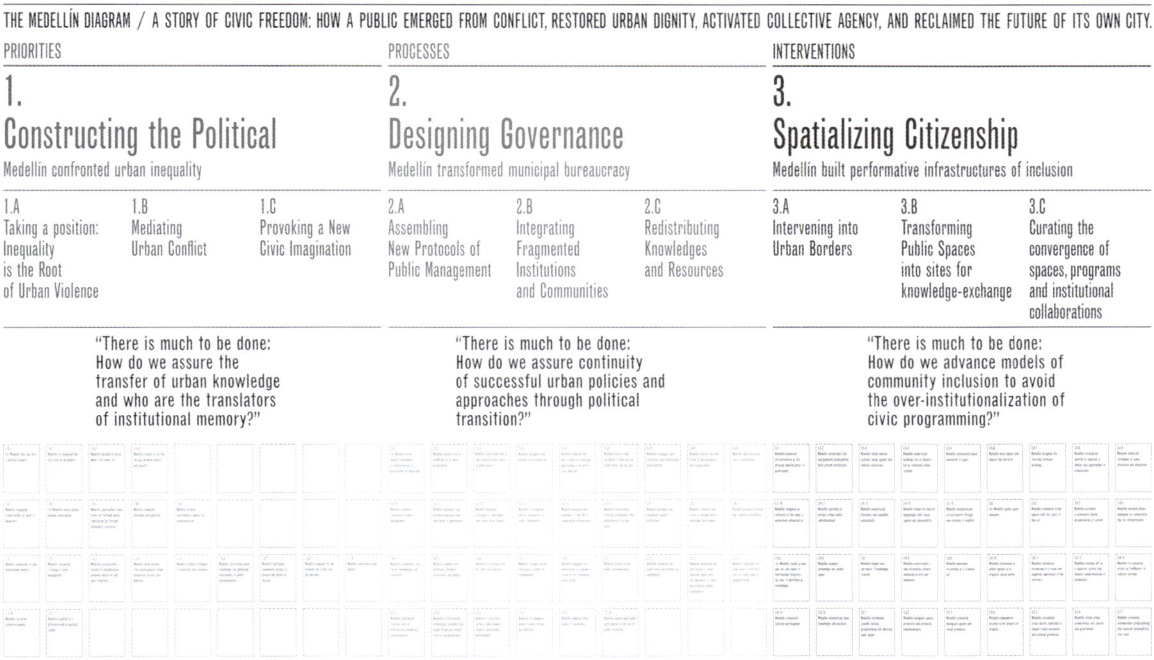

THE MEDELLÍN DIAGRAM / A STORY OF CIVIC FREEDOM: HOW A PUBLIC EMERGED FROM CONFLICT, RESTORED URBAN DIGNITY, ACTIVATED COLLECTIVE AGENCY, AND RECLAIMED THE FUTURE OF ITS OWN CITY.

PRIORITIES	PROCESSES	INTERVENTIONS
1. Constructing the Political Medellín confronted urban inequality	**2. Designing Governance** Medellín transformed municipal bureaucracy	**3. Spatializing Citizenship** Medellín built performative infrastructures of inclusion
1.A Taking a position: Inequality is the Root of Urban Violence	2.A Assembling New Protocols of Public Management	3.A Intervening into Urban Borders
1.B Mediating Urban Conflict	2.B Integrating Fragmented Institutions and Communities	3.B Transforming Public Spaces into sites for knowledge-exchange
1.C Provoking a New Civic Imagination	2.C Redistributing Knowledges and Resources	3.C Curating the convergence of spaces, programs and institutional collaborations
"There is much to be done: How do we assure the transfer of urban knowledge and who are the translators of institutional memory?"	"There is much to be done: How do we assure continuity of successful urban policies and approaches through political transition?"	"There is much to be done: How do we advance models of community inclusion to avoid the over-institutionalization of civic programming?"

▲ Figure 2.11

Medellín: a story of civic freedom © estudio teddy cruz.

Notes

1. Caltrans is the state agency that governs the freeway system in California.
2. For reference see: www.sesc.com.br/ (Last accessed on February 15, 2015).

Conversations 1

AUDIENCE (for Teddy Cruz): I am curious about the examples of the skaters and how they navigated and negotiated the space and articulated the process. As a designer, how do you propose that, how do you say to a community, "this is how we are going to do it". How do you initiate the process? How do you communicate that to people?

TEDDY CRUZ: Lorenzo (Romito) too has been involved in the process of engaging the government, particularly his running for Mayor of Rome. At this moment, the Mayor of San Diego who has attempted to engage in a very different approach to the border region, has invited a few of us to carve a space within the municipality of San Diego, to bring some of these lessons and procedures. One aspect of the project that may not yet pertain to the process of design—in which we begin to anticipate spatial and formal configurations—is simply about reconvening the conversation. One point of entry is for us to serve as urban curators of sorts, in which we assume the role of convening a new type of conversation. When I imagine the project in Medellin, I think it must have started with that kind of possibility, when a mayor says, "Wait a minute, we can be producing a think-tank inside our government, a creative engine of ideas." This may sound overly simplistic, but let me assure you that over 80 percent of municipalities around the world act as reactive institutions, managerial in the very production of regulations, and never aspirational. Design never happens in governmental space. The criteria by which the city evolves is never assembled creatively within that space in order to enable the creative intelligence of all the groups who ought to participate in the production of the criteria. The point of departure is to summon a new platform of knowledge exchange between the institutions and communities. We can serve a huge role if we ourselves and our (educational) institutions become representatives of this type of new engagement.

AUDIENCE: Given your notion of "colliding ecologies" in the context of social justice, and the need to create a narrative, how do you engage in the transference of knowledge when you work with less-defined, amorphous and nonlinear ecologies?

CRUZ: I am very interested in the construction of narratives, of other scripts that begin to reorganize our thinking: The 60-mile cross-section that I did at some point was a way of narrativizing global conflict as it hits the ground and bring up physical manifestations in the landscape. Retroactively looking at that condition and asking "what produced that collision" through some kind of forensics of urbanization, the narrative begins to emerge with particular aspects of imagination that begin to enable my thinking about the procedures of interventions as well as its potential: first, the exposure (the reorganization of the systems) and then the procedures. For me the narrative is the point of departure, about how to transcend and transgress the problems we face, and unmask what has been hidden from us.

AUDIENCE: How has the walk through actual territories around Rome changed the political, and has it changed the perception people have of the municipal and local politics?

LORENZO ROMITO: For us the idea of walking is about establishing a new set of relationships with other people and with the territory. This is the largest absence we face, that prohibits the emergence of new narratives, new ways of thinking, new possibilities, and new ways of organizing. As soon as we establish these relationships, we begin to discover the potential, the magic of it, and its capacity to produce new knowledge about the city. Then you start to reflect upon the layer of organization you produce by doing this work, and you realize that what you imagine can actually become possible, and it can become socially acceptable. The idea to take part in the political elections in Rome is evidently not to be elected, but to establish the concrete possibility of it happening, of turning things this way, that it exists as a concrete reality if it recognizes itself. The act of walking is the beginning of the reshaping of the unsustainable positions we all occupy in the world and in the society. When you start to feel the possibility that this process opens up, people begin to identify with it and join it. It is a slow process and you begin to think how to preserve it from the outside forces. It is very harsh to imagine what and how to do before you do it, as it becomes very natural once you begin to do it.

AUDIENCE: We heard a lot about working with small communities, but in the context of the paternalistic public housing situation where huge populations have lived under large public authorities, and institutions that exhibit the lack of willingness to change their practices, how do you imagine "the new political" in that context?

CRUZ: I have been thinking about that as I recently participated as a juror of the Pruitt Igoe competition. I wasn't that familiar with the history of the massive public housing projects, but that particular one has become so emblematic of the demolition of public housing as a topic to be debated in this country. The famous image of implosion of the Pruitt Igoe buildings had demonized modern architecture and that housing typology, but it also particularly demonized public housing in the United States. Even though those buildings were badly designed, the problem wasn't architectural. A part of the problem was that at the moment in the history of this country when at least we had agreed to invest in public imagination, unfortunately that decision was followed by bad planning. Most importantly though, the decay of that project was because of the deliberate unplugging of the economic, social, and political support systems. De-taxation and the processes of demonizing began to erode it. As we reimagine public housing, which we must, we must realize that the longevity of the welfare state is counted, we must reimagine what the public housing can be without the top-down support of the state. Perhaps not on the scale of Pruitt Igoe, but in other modalities, jurisdictions, and communities. This is a very important question today. When the public has in many ways disappeared, in what other ways can we imagine the relationship of housing to such economic and cultural support systems?

Chapter 3

Walking Out of the Contemporary

Lorenzo Romito

We are living in a time that, for too long, has been exhausted and that has exhausted us. Despite the strong critique of the political and social aspects of our cultural moment, it persists. The crisis of representative democracy is evident today, as are the problems with both social and economic technologies of power. Despite a heightened awareness of social inequality and a strong criticism of neoliberalism, there is inadequate critique of the dominant cultural model. This model unmistakably and deliberately inhibits the construction of cultural movements directed at overcoming it. In order to define itself, this enduring cultural moment has seized the term *contemporary* and has reversed its original meaning. Originally conceived as the "negative instrument" employed to critically interpret modernity, the *contemporary* has turned into a dominant cultural ideology, an apparatus with absolute rule over the production of language. The principal goal of such a rule is the enslavement of cultural practices, and thereby, the inhibition of any meaningful transformation of the dominant economic, political, and social models. In this way, the development of culture outside of its sphere of control has been rendered impossible.

Today, the *contemporary* has become a bombastic autonarrative apparatus of the present, an apparatus that dislodges spaces, time, social and cultural organizations as well as any creative, innovative, or resistant language or expression on the horizon of its reign over the present, impeding their becoming, uprooting them from the past. It is from this efficacious apparatus for the production of the *contemporary* that we must extricate ourselves, at the moment when its meaning is reversed from that of expressing critique and renewal, to that of scaffolding the production of social oppression. On the other hand, the *contemporary* is neither a homogeneous cultural movement nor an avant-garde practice. We could conceive of it as a cultural period, but unlike the postmodern it has not been defined in relation to a preceding historical period; it rather seems to occupy boundaries that are simultaneously present and metahistorical.

I believe that the *contemporary* today has become a governing apparatus—political, economic, and social—of the production of language, and it entrusts the control of technological innovation with its ostensible renewal. The absence of its unique and recognizable language allows the *contemporary* to appropriate any vocabulary—be it conservative, progressive, or subversive. Any language can be bent to its will and turned into capital, as long as it embraces media success and economic profit as measures for the attribution of value, and thus the *contemporary's* ultimate logic as the universal truth. In this way, the *contemporary* dissolves every bond with history and geography as it colonizes by plundering them of vital resources. It also thereby erases all that is public as well as the commons as the only loci that might accommodate the elaboration of a critical discourse.

Stalker

Stalker was initiated in October 1995 with a walk on the outskirts of Rome organized by a group of young architects and artists who transgressed forty-three miles of paths never walked before.[1] Stalker[2] is not a group, it is an inter-related open system that grows and emerges through its continuously evolving praxis; it is a collective subject engaged in territorial and spatial actions and research with the aim of catalyzing and instigating the coproduction of self-organized places, environments, and situations (Careri and Romito 2005). Stalker proposes experimental strategies for intervention founded on exploratory spatial practices, using playful, convivial, and interactive tactics that relate to an environment, its inhabitants, and their local culture. Such practices and methods are conceived to catalyze and develop evolutionary and self-organizing processes through the social and environmental fabric specifically in the areas where, through abandonment or impoverishment, basic necessities are lacking. The traces of these interventions constitute a sensible mapping of the complexity and dynamics of the territory realized through the collective contribution of individuals from different backgrounds and disciplines. These contributors investigate, document, and co-create processes of urban transformation.

For Stalker, it has been important to ponder the following questions: How can we find ways out of the overwhelming and totalizing reach of the *contemporary*? How can we weave the connections between texts and contexts, between normative and alternative identities that can bring back meaning to our location in space and time? How can we reactivate the processes that reconnect our current positioning to the past and reopen our gaze toward the future? How can we reconstruct the ranges and the gaps that enable individuals and cultural groups to (re)acquire meanings and specificities that recognize and celebrate difference? How can we reconstitute democracy on the ground by operationalizing such differences as a political vehicle in pushing against the dominant political and economic models in specific urban territories? Is it possible to produce a language that exposes this tyrannical and regressive apparatus, reopening the way to dialectics and to debates among different cultural realms, putting back into motion both history and the very possibility of the future? The linguistic laboratories of neoliberal propaganda have transformed the society of the spectacle (Debord 1994) into an ostensibly perfect apparatus, a virus that has contaminated all reality, not just by controlling and repressing but by producing consensus and delegitimizing dissent as well as by aestheticizing and commercializing counter ideologies.

I see three domains of affirmation for the languages of present-day urban societies: art, architecture, and the city. They are all based on the same distribution model: neighborhoods that become impermeable and homogenous enclaves and architectures and works of art that clash with natural, social, ecological, and cultural contexts inhibited from the possibility of transformation. Our main point of focus has been the present-day city, since the city is the most pervasive of these systems of knowledge, power, and experience. It concerns the life of all urban citizens, and it is endowed with spatial and cartographic representations that are immediate and multi-scalar, updated in real time and used widely. I see the present-day city as the locus for the only possible, real critique of the *contemporary* and of neoliberalism, by means of crossing it, step by step, on foot. I have argued—through my twenty-year experience with Stalker—that this particular praxis, and the lessons learned from it can help us to walk out of the bounds of the *contemporary*.

Walking Through, Constructing the Commons

Stalker had its beginnings in action, a simple but paradoxical action, a unique experience: taking a stroll around Rome through the abandoned urban spaces, within the circuit of highways that surrounds it, and avoiding familiar spaces (Figure 3.1). It took us five days to do it, and we spent four nights in tents (Figure 3.2). We called that first expedition "Stalker Through the Actual Territories." With the expression *actual territories* we sought to identify and name

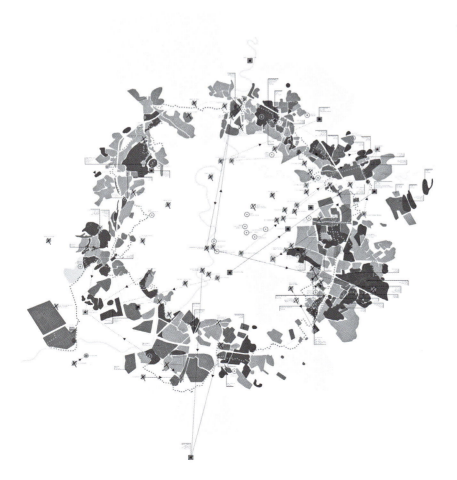

◀ Figure 3.1

Primavera Romana Experience map © Stalker archives.

▶ Figure 3.2

Walking across actual territories © Stalker archives.

▲ Figure 3.3

Map of Rome © Stalker archives.

an alternative space, and also to juxtapose it to the space of the contemporary city. We called artists, architects, and scientific researchers to participate in order to understand this space and to interpret its dynamics through their means and with their own actions, just as we sought to do with our own walking through. Coming back into the contemporary city after transgressing the *actual territories*, we developed a cartography of the experience. I also compiled my own personal diary together with a list of reflections that resulted from this collective experience. From that first stroll around Rome we have attempted to contrast the *actual* against the *contemporary*. Namely, walking—or walking through—was a founding principle of Stalker. The design of the contours of collective experiences, paths of space–time continuity, margins and boundaries that separate the spatial islands and archipelagoes, the continents of widespread urbanization adrift, reconnecting spaces that, although close to one another, are disconnected. Stalker constructs a vision of becoming urban that begins at its negative, from the background where memory is by now unconscious. It is the spontaneity of reappropriation that gives the future the chance to become something different, to emerge ruggedly and inconceivably from the *actual territories* without planning and without supervision. We created a map of Rome in an attempt to describe the emerging urban dimension in the cracking of the contemporary city (Figure 3.3). In this map, we marked the islands of the *contemporary* in yellow, like land above sea level in a world atlas. We then began to perceive that some other dimension was emerging within the city. We marked all the abandoned urban spaces in blue—left over infrastructure spaces, spaces abandoned as a result of the economic crisis, "non-places" and "non-sites"—and we defined these spaces as critical for the city of Rome. To us, these were the most interesting spaces where we tried to understand the becoming of the city. We call these spaces *actual territories*, to counterpose those spaces to the contemporary city. On the

CHAPTER 3 Walking Out of the Contemporary   27 map, the *actual territories* are like blue oceans that surround the inhabited spaces and give visibility and form to an alter ego of the contemporary city. Walking through the *actual territories* becomes a means of access that allows us to look beyond the inanity of contemporary spatiality while seeking to seize the lost meaning of places, to put back in motion the possibility of a different future, beyond the omnipresence of the *contemporary*.

Walking through is at once an aesthetic practice and one of freedom and of awareness. It is a practice aimed more at changing those who enact it than at things themselves: a change of perception that prompts a transformation in behaviors and their coercion to transform places. It teaches us not to make predictions and plan, but to experiment, to think about a project as a process. Walking draws a line: It is itself the most elementary of processes that a human being can undertake; it displaces onto a single experiential fragment the perception of space, the sensation of one's body living that space, and the conception of its transformation (Figure 3.4). Walking through means living the distances between things, backing out of the real time of the *contemporary*, desecrating the walls that protect its synchronicity and indifference. It brings about a spontaneous, unexpected encounter between people and spaces via

◀ **Figure 3.4**

Beyond City © Stalker archives.

◀ **Figure 3.5**

Walking across actual territories © Stalker archives.

inhabiting boundaries as well as distances. These distances to be lived, the distances in which we might linger and in which these encounters might take place, differ. Erasing them to replace them with tidy, exclusionary borders is an obsession of the *contemporary*. Born under the regimes of difference, these borders have sanctioned the incommunicability between the various forms of diversity, negating the spontaneous encounter at its inception, and designing geographies of exclusion and exclusivity. By way of such exclusivity, the threshold becomes normativized, made into a spectacle, and rendered a chance for economic speculation on and social exploitation of the differences that it sanctions (Figure 3.5).

In 1999, we lingered on one of these borders. We decided to live it, to allow it to go back to being a distance to be crossed, as a way to get to know each other, to understand each other, to coexist. In this way we transformed that distance into an experimental space of possible relation that we could construct together. More specifically, we organized a new experience of creating the commons through the design of a game at Campo Boario, on the premises of Testaccio's ex-slaughter-house in southwest-central Rome, in the vicinity of the Roma Ostiense train station. As the area has had no land-use destination since 1975, the sedimentation of time and the absence of any proposal for future use have made it an example of self-organization and cohabitation of different cultures, communities, and civic groups. Campo Boario is a rectangular courtyard measuring about three hectares where different communities, extraneous to the "normal" life of the city, live together. In this large space, the caravans of the Roma Calderasha community are settled for almost the entire year. The Roma Calderasha are a nomad community inhabiting the region since the 1500s, and specializing in working with raw metals. The stables within the camp are occupied by the *cavallari*, the conductors of tourist horse carriages and their three hundred horses. On the opposite side of the lot is Villaggio Globale, the prominent, self-managed Roman social center where intercultural activities take place yearlong. Other parts of the camp are inhabited by immigrant communities, especially from Senegal and North Africa, and by the many homeless citizens.

In May 1999, Stalker joined the Biennale dei Giovani Artisti exhibition that took place in an area adjacent to Campo Boario. Our proposal for the Biennale was a workshop titled From Cartonia to Piazza Kurdistan aimed at integrating the Kurd refugee community arriving at the time from Turkey into the multicultural context of Campo Boario. The workshop involved the Kurdish organization Azad, the Kurd refugees, as well as architecture students from the University of Reggio Calabria. A part of our long-term project was to inhabit and restore the abandoned veterinary building on the site (Figure 3.6). We called the building Ararat, the name of the sacred mountain where Noah landed after the Flood. During the following months, Ararat became the gathering place for the Kurd community and a working space for artists, architects, researchers, and citizens invited to cohabit the space (Figure 3.7). Ararat provided us with an opportunity to comprehend the complexity of dynamic urban transformations taking place in Rome via the material and cultural enclosures of the building and the Campo. Without any assistance from public institutions, the space in front of Ararat was transformed into a giant playground, a blackboard used to freely imagine and

◀ Figure 3.6

Campo Boario © Stalker archives.

◀ Figure 3.7

Campo Boario © Stalker archives.

draw actions and interactions among the different communities who lived there. From 1999–2002, we co-designed collective games[3] that engaged the community and contributed to the transformation and emancipation of this shared space.

Today, Ararat is a mandatory stop for thousands of Kurd refugees passing through Europe, and also the center of the entire Kurd community in Rome. Part of the playground was transformed into Ortoboario, a public garden where sunflowers and fruit trees were planted. This is also the site of the annual Newroz celebration where Kurds celebrate the time when Babylonians were forced out from the territory of Kurdistan by lighting up fires and dancing. Events like these are designed to catalyze processes of transformation, try to eliminate idle prejudice and conflict, and direct group energies towards change by means of playful devices. Design is here employed subversively, via the process of *détournement*, in defining new social configurations from the self-defined relationships that arise in this process. This project exemplifies Stalker's philosophy and approach: it generates an ethical, political, and aesthetic space; a real, autonomous, living space; a territory made up of environments, situations, and places designed to reestablish a creative circularity which has been taken away from us by the commodification of everyday life. We designate places for encounters and spaces for possible relations; as in a game, a space of safe relations where one feels invited to take on a risk but also to attempt to reconcile seemingly irresolvable conflicts. This space is an open, experimental theater where one learns how to affect change, and how to change oneself by experimenting with different forms of coexistence.

Before designing the rules of our games, we first instigate the aspects of the game that stimulate the will to "waste time" and immerse oneself in the distance between the self and the other. This is precisely the type of relationship—a type of spatial and temporal experience—that the contemporary city refuses to concede to us. It can only be realized beyond the disciplinary and normative obsessions of the state and the blind and rapacious interest of private capital, in an uncertain, undetermined space that becomes the theater of the commons to invent and cohabit. Stalker-ing is thus a process of building relationships with the inhabitants of the urban territories where we work. We never plan our actions. We design devices meant to open up possible ways of establishing such relationships, and then we try to keep track of the action; sometimes, our process develops into a concrete project, like the making of Ararat. We believe that instigating the processes of self-organization on a small scale marks the creation of the process of reorganization of the society as a whole. Particularly since 2008,[4] our projects have moved beyond research and investigational practice towards more explicit practices of engagement of individuals and groups representing different strata of society. The processes of cooperation and knowledge production, which our walks have enabled, have also charted the spontaneous practices of urban and civic self-organization emerging in Rome. We began to focus on sites of speculation and discrimination, and besides walking our practice expanded into gardening in abandoned areas and squatting in abandoned public buildings and transforming them into cooperative housing. All these practices also invented and introduced alternative urban micro-economies in contrast to the dominant models imposed by the capitalist system.

For example, through the project we call Urban Agronomadism we have attempted to move social action from raising awareness to urban commoning as a way of producing new ways of inhabiting the city and creating new urban economies. Our mapping of the abandoned public land in and around Rome indicated that many public gardens, archeological sites, and forgotten public lands are covered with olive trees. In 2010, via our web site and word of mouth, we asked people to mark the public lands where olive trees were on our map. Together with our partners, collaborators, and volunteers we collected olives from public lands and produced over three hundred bottles of olive oil (Figure 3.8). The Roman Public Oil (Olio PU.RO/Olio Pubblico di Roma) was distributed through the solidarity network to buyer groups across the city of

◀ **Figure 3.8**

2010 olive harvest © Stalker archives.

◀ **Figure 3.9**

2010 olive harvest © Stalker archives.

Rome (Figure 3.9). The income was used to create new programs and support immigrant groups. Similarly, our 2011 project Oranges Don't Fall from the Sky (Le Arance Non Cadono Dal Cielo) was done to raise awareness of the horrifying living and working conditions of orange pickers in South Italy (Figure 3.10). These mostly illegal workers from Sub-Saharan Africa collect oranges with no shelter, no health insurance, and no housing provisions. Moreover, they are usually economically exploited because they lack legal working permits.[5] These workers' attempts to organize public protests were forcefully shut down by the police, the mafia, and regular citizens. We announced the date for collecting all the oranges from the public gardens and lands of the city of Rome, and around four hundred people took part in the event. We collected a few tons of oranges and produced more than a thousand jars of bitter-orange jam (Figure 3.11). These were distributed and sold, and the proceeds were used to build a social center for the African workers in the small town of Rosarno, where all the migrant workers from Africa were beaten with iron bars in 2010. This project is more evidence of how a design of a social network generates collective action, creates a new consciousness, and creates anti-institutional paths by coproducing a new political dimension in our world.

▶ Figure 3.10

Le Arance Non Cadono Dal Cielo campaign © Stalker archives.

▶ Figure 3.11

2011 orange harvest © Stalker archives.

◀ Figure 3.12

2011 orange harvest © Stalker archives.

The Beyond-the-City

Our work of walking through and tracing the lines desecrates the exclusionary boundaries of the contemporary city and lucidly lives the distances that divide us in order to reestablish an unprecedented urban commons and an unprecedented urban community. Lines and circles begin to weave networks, to draw unexplored cartographies in which we all act as explorers, inhabitants, and mapmakers. In this way, against the backdrop of the contemporary city, there emerges a complex, dynamic design whose cartographic representation is no longer a device of planning and control, but the realization of an attempt by collective consciousness to redesign coexistence in the beyond-the-city. By beyond-the-city I mean the perspective of meaning in which the *contemporary city* can no longer withdraw from a confrontation with the *actual territories*. It is there that boundaries and conflicts between city and countryside, between past and future, and between inhabitants and institutions become laboratories and theaters for the reinvention of the commons. It is an unprecedented space to be constructed between public and private, between spontaneity and planning, between local and global; a design that renders the margin as the center of transformation provided that the project ceases to be constituted of violent and abstract top-down planning to allow for the bottom-up emergence of a collective consciousness. Finally, it is a taking of form and consciousness of an emergent awareness that surpasses the contemporary city.

We hold this to be true, that the current economic, political, and social crisis will necessarily bring about a structural transformation of the dominant socioeconomic system. We do not intend to engineer this necessary change for we do not desire to do violence upon this system; nor do we want to endure violence from it. We would like to face it with spontaneity, seeking to avoid conflicts and help the failing system evolve through the design of complex, innovative, and creative relations. To understand and to give rise to such a transformation means to oppose change and be ready to discover the opportunities brought by this crisis. In that respect, our work attempts to facilitate the emergence of a communal awareness—a collective consciousness that could define a profound transformation in the self-organizing processes of human society. Such a change in social organization can only occur through a foundation of consciousness that is indeed collective but emerges out of individual struggles for change. Society will not change if we ourselves do not change.

From Saturday, March 21 through Saturday, June 21, 2014 we organized a series of walks in Rome titled The Great Ring Junction (Grande Raccordo Anulare). The walk took the form of a ring-like junction seeking to become an itinerary within and through social transformation by way of which we attempted to coexist, imagine, and devise a different way of life. We invited organizations and communities as well as individual citizens to participate, to share, and to promote this walk as the conjoining of all those who believe in the practice of sustainable change. To activate and to share this self- and co-evolutionary measure is the current task of Stalker in the face of the need for a profound social transformation.

Notes

1. For more information about the formative 1995 walk on the outskirts of Rome, see Romito (1997) and Lang (2007).
2. As Peter Lang writes,

   The action, conceived to document Rome's local periphery and record experiences along the way, drew considerable attention from Italy's local and national media. The name that stuck with the group was almost an afterthought, when a news reporter who had seen the 1979 film Stalker by the master Russian director Andrei Tarkovsky suggested similarities between the film's enchanted "zone" and the areas traversed during the Walk about Rome.

   (Lang 2007: 183)

3. Among numerous games, the most popular were Carta di Non-Identità (Non-ID Card) which was distributed to all the inhabitants on the occasion of the Clandestino Day; the Pranzo Boario (Boario Lunch), a big circular dining table where Kurdish food, Gypsy gulash, and Japanese seaweeds (cooked by Asako Iwama, Japanese artist and architect) were served together; the Globall Game, during which two thousand soccer balls were used to write the stories of Campo Boario; the Transborderline, a spiral space which symbolically represented a permeable and inhabitable border, which was then installed on the Italian-Slovenian border without the necessary permits; and the Tappeto Volante (Flying Carpet), an itinerant ceiling which traces the mucarnas of the Palatine Chapel in Palermo using ropes and copper.
4. 2008 Venice Architecture Biennale titled *Out There: Architecture Beyond Building* was curated by Aaron Betsky. Stalker presented work in the Italian pavilion and also took part in the *Experimental Architecture* exhibition curated by Emiliano Gandolfi.
5. For the coverage of these events, see: www.theguardian.com/world/2010/jan/08/standoff-italy-four-africans-wounded (Last accessed on February 15, 2015).

Bibliography

Careri, F. (2001) *Walkscapes: Walking as an Aesthetic Practice*. Gustavo Gil.

Careri, F. and Romito, L. (2005) Stalker and the Big Game of Campo Boario. Jones, P. B., Petrescu, D. and Till, T. (Eds.) *Architecture and Participation*. Spon Press, pp. 227–234.

Debord, G. (1994) *The Society of the Spectacle*. Zone Books (Originally published as *La Société du Spectacle* in 1967 in France).

Lang, P. T. (2007) Stalker on Location. Franck, K. A. (Ed.) *Loose Space: Possibility and Diversity in Urban Life*. Routledge, pp. 193–209.

Recchia, F. (2011) Radical Territories of Affection: The Art of Being Stalker. De Cauter, L., De Roo, R. and Vanhaesebrouck, K. (Eds.) *Art and Activism in the Age of Globalization*. NAi publishers, pp. 160–171.

Romito, L. (1997) Stalker. Lang, P. (Ed.) *Suburban Discipline*. Princeton Architectura Press, pp. 130–141.

Romito, L. (2001) Observe and Interact. Koolhaas, R. et al. (Eds.) *Mutations*. Actar, p. 433.

Romito, L. (20051 The Surreal Foil. *Architectural Design*. "New Babylonians." Vol. 71, No. 3. June 2001, pp. 20–22.

Romito, L. (2007) Campagna Romana, the Formation of the "Oltrecittà." Swenarton, M., Troiani, I. and Webster, E. (Eds.) *The Politics of Making*. Routledge, pp. 87–92.

Chapter 4
Walks On the Wild Side
Ana Džokić and Marc Neelen

In the late 1990s, we envisioned an architectural practice that would address the complicated and, at times, radical developments in urban conditions unfolding around the world. It was clear that a different approach, a different toolset, and a different mind-set were needed in order to understand such conditions, detect what remains under the radar of the architecture profession, and engage with the stealthy processes that transform cities. With this in mind, STEALTH.unlimited emerged. At that time, we felt the urgency to address the ferocious urban transformations that had been taking place in Belgrade, Serbia[1] since the early 1990s.

    Amid the gradual disintegration of Yugoslavia in the 1990s, the Yugoslav civil war, and, most crucially, the United Nations (UN) economic embargo of 1992–1995,[2] Belgrade turned into a "wild city." During the decade of economic and political instability following the imposition of the embargo, the grip of the

▶ Figure 4.1

Wild City: Street commerce © STEALTH group, wild city project archive.

public institutions on society weakened dramatically due to successive economic, demographic and social crises. As the centrally-run socialist government and its civic institutions rapidly dissolved, individual initiatives and informal organizational forms appeared as the only way to fulfill the increasingly complex demands of urban living. For ten subsequent years, countless emergent urban phenomena and processes started substituting the city's primary urban systems: institutionally organized collective housing provision was replaced with semi-legal, unplanned, self-constructed housing; the state controlled market with grey-market "street commerce"; municipal transport with semi-private "one man-one bus" companies; and the state-monopolized petrol provision with smuggled petrol sold in plastic 1.5-liter Coca-Cola bottles on the streets of Belgrade (Figure 4.1). Though self-organized and informal housing provisions had been recorded even under the strict control of the socialist welfare state in the years prior to 1990, the number of such structures began to grow greatly following the 1992 UN embargo. In 1975, 17,903 illegal or semi-legal buildings were registered in Belgrade; in 1995, the number nearly doubled, reaching 33,594. In the year 2000, over 10,000 housing units were built, over ninety-five percent of which were self-constructed and built without building permits.[3] In 2001, 95,419 wild buildings were registered, while unofficial estimations reached 200,000 illegal constructions.[4] These numbers show that in the gaps left open by previously dominant public and civic institutions

◀ Figure 4.2

The Kaludjerica settlement
© STEALTH.unlimited.

▲ Figure 4.3

Kaludjerica from Šklj to Abc
© Vahida Ramujkić.

of the socialist state, new constellations of actors formed to open up the process of envisioning and cocreating the city.

Such frenetic construction activity went on without much public discussion. It only began to get noticed with the media attention given to "the two brothers" phenomenon that illustrated the "wild urbanization" of Belgrade in its clearest form.[5] Feeling at odds with the resulting response among colleagues, many of whom evidently lacked the understanding and tools to engage within this emerging unruly reality, while simultaneously witnessing the immense energy created by urban movements initiated by citizens and civic associations, in 1998 we decided to begin to observe and learn from these emerging conditions. Among the outcomes of this multi-year research are *Wild City: Genetics of Uncontrolled Urban Processes*[6] and *Kaludjerica from Šklj to Abc: A Life in The Shadow of Modernization*. *Wild City* forged much of our professional stance towards the role of architects and the capacity of citizens in creating their own urban environment. The urban transformations occurring in Belgrade were powerful, unparalleled, and, in a crude way, ingeniously creative. Much to Kevin Kelly's point in *The Nine Laws of God* (Kelly 1995), the city of Belgrade has acted like a dynamic living system, and what only appeared to be chaotic development was *de facto* a systemic evolution, based on clear emergent rules and principles. Most importantly, Belgrade's wilderness began to reveal an ad-hoc, almost collateral democratization of urban space, in which urban innovation was no longer limited to the work of urban professionals.

CHAPTER 4 Walks On the Wild Side

Kaludjerica: A Green Area on the Planners' Drafting Board

South-east of downtown Belgrade, along the E-75 European highway, nests Kaludjerica, a settlement of incomplete individual residential objects in the hilly landscape. Today this suburb, known as the "largest wild settlement in the Balkans," officially houses over thirty thousand inhabitants, largely in brick and concrete buildings erected without legal building permits (Figure 4.2). Kaludjerica began to emerge as an informal settlement during the late 1960s. At that time, even though most citizens enjoyed the enthusiastic modernization that accompanied socialism in post-World War II Yugoslavia, not everybody shared the benefits and advantages of its welfare housing policies. Although state laws formally guaranteed the right to housing for each worker and his or her family[7], this promise was not always fulfilled. The lack of "housing for all" had triggered construction of nearly eighteen thousand illegal and semi-legal residential buildings by 1975 in Belgrade alone. In subsequent years, the housing shortage was exacerbated by an influx of opportunity seekers, who came to the capital, following a series of important economic reforms, in search of seasonal and general work, education, and professional careers. Living and working conditions in Belgrade were far better than in many other regions of Yugoslavia, and such conveniences made many of the ever-growing number of urban newcomers decide to settle within the metropolitan region. However, the numbers of newcomers far exceeded the capacity of housing provided. Marginal metropolitan sites like Kaludjerica therefore became a desired destination for those who had to settle at their own expense and in their own right (Figure 4.3).

The methods of parceling agricultural land, organizing building lots, designing houses, establishing and maintaining streets, and improvising water and sewage infrastructure in Kaludjerica, all trace the history of a negotiation between a rapidly urbanizing and modernizing society, and the civic governing structures. In the late 1960s and early 1970s, unrealistic loan terms motivated citizens to buy plots of agricultural land not intended for construction, in Kaludjerica and elsewhere in the Belgrade metropolitan region. The vicinity to a large city, the lack of public infrastructure and municipal utility fees, and low land prices attracted many. As soon as the concrete slab for a structure's first elevation was laid, the house was inhabited. Owners only continued building as savings allowed. Hence, the construction of individual houses took decades.

The first settlement was built away from municipal roads in order not to attract attention. The pattern of eight-meter-wide streets was established by each of the neighbors contributing a piece of their land for this new, shared infrastructure. However, not everyone followed suit, causing the streets to be curvy, and to occasionally vary in width. Plentiful land allowed for agriculture and the construction of small gardens surrounding the newly-built houses (Figure 4.4).

Even though the initially cheap prices were attractive for people to decide to construct here, the lack of paved roads, running water, sewage, electricity, public schools, and transport made many of Kaludjerica's settlers question their choice. In the early 1970s, the settlement consisted of 6,000 inhabitants, and

▶ Figure 4.4

Kaludjerica from Šklj to Abc: Collective action © Vahida Ramujkić.

about 10,000 new houses were under construction. By that time, the individual well-based water sources, one paved road, and an old village school with three classrooms could no longer sustain the area. The settlement could no longer afford to stay "invisible." An important turn came through a local demand to establish a community organization, a political unit, which would represent the interests of its citizens. Even though this community organization represented the people who built a settlement largely without any permits, it managed to negotiate successfully with the municipal government. In turn, between mid-1970s and mid-1980s, municipal authorities supported the introduction of the first public bus line, running water supply pipes, the construction of a public primary school with adequate capacity, and a local health center. This process also brought close to thirty professional engineers to the settlement, including architects and civil engineers. The enthusiasm these events unlocked contributed to more solidarity among the inhabitants, who collectively began to invest in paving the streets, constructing street lighting, building parts of a new sewage system, and bringing in the first food stores.

According to a much-retold anecdote, while driving by Kaludjerica along the highway in the 1970s, Yugoslavia's then-president Tito was apparently informed about the "problem" of this informal settlement, and of the imminent demolition of such suburban neighborhoods. As the anecdote goes, Tito ordered that people living in such conditions should be spared the demolition, and that the "will of the people" deserved respect. In fact, neither public authorities nor planning institutions were aware of, or unconcerned with, the possible consequences of such an emerging, informal urbanization. As a prominent urban planner of the period recently revealed, ". . . we would draw Kaludjerica on the masterplan like a green area—which it wasn't, obviously."[8]

Until today, an institutional way to engage in a comprehensive inclusion of Kaludjerica into the urban plan of Belgrade and to legislate the majority of its housing assets has not been found. When we began our research in Kaludjerica in 2011, we set out to explore the gap between institutional and practical thinking—an existential void in which, meanwhile, tens of thousands of Kaludjerica's inhabitants have lived for decades.[9] In *Kaludjerica from Šklj to Abc*, we argued that over the last fifteen years Kaludjerica-like developments have spread over the entire Belgrade metro region, with over 350,000 people living in suburbs of a similar kind. In many ways, Kaludjerica has become a model of urbanization at the local level, and thus worth learning from. Moreover, the events of the previous decades described above opened a completely new space for negotiations between the concepts, notions, and practices of legal and illegal urbanization. Unlike in the 1970s, in the contemporary political and economic context citizens are frightened by the threats and challenges intrinsic to such negotiations. The older forms of solidarity, innovative initiatives, and grass-roots organization have diminished as citizens choose to remain passive. Therefore, there is an urgent need to find modes of communication between citizens living in informal settlements and civic associations, municipal governments, and other institutions with the capacity to contribute to solving the specific challenges facing such urban communities. Also, citizens in such informal settlements are commonly detached from the professional organizations of architects, urban planners, and civil engineers, indicating a need for knowledge transfer between these communities. Finally, and possibly paradoxically, another reason for our involvement has been to create an awareness and an understanding that whereas socialist ideology left a considerable group of citizens "out in the cold" during the socialist era, today it is the highly regulated free market-driven conditions that leave out many more. Namely, under the conditions of parliamentary democracy, free market, and unapologetic neoliberal policies in place in Serbia today, a growing number of citizens are unable even to construct "wild." Where will they live?

Housing—Fiction or Reality?

In the early 2000s, private housing loans were for the first time introduced in Serbia. Private developers took the stage, together with the rather ad-hoc speculative investment schemes and with price gouging that became the rule of the game. Besides, numerous criminal schemes were executed daily where one and the same apartment in downtown Belgrade, still under construction, was sold multiple times to several buyers, driving desperate new housing "owners" toward criminal courts, bankruptcies, and poverty. In the wake of this, associations like "1000 Mistreated" were formed, representing citizens who camped in incomplete buildings while waiting for their legal rights to be upheld. In some instances, associations of homebuyers seized the incomplete buildings from developers in order to complete them on their own. By 2008, just before the beginning of the global economic crisis, prices per square meter in Belgrade had skyrocketed. Today, with the median monthly family income at 50,820 Serbian dinars[10] (about US$600) and the average price of real-estate ranging from US$1,300 per square meter in the suburbs to well over US$2,600 downtown, housing buyers have found themselves in unrealistic long-term debts, and, in more severe cases, in poverty.

In Belgrade, as in many cities across the region, where a transition to the market economy was made in the early 1990s, subsidized public housing does not exist. The main reason for this is the reform covered by the Housing Relations Law of 1990 and the Residence Law of 1992, which *de facto* first nationalized the societal housing stock and then enabled the privatization of the entire, now public, housing stock in Serbia (Bartlett 2007: 156). The Residence Law demanded that public sector housing be first offered to current tenants at heavily discounted prices, which turned over ninety three percent of citizens living in the former societal housing into home owners by 1993. Today, an estimated 140,000 people in Belgrade cannot resolve their housing situation, over 350,000 live in informal settlements, while those who became homeowners during the last decade struggle under the burden of heavy mortgages. Understanding that neither market forces nor the state are capable of addressing this issue systematically, we made the decision to position ourselves amid this housing challenge with a number of unusual associates.

Smarter Building

Are you interested in building a decent apartment in Belgrade at US$400–700 per square meter without getting yourself into debt and unpayable loans, living in impossible conditions, or waiting for your relatives to move to the countryside or to Heaven? Impossible?

It was with this announcement in 2012 that, through the "Who Builds the City"[11] platform, we took the first step to address the housing deadlock (Figure 4.5). The basic idea of the Smarter Building project is to invent a method of conceptualizing, designing, and constructing housing units that will be available to those who cannot otherwise afford housing under the current economic conditions. The approach is to construct a community of future co owners that will deconstruct the existing market-driven norms and models by disentangling them from unsustainable credit debts, economic and social enslavement, and gender-based dependence. From its inception, the project was open to people seeking to jointly engage—in a "smarter" way—by planning and designing collectively, investing their time, knowledge, skills, and financial resources responsibly, and building intelligently.[12] The start of the project was covered in the local media confirming both the urgency of the topic and the widespread disbelief in an out-of-the-box solution, or any solution at all. Smarter Building intervened in the speculative housing market by introducing the format of public working sessions to discuss, self-organize, and construct a prototype of a collective housing solution that can serve as a model. Through a number of working sessions, the Smarter Building group was constituted, and began to dissect housing pricing, explore forms of direct democratic decision making, outline the legal aspects of a collectively run organizational model, and imagine possibilities for introducing the notion of equality to a society largely based on inequality. Within the first year of working together, we designed a model of a

◀ Figure 4.5

Who Builds the City: Smarter Builing working session © STEALTH.unlimited.

cooperative organization that included a wide variety of participants with very different skills and resources to be employed in the realization of Belgrade's first contemporary cooperative housing settlement. In December of 2013, a large centrally-located municipality announced a design competition for low-cost DIY housing;[13] eager to get to a "proof of concept" following one year of preparatory work, we entered the competition and won.

We took an unconventional approach to an architecture competition by first setting the price level and coinvestment model for the affordable housing unit, from which everything else was to be determined. Namely, an average household in Belgrade currently spends US$110 a month on housing, a large percent of which goes to pay for the utilities (Figures 4.6). Our model was devised to keep the utility expenses very low, allowing for a more substantial monthly investment in housing construction. From there, Smarter Building started working according to PassivHaus standards[14] and producing energy on site with DIY solar panels and ground source heat. The buildings themselves are based on a modular system of prefabricated load-bearing panels made almost entirely from renewable materials: The insulating core is made of straw bales fitted into a structural wooden frame and produced based on open-source technology in the community workshop. The panels are also appropriate for DIY installation by existing and future residents. Housing units are based on a low-risk strategy with about forty apartments built in sequence, mitigating the risk of the individual investments made by each of the cooperants (Figure 4.8). Such cooperative strategy also makes it possible to include coop members with different investments capacities (in finances or time of DIY construction), from diverse walks of life, and from all social strata (Figure 4.7). Each such 40-apartment unit is a self-contained community and can optimize the design to its specific needs. Besides, each unit invests in, and produces, a common facility such as a workshop for the construction of prefabricated panels, a coworking space, a social center, a

▶ Figure 4.6

Smarter Building, competition entry: pricing
options and alternatives
© Smarter Building team.

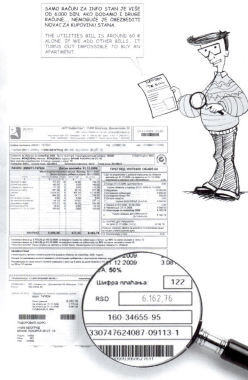

▼ Figure 4.7

Smarter Building, competition entry: social stratification
© Smarter Building team.

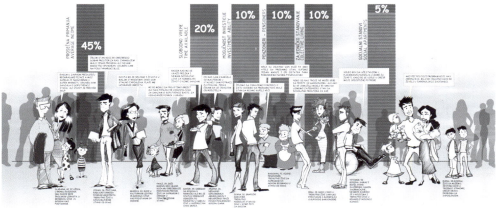

CHAPTER 4 Walks On the Wild Side

◀ **Figure 4.8**

Smarter Building, competition entry: settlement plan © Smarter Building team.

restaurant, an organic market, or an open air sports complex with educational and learning spaces (Figure 4.9). In addition, each unit contains 1,000 square feet of shared facilities such as the laundry room, a communal space with kitchen, and a guest apartment (Figure 4.10).

The Smarter Building project brings to the fore serious and systemic issues that cannot be resolved by the competition entry alone, such as the vast impact of land values, the excessive construction taxes, and the still delicate financing model that will support this approach. However, the point is not merely to solve technical, legal, and administrative issues, but also to empower citizens to engage in the processes of urban commoning via the formation of housing cooperatives based on the proposed model. In societies that increasingly depend on the collective action of urban citizens, there is an increasing pressure on professional architects and urbanists to acknowledge the necessity of such action

▶ Figure 4.9

Smarter Building, competition entry: communal spaces © Smarter Building team.

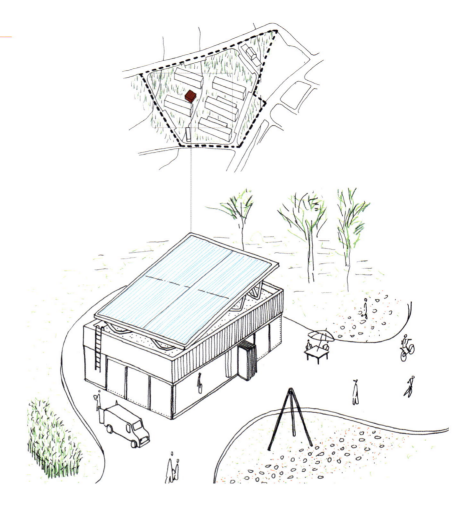

▶ Figure 4.10

Smarter Building, competition entry: communal spaces © Smarter Building team.

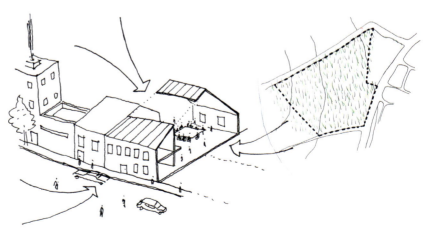

CHAPTER 4 Walks On the Wild Side   47

as well as to help imagine and coproduce social, economic, and spatial models that would facilitate it. While at first glance it may seem that citizens' urban movements may render our involvement obsolete, nothing can be less true. Our evolving expertise is increasingly relevant in the face of complex challenges our societies face and the urgent need for changes in the urban socioeconomic systems of power we have inherited. For this to happen, we have worked hard to introduce modes of activist practice to designers across the world. Exposure to radically different approaches; toolsets; and mind-set collapses of our roles as designers and citizens into codesigners of the cities we act upon.

Bibliography

Bartlett, W. (2007) *Economic Reconstruction in the Balkans: Economic Development, Institutional Reform, and Social Welfare in the Western Balkans.* Routledge Studies in Development Economics, p. 158.

Bojović, B. (December 7, 2000) "Kome Odgovara Haos?" In: *Vreme*, No. 518.

Džokić, A. and Neelen, M. (2009a) "Clones and the Fashion Book, New Belgrade." In: *SPAM_mag*, Vol. 6. SPAM_arq Ltda.

Džokić, A. and Neelen, M. (2009b) "Two brothers in the Wild City." In: *SPAM_mag*, Vol. 6. SPAM_arq Ltda.

Džokić, A., Neelen, M. and Milikić, N. (2012) Kaludjerica from Šklj to Abc: A Life in the Shadow of Modernization. In: Mrduljaš, M. and Kulić, V. (Eds.) *Unfinished Modernizations: Between Utopia and Pragmatism.* Croatian Architect's Association. Drawings by Vahida Ramujkić.

Džokić, A., Neelen, M. and Sekulić, D. (2010) New, Newer—the Newest Belgarde. In: *New Towns for the 21st Century: The Planned vs. the Unplanned City.* International New Town Institute. SUN publishers.

Džokić, A., Topalović, M., Kucina, I. and Neelen, M. (2002) Wild City: Genetics of Uncontrolled Urban Processes. In: *Hunch #4.* Nai010 Publishers.

Džokić, A., Topalović, M., Kucina, I. and Neelen, M. (2003) Belgrade: Fragments for Wild City. In: *Beograd—Den Haag, about the Impossibility of Planning.* Stroom.

Džokić, A., Topalović, M., Kucina, I. and Neelen, M. (2005) Belgrade: Evolution in an Urban Jungle. In: Read, S., Rosemann, J. and van Eldijk, J. (Eds.) *Future City.* Spon press.

Kelly, K. (1995) *Out of Control: The New Biology of Machines, Social Systems, & the Economic World.* Perseus Press.

Poulter, A. (1992) The Use and Abuse of Urbanism in the Danubian Provinces during the Late Roman Empire. In: Rich, J. (Ed.) *The City in Late Antiquity.* Routledge, pp. 99–135.

Notes

1. Belgrade was the capital of the Socialist Federal Republic of Yugoslavia from 1945–1992, and then the capital of the federation of Serbia and Montenegro from 1992–2006. As of 2006, Belgrade is the capital of Serbia with a population of 1.65 million.
2. In May 1992, the United Nations Security Council imposed strict trade, financial and political sanctions against the federation of Serbia and Montenegro for their role in the Yugoslav civil war.
3. Branko Bojović in weekly *Vreme*, Belgrade, December 7, 2000.

4. *Glas Javnosti*, Belgrade, January 22, 2001, p. 13.
5. In 1997, in the downtown Belgrade, two rural-like houses, nicknamed "the two brothers", were built on top of a flat-roof modern apartment building overlooking Sava river.
6. "Wild City: Genetics of Uncontrolled Urban Processes" was the title of the research by STEALTH group—Ana Džokić, Milica Topalović, Marc Neelen and Ivan Kucina, conducted at the Berlage Institute, Amsterdam/Rotterdam (1998–2001). The title plays with the notion of "wild construction" as used in the Serbian language to indicate informal and illegal construction activities. The research involved a group of about eighty of the students from the School of Architecture, University of Belgrade. Together, we created an unprecedented database of the city's (semi-)legal transformations in the 1990s.
7. This societal housing was financed through collective housing funds invested in by the workers of individual socialist companies.
8. Public interview with urban planners Miodrag Braca Ferenčak, Dragomir Dik Manojlović, and Branislav Jovin at the panel titled The Protagonists of the Socialist Construction, moderated by Ivan Kucina, as part of the "Unfinished Modernizations" conference. Belgrade, Serbia, May 7, 2011.
9. This resulted in the research project and publication *Kaludjerica from Šklj to Abc: A Life in The Shadow of Modernization* (2011–2012), made in collaboration with Nebojša Milikić, researcher and cultural worker, and drawings by artist Vahida Ramujkić. Made as a part of the project "Unfinished Modernisations: Between Utopia and Pragmatism" (2010–2012).
10. According to the Statistical Office of the Republic of Serbia. For reference see: www.politika.rs/vesti/najnovije-vesti/Prosecna-zarada-u-decembru-u-Srbiji-50_820-dinara.lt.html (Last accessed on February 15, 2015).
11. In 2010, STEALTH teamed up with the Culture Center Rex and Marko Aksentijević in Belgrade, to organize a series of open talks titled "Who Builds the City." A wide range of participants from various fields and positions took part in these events: representatives of public institutions, non-governmental organizations, private investors, academics and professionals in the fields of urbanism, architecture, urban economy, law, as well as urban activists, artists, journalists, and fellow citizens alike. The event, the first of its kind in Serbia, discussed the mechanisms of urban transformation and the role citizens played in them, particularly in relation to the citizen-organizations' fight for the right to the city. Since then, "Who Builds the City" has developed into a platform oriented toward activvist urban research.
12. In a twist on the notion of "smart house," "smarter building" suggests that housing should—through a collective process—be much more a social response, rather than delving into smart materials and energy efficiency.
13. Belgrade's municipality Savski Venac ran the competition of ideas for architectural and urban design of Eco Green Village composed of MILD Home housing units (My Modular, Intelligent, Low cost, Do it yourself, nearly zero energy house, for Eco Green Village) between December 2013 and February 2014, as part of a two-year project funded by the European Union, within the SEE Transnational Cooperation Programme South East Europe, which was simultaneously implemented in six countries. See: www.mildhome.eu/ (Last accessed on February 15, 2015).
14. For more information on the PassivHaus standards, see www.passivhaus.org.uk/ (Last accessed on February 15, 2015).

Conversations 2

JOSEPH HEATHCOTT: I will focus on a few questions we should be asking at this moment in thinking about design and urbanism. The first question I have is just a basic one, which is "what is design knowledge and how do we come by it." There is an implicit notion in all of the talks that there is something called "design knowledge," which we are trying to apprehend, but I am not sure what that is, where it comes from, and how we get to it. Are there critical differences between what we might call a vernacular design practice and an academic design practice? To me an academic design practice is a vernacular practice, and people figuring out how to make oil lamps out of discarded, rusted metal in informal settlements is a formal design process, as well. Here I use "vernacular" and "academic" as heuristic terms. Nevertheless, there are differences in the way people think about how to transform the material world into something useful in day-to-day life. What are the opportunities in conjoining those kinds of practices on the ground? And what are the challenges and the limits to that sort of conjunction? The other question I have is really about the purposes of design, particularly in this collaborative moment, and I wonder is the community collaboration a kind of dressed-up uni-directional design practice, or is there really a real collaboration happening at this level? And what I mean is do the communities that designers work with merely inform exogenous practices of design, or in fact are we managing to transform the root understanding of what constitutes the form, content, and process of design itself? That is, are we really changing design as we think of it in these processes? I really appreciated Deborah Gans's assertion that our discursive notions of design that we carry with us often into the field are themselves metaphors. They are deeply problematic, and we need to rethink them—that is, the metaphors of scale that we use to talk about design, the idea of top-down and bottom-up as kind of metaphors of location for where design emerges and where it's practiced. All these are discursive distinctions that I think have to be taken apart and put back together again in all kinds of ways, and I wondered if these collaborative practices are locations for that sort of critical work. Also, how can we bring these practices into the academy? How does this inform our curriculum? How does this inform the way we teach our students?

Perhaps a more speculative question on my part would be are we actually in a moment of "design revolution?" Is there something really significant going on? What sort of stage are we in in the rethinking of our design practices? Are we looking for lots of different sorts of practices around the globe, or do we see an emerging set of best practices that we can then begin to organize around and teach in the classroom? And the very last thing I will say is the question of ethical norms in design and ethical codes. It is still amazing to me that there really aren't too many conventions in the various design fields. So the question is do we design to ameliorate the worst aspects of a sick world, or is design itself a change agent?

ANNE FREDERICK: I'll talk about collaboration: whether you come to the table with knowledge of what the collaboration is beforehand and what the collaboration brings to the design knowledge. I think from our perspective, the process itself and the collaboration is what informs the ongoing kind of research and project ideas. And we see ourselves just as much as learners in the process as designers with expertise or knowledge that we can bring to bear upon some of these community development issues. I think that's a really important perspective to have going into the practice, and it's not necessarily one that I came out of school with. I learned very much from partnering with community-based organizations, where that is much more the norm, or with social justice organizations that would never think of coming to the table with all the answers. There is a lot to learn from collaboration with other practices and other disciplines. There's just something also very humbling about not having it all figured out from the beginning. Also, if we look at the distinction between planning and design professions, planners have been employing collaborative planning tools for much longer than designers have. There's often a false distinction between planning and design, and coming out of school, I wondered why do these fields have to be so distinct and separate? In fact, planners have been using community engagement tools for gathering input for years. How can we, coming from the design side, employ some of those tools or build on them?

ROSTEN WOO: I have no formal design training so I didn't come to this from having a set of design skills. One thing that is always funny to me when I interact with the design community is that people are interested in this question of "What is design, really?" And I am not interested in that question at all. I think if it's designing the way that people interact with the communication system, then that's kind of design. At Center for Urban Pedagogy (CUP), our approach is that the expertise designers bring to the table is about making stuff, and there are other kinds of expertise that are out there that are equally valuable in a given situation and are about collaboration. There is also a specific role for designers to have, it's not that we all become an undifferentiated mass of designers, or that we call everything design. I certainly think that there is place for expertise in our work—people have kind of their practices and the way they approach a problem—but I think that there is something productive about that melding of knowledge and approaches, and I think a lot of the value in our projects comes from that overlap. As to "community," we really don't work with the community in any sort of undifferentiated way; we work with institutions and with organizations, and we would never try to produce a project, say, for street vendors in general. We rely on having relationships with specific organizing bodies that do all this work to produce specific communities.

MARC TURKEL: I'm interested in the idea of design knowledge and how it forms a kind of literacy. I was having a conversation the other day with a middle school educator, who was remarking to me that there's nothing in the curriculum that any of us have had growing up—there's not even art history in middle and high school level. There is nothing to acquaint the average individual to issues that pertain to the fields of design in the broadest sense to introduce anybody to those issues precollege. You might go to a specialized high school, specialized public or private high school, and that might be brought to the table. But in general, across the country, that's not part of the foundations of our learning today. What I'm struck by is that if you take that to the academy, if you go to the architecture schools, there's still this heroic model of the practitioner. And when I graduated from an architecture school, I had my marching orders, and between not having any introduction in the primary school and through high school, and then having this distorted introduction in college, you can clearly see where the problem lies. You can see where we are, and what I was struck by was that there's this idea among us here of empowerment through education, through educating the public. But shouldn't that education process also be in the various levels of the academy?

WOO: I'd like to talk about specifically our education programs. It is something where we really collaborate with high school students, and there is a specific way we are nested within the world of arts education. At first, those of us who were working on these projects felt a little bit embarrassed, because maybe we were doing it wrong? Because the arts education curricula are typically for high school students, and it's fairly robust and materially-focused. The most important thing is that the final thing is something that you've produced from dirt to dinner, you know, and that's the most privileged aspect of it. So the value of this thing comes from the fact that a kid made it and that's a wonderful thing, so we had to find ways to articulate this kind of work. We do use design in a lot of ways as a means to different ends; the design process is something where the fact that you have to build something halfway through the semester allows students to access questions, locate things that you're missing, figure out ways to articulate what you know. It is a real civic education process to engage in design. At the same time, people are bringing lots of different things to the table and sharing them, and I think it's important to recognize the differences, but also what's gained by the sharing.

VYJAYANTHI RAO: Both your points are so valid that what we need to rethink is the place of expert knowledge, not doing away with expert knowledge. Because, there are all kinds of rapid prototyping tools that are available to "the public," and there's proliferation of design tools, but where do they all go?

AUDIENCE: This question of where do you go, or the idea that you have to think about how everybody's involved and about a collaboration, as well as the idea of inviting students into professional collaboration actually relates to the idea of "middle scale" that Deborah Gans mentioned. I was wondering if the panel could talk more about the middle scale. I think that's really interesting. What I find missing here about the middle scale is we've got the big picture and little picture. We don't have the picture in between.

DEBORAH GANS: I think that is serious, but the one thing that actually does play into your provocation has to do with time. Because scales of effect have to do with time. CUP is dealing with the issue of time, and it's going to achieve the middle scale over time because the educated citizen has an effect beyond the individual in terms of other educated citizens. Now, one of the things that gave me this idea was dealing with the landscape in New Orleans, because I think landscape architects and landscape planners really understand this because there's no such thing as an immediate landscape. It doesn't exist. And as it affects itself, it changes its scale, changes its complexity, and re-prototypes itself. So if you're looking for an analogue or a kind of metaphoric model, I would say look at "landscape" because of the element of time.

AUDIENCE: The one question following up on this, we keep framing it in terms of little and big, local and global, bottom-up and top-down; I wonder if it's not all "middle," and that if you look at the language that we use, if pedagogy is too big a word, I think there's still the observer and the observed, the colonial status of professional and amateur, of local wisdom versus educated knowledge. If we change the word from "teaching" and "learning" to just "learning," it is problematic because it de-institutionalizes the very institutions that run themselves based on the right to be teaching others. If you frame it as learning, than you immediately engage that "middle ground" which is at once political, specialized, because you do need special wisdom, but you have to think outside of your discipline, it's not just interdisciplinary collaboration. I would just propose that we just call it learning and that might take away that window of the observer versus the observed.

WOO: I'll just make two little windows here out of things that I have found useful in thinking about the role of education, design, and social movements. One is the work of Myles Horton and the Highlander School: He has a concept of the "long haul" and how arts and culture can develop a social infrastructure that engages people and a social movement for this long haul. And so you aren't always going to get an immediate result by the product that you produce, but you produce kind of a continuity of experience that eventually, like when the time is right, connects into a movement of social change, and you can actually then push everything forward. And when I talk about the two time scales that CUP is working on, I think one of them is really actively trying to think about this long haul framework. We're not getting to the massive change that I think all of us here probably want to see tomorrow, but it's building this larger network. The other thing specifically about education that has been inspirational to a lot of us at CUP is *The Ignorant Schoolmaster* by Jacques Ranciere, and the idea of the role of the teacher as taskmaster, someone who organizes the learning experience for everyone and pushes people to work together. That's the role of the teacher, much more than being a vessel of knowledge, and that's a part of what we do in our youth education programs. The folks that we have as the teaching designers frequently are people who don't have a lot of knowledge in the question that's being investigated. It's actually more interesting to have someone who's just an engaged educator or interesting designer work with the students and be learning alongside with them. We think there's something valuable that happens in that learning environment.

FREDERICK: I also want to just come back to this idea of "outcomes." Because we have to define what we're talking about when we look at outcomes. Are we looking at the big sea change, or are we looking at the steps in the process of that sea change? I think it's really important to define for ourselves what some of those benchmarks might be and how we can start to look at them. For example, for us with the toolkit, it's not that overnight every community is automatically involved in the design of their park, and we get fabulous new parks overnight. That's obviously not realistic. But if we can start to crack open a city agency or begin to see a different kind of receptivity towards this kind of work, that's a big first step. I think when we're talking about this work we have to be curious by what we mean by "the outcomes." Does the outcome always have to be framed as a product or a built object? Can it be framed as policy change or as culture change within city agencies or new kinds of knowledge, new kinds of understandings of the world?

RAO: What I find so interesting is that these processes that you all are speaking about involving communities are really global processes that one can find in numerous cities today. At least over the last decade, there has been an increasing interest in participation in design processes even if people don't quite perceive them as design processes. That's of great interest to me as an anthropologist who studies urban processes. The question in my collaborations with designers has been, what it means to study these processes that people are engaging in as design but without really quite naming it as design. Here I mean the distinction that Deborah Gans brought up between form and process, and another sort of dualism which is the relationship between form and content, and specifically the content of cultural meaning or of social life that is generated through these various forms. In anthropology today, the interesting thing that's come to the fore is a return to an engagement with material life. As Bruno Latour particularly points out, an engagement that was really embedded in an anthropology that was colonialist, imperialist, but one that looked at societies as pre-modern societies, labeled them as pre-modern and primitive, and really engaged them through the human/nonhuman material into sections. As the fields in which anthropologists have operated have changed radically and are things of the past, particularly due to the urban demographic revolution, even the phrase "the other" is rarely used in anthropology today. I do think that the whole explosion of urban life and the kind of symmetries that it establishes across the globe have something to do with this changing vocabulary. I've been collaborating with my colleagues whose work ranges from product design to urban planning scale, and my focus in that has primarily been on trying to understand how my research methods can be transformed in the process. The notion of participation is of great interest because the primary method of anthropologists is ethnography, and more specifically its participant observation. And there's something mystical about participant observation: Nobody really quite knows what it is. In deconstructing this term, we are wondering what they mean by "participant observation?" How can you be both at the same time? Of course, the fact of the matter is that the discipline presumes a split between observer and observed, a critical distance between the two in order to facilitate the production of knowledge. So let me just briefly speak specifically about new forms of knowledge that might emerge in collaborative processes where that divide is pushed in particular ways. The new design initiatives that focus on participatory learning and user participation in the design process were very well exemplified by the presentations today: For example, pedagogical initiatives that involve urban youth potentially challenge and transform this traditional observer/observed relationship between the anthropologist and her subjects. How then should anthropology respond to these challenges? Our question was whether or not research into "the anthropology of design" or an "anthropology of design practices" can affect the design of anthropology's method of ethnographic observation and representation. The second related question concerns the fields of change in our subjects' lives: How might design practice enable our subjects to understand change differently, how might certain design practices help them to understand change as an open-ended process rather than one geared toward efficiency and problematizing? And also, toward an equivalence between development, productivity, and good citizenship?

One aspect that anthropology brings to that conversation is how we can dislodge that commitment without losing the ethical impact of that opposition. One of the ways to do that would be to turn to the literature within anthropology that has problematized the development and transfer of technology. Anthropologists often operate in conditions of flux and change. The modernizing process itself has provided the most fertile of research fields. Designers are implicated quite explicitly in that process. What happens when the subjects of that process become designers themselves, as all of you are suggesting through the participatory method? How might anthropologists study their subjects as they themselves become active participants rather than recipients of the processes under study? These ethical questions can be fruitfully brought to the design table as it were to critique ideas of intervention for its own sake. For instance, in a course I cotaught with two colleagues from Parsons, we literally had a Mason Dixon Line: We had a serious divide over the question of intervention, with anthropologists falling on the critique side and designers falling on the practice side, or in other words, on the side of knowledge whose implicit norms are sensible to practitioners within the field without requiring explicit critical analysis. This was my interpretation of the divide. That the designers seemed to be invoking a kind of knowledge practice in which there is a set of norms, but it is implicit and sensible to the practitioners, while for the anthropologists it's always a matter of distance and critique and a constant reflection on the content. The reason for this divide might also be that the practice of anthropology has been committed to a certain ontological stability of its subject. It always begins with the apprehension of what is there, and a commitment to what is, rather than what can be, or what might be, and the processes that would involve that becoming. So that's the observation part of that "participant observation" hyphen. You are really referring to an object that seems to be there, even if you critique the ways in which it has come into being from a retrospective historical–critical practice that so far has been dominant within the discipline. The other interesting thing is that other professions, like law or medicine, have a codified set of ethical norms: for instance, the Hippocratic Oath. The anthropology students in my seminar were constantly asking the question, "Where does design rest in relation to such a code? What is your code for intervention? Are there any sort of limits? And how do you come up with those limits?" Because often they saw their design colleagues as just parachuting into situations and producing various kinds of prototypes and interventions. The populations that designers interact with are rarely defined *a priori*, but they seem to emerge in the design process itself. This was one of the discoveries of the seminar and I think that the work discussed earlier precisely speaks to this point, that it is a community of the future, and it is a community that is produced in the process.

I think one way to think about the intervention process is to foreground the sort of *becoming* quality of what might come into being from those intersections. The interpretation of intervention actually brings us closer to the ethical struggles of anthropology as a discipline whose subjects are also always defined in process, despite the fact that they do have a kind of ontological commitment to the community that is being studied. The evolving relationship between design and anthropology as it has emerged in my own collaborations could be summarized by making a tentative connection between processes of *understanding* and of *making sense*, that is, making sense as a way of producing knowledge. These connected processes are often disconnected in my own disciplinary field. Working with designers has revealed the multiple meanings and the richness of the phrase "making sense," of producing understanding through an involvement of the senses and the media forms through which our senses are constructed. *Making sense* and *making sensible* also foregrounds a broader and more inchoate field of knowledge whose norms are sensed and felt in processes of designing rather than brought to light through explicit and relentless critique. As an anthropologist, I think about design as itself a process of knowledge generation rather than as a consequence and reflection of scientific protocols of knowledge production. The movement from participant observation and ethnographic techniques to engaging explicitly in collaboration with designers has actually foregrounded another thing, which is thinking about knowledge through making propositions in the world, and using the whole idea of the prototype as a tool of research. So there's this kind of iterative process, as it were, becoming a research tool instead of working as anthropologists have done in the past with *a priori* constructed conceptual models which have a coherent relationship to reality as it emerges through the process of knowledge generation. So that was I would say the big shift in my own thinking.

[. . .] In the panelists' work I also found that there was a call to recognize self-organization as a model, particularly as a model for architects to take into account. This led to a number of speculations and a whole set of inversions where you are now looking at a city like Belgrade or Mumbai from the point of view of the slum and not from the point of view of the supposed normative form. This shift is necessary because in these cities this condition has spread to such an extent that it calls into question really the relationship between what is *normal* and what is *normative*, in relation to what is on the ground and how we deal with it. The second set of inversions has to do with the relationship between legality and illegality, which is again reversed in this whole explosion of the so-called informal forms of building. Formality is nothing more really than a condition that exists only dialectically with regulation, so that we can only understand it in relation to regulation but we can't actually conceive of that relationship as being no longer illicit. In the first place, you have a set of conditions which if they were looked through the lens of being problems, then you would have to conclude that these conditions are illicit. But once you remove that lens of the problematic, there's something very productive that opens up. And this is the relationship to regulation and what these forms are doing with regulation. When the planner becomes a hunter, as the STEALTH group suggests, and researching becomes an activity of discovering of processes that are no longer viewed as exotic but as conditions that are establishing relationships to existing or original conditions, we then begin to see what can be done with regulation. I find very provocative the STEALTH group's question whether "found processes" can become more sophisticated through support. Once we no longer think of this as a problem, then we get out of the logic of emergency life support as we see such conditions as becoming increasingly normal, to discover their genetic codes, to map them as atlases of forms, and to speculate through them. I also found it very interesting that there's an inevitable kind of logic of capitalist urban development in cities like Belgrade and Bombay, but mapping out the possibilities for capital investment can direct you to places where you can speculate on urban growth. That's exactly what has happened in Mumbai with an instrument called "tradable development rights," where in exchange for slum development and building social housing, private developers actually get to use space as a currency, they get to trade it and build on another plot or another building, often by putting like an exoskeleton and mutating existing buildings. In this way, space is mobilized through such currencies through the entire city. That's one form of speculation. The other form of speculation would be to think of architecture that ought to confront these conditions not as problems but as norms after they have somehow established new normative standards.

RADIKA SUBRAMANIAM: I am thinking about another discursive frame, that of translation and whether that might be another way to enter this discussion of design and the transfer of knowledge. I'm thinking of Vyjayanthi's very illuminating discussion about the Mason-Dixon line between design and ethnography. One of the interesting debates in this culture that has come out of the anthropological notion of cultural translation, and also linguistic translation, which gives us that attention not only to the form of the thing as well as the content of the thing: That is, you must transfer not only meaning, but you must transfer some active sensuous sense of the original, and that also allows us to pay attention to the fact that things, objects, communities, people, are created in that process of translation. One of anthropology's greatest legacies is that people have been created precisely in the process of that monographing, no?

ANA DZOKIC: If you observe the process of street vending in Belgrade in the 1990s, you find out that through the process people who lived in a secured social system that has failed have changed their view of what is possible and what they can do about it. By going out to the streets, they became more engaged with the reality of the city. When you speak with people who were office workers earlier and then made a living as street vendors, they tell you that they will never again go back to work in an office. So through this process of transformation, the physical transformation of the city is as much at stake as the process of change for the people who instigated the process in the first place.

RAO: Can I just add one thing to this, the STEALTH group's observation about these conditions jumping out at them because they were bypassing the architects. So this to me has a very, very sort of poignant ring insofar as it's all about the status of expert knowledge, which I think as Ivan Kucina was pointing out, it's not necessarily Western, so it's not outside of the discourse of Western urbanism at all, nor has it ever been from its conception.

DZOKIC: For us as educators working in academic settings with students, the impact that these kinds of projects have on students is very important. In the project Ivan Kucina was working on in Belgrade, for example, students would otherwise really not get in touch with thinking about their own city. When we worked on the project about Roma settlements across Europe, the TU Delft students who were involved in that project and working on the site in Rome were deeply impacted by having spent three weeks engaging with the Roma community. I think that such an impact should not be underestimated and that you get different kinds of professionals after these kinds of hands-on experiences. Equally, our Wild City project changed students' view on the processes of spatial production in the city.

IVAN KUCINA: Let me say a few words about the Roma project from last year. Students from Rome and Delft were involved in the research projects on the Roma case studies in Italy. Given that many of the Roma people living in Rome came from Serbia, they visited Belgrade in order to conduct research and understand how the Roma culture has spread across Europe. I joined the group together with my own graduate students from the Faculty of Architecture at the University of Belgrade, as well as with a group of students from KTH Stockholm. A group of fifty students of twenty different nationalities travelled together for about ten days visiting Roma settlements and camps, talking to people and trying to understand their ways of life. The number of Roma people in Europe is estimated to be around fifteen million, even though official census data indicates that number to be three times lower. Roma see themselves as a nation without state and without national institutions. Their culture is nomadic and in many ways has been formed through the reflections on their host cultures over centuries of existence in Europe. They have absorbed and amalgamated elements of different cultural and economic models and have somehow produced a recognizable Roma way of life as a mirror of the social and cultural norms that govern Europe. What we learned in the process is that most of the European countries that discriminate Roma people in fact discriminate their own mirror image. The European Union founded the Roma Decade (2005–2015), initially as a collaboration between twelve European governments that attempted to deal with "the Roma problem" in a top-down manner. By institutionalizing the Roma problem, they expected to find solutions, which in most cases resulted in semi-temporary social housing schemes. We asked, why is it that we are not able to do something else? We framed our project as a learning challenge, that of accumulating the knowledge and finding the way to intervene in the volatile social structure of the Roma. However, what we discovered was that, in many significant ways, Roma are much more advanced than the host societies: For example, the most advanced strategies as well as tactics that came out of the lessons of information technology and networked society have actually been a fundamental part of the Roma life for centuries. We thus approached them as a creative community we need to learn from in four major categories of urban knowledge and urbanist practice: integration (antidiscrimination), sustainability, self-organization, and contentment. Self-organization presented to us new ways of understanding both community and society, and avoiding the conventional top-down and bottom-up view of social processes, while contentment related to a particular kind of activism characteristic for the Roma people and their ability to inhabit in the present creatively. In addition to these four categories, we also discovered and mapped out a set of rules that transgressed national boundaries and shaped the daily life in Roma communities across different urban geographies. We created a series of urban strategies, tactics, and scenarios, and have used the tools invented or discovered in the Roma project to understand and intervene in other situations and other locales beyond Roma settlements. For example, in our Wild City project, we employed them to frame a situation of profound institutional, economic, and political crisis in Serbia when the entire society most literally collapsed and the adequate urban survival strategies were the only way to stay afloat, both for individual citizens and for urban communities. This newly faced situation grounded in extremes had created for us a field open to producing new models of understanding, new urbanist instruments and tools, all based on the lessons learned from studying the creative praxis of the Roma community. The significance of this work is that the Roma have become both the metaphor and the operational model for organizing many urban communities across the world living in the situation of ongoing economic precarity, political instability, lack of governmental support, and absence of public services.

Chapter 5

Hester Street Collaborative: Developing a Model for Community-Led Design

Anne Frederick

In 1998, East New York Urban Youth Corps (ENYUYC), an affordable housing developer in Brooklyn's neighborhood of East New York, sought to engage the future tenants of a new building on Sutter Avenue in the process of designing its ground floor. The space was slated to become a community center that extended into an outdoor public courtyard. The architecture firm Leroy Street Studio was invited to facilitate the residents' participation in envisioning and creating these community spaces. Each week, a team of volunteer artists and architects hosted art and design workshops. Local children regularly flooded the courtyard to carve and fire clay tiles, develop color palettes, sketch plans of the building, mix concrete, sculpt ferrocement planters, and lay out mosaics. The energy and joy of making was contagious, and the result was a transformation of what would have been a bare, institutional space into a radiant community area that reflects the creative vision and personality of the residents.

In 2002, Hester Street Collaborative was founded by the partners in the Leroy Street Studio. The studio moved to Hester Street in the Lower East Side (LES) after the events of September 11, 2001 brought the professional architectural practice to a halt. It was a moment of reflection during which the studio worked to reimagine its professional design practice as one more acutely oriented towards catalyzing social change. We began on the premise that creative community engagement is a powerful tool for community-led change, and looked back at the ENY experience to shape our approach to the entire lifecycle of each future project, starting with how such opportunities were identified.

We discovered that it was essential for a community-led design project to be initiated by a deeply rooted community-based organization. By the time we joined the ENY project, ENYUYC had already cultivated relationships with the future residents through social and cultural programming. It was this organization that had identified an opportunity for deeper engagement with the future residents, leading to the creation of participatory workshops for the design of shared spaces. ENYUYC had developed the high degree of trust with the members of the community and the developer that was necessary for the project to succeed. Coming from the outside, our relationships with the residents relied fully on having an established grassroots partner that understood local needs and opportunities.

Once we successfully completed the ENY project and decided to grow our practice in the direction of community-led design transformation, we did not know how to begin our next project without an explicit invitation by a grassroots partner. We decided to visit the principal of the Dr. Sun Yat Sen Middle School (M.S. 131) across Hester Street to ask what opportunities for community development were present. The principal emphasized the importance of being committed and reliable if we were to initiate a program with their school. She had seen many well-intentioned partners come and go to the detriment of the students' learning experiences. We decided to make a commitment to a long-term partnership with the school. Our partnership with M.S. 131 started small, with one class of students making hands-on collaborative improvements to the shared spaces in the school building. Based on this experience, we initiated the design education program Ground Up. We developed Ground Up to involve larger groups of students in projects that visibly and measurably improve their school campus and community spaces. As in the ENY project, we witnessed the pleasure of cocreating and participating in a hands-on making and building process that kept students coming back week after week. Students explored materials, developed tactile experiences through making, and ultimately, collectively created lasting transformations of their school. Thus, another principle of our community-based design process was solidified: All of our projects would involve hands-on, tactile experiences that make participation and codesigning accessible to people of all ages and linguistic abilities.

In 2004, when the Hester Street Playground in Sara D. Roosevelt Park (in the vicinity of M.S. 131 and our offices) was slated for reconstruction, we organized student participation in the capital redesign and in making a permanent mosaic installation for the playground. The park, a 7.8-acre (32,000 m^2) space measuring three blocks in size, stretches north-south between East Houston Street on the Lower East Side and Canal Street in Chinatown, and between Chrystie Street to the west and Forsyth Street to the east. The park is operated and maintained by the New York City Department of Parks and Recreation (NYC Parks). Through the process of working on the playground with students, children, and residents from the neighborhood, we also began our long-term relationship with NYC Parks. The department has a very complex internal structure and is responsible for maintaining the city's parks system, preserving and maintaining the ecological diversity of the metropolitan natural areas, and providing recreational opportunities for the city's nine million residents and over fifty million visitors.[1] It maintains a total area of over 29,000 acres (113 km^2), or fourteen percent of the total area of New York City,[2] which includes over 1,700 parks, playgrounds, and recreation facilities across the five boroughs.

We quickly realized that NYC Parks did not have the resources to do the kind of in-depth community engagement that had been so effective in the ENY project and in the projects at M.S. 131. Besides, public agencies do not collaborate and partner with individuals and communities; their constituencies are the registered civic and citizen organizations that represent the views and vested interest of some citizens. Official protocols for participation in the decision-making processes consist of town hall-style meetings and community board meetings. Even with the more recent online tools, digital platforms, and social media, the experience of community participation tends to consist of a few touch points where community stakeholders share their input with decision makers within a typical discursive format. Such traditional opportunities for feedback are important and necessary, but it is also useful to qualitatively distinguish input-gathering opportunities from the processes of creative engagement. Input gathering tends to be one-directional, difficult to qualify, and impossible to trace all the way to final designs and policies. We saw an opportunity to implement a design process that would foster greater local ownership for the participants and result in a more responsive design. We conceived of our agency as creating the bridge between, on the one hand, NYC Parks and other public agencies, and on the other, the communities and constituencies they serve. The hands-on creative making process we put forth is qualitatively different from traditional input gathering: Making and building prototypes and models is iterative, process-oriented, reassuring, and highly rewarding, because participants can directly experience the results of their efforts in a tangible outcome, be it a prototype of a communal facility or a policy proposal. An iterative process is a process of learning, working with others, and negotiating the issues that matter and stand at the heart of the community. Codesigning is capable of developing skills and relationships equally; it strengthens ties between community members as well as between the community and city administrators. Through working side by side, an acute understanding that the whole team needs to collaborate for the project to be realized is developed.

Our approach to the design process embeds critical issues of social justice, inclusion, and cultural equity into the practice of making public spaces. Therefore, our design process is attuned to issues of inequity in the distribution of decision-making powers and driven by the goals of those who stand to be affected and yet are not included. On the other hand, since there is no such thing as "community consensus" on key issues, and no right or wrong decisions when one works on complex social and communal challenges, we employ adesign process to simultaneously internalize the embedded contradictions and likewise create a space for the inclusive, community decision-making processes. We employ our participatory tool kits, design charrettes, and visioning sessions in order to engage all stakeholders who take part in these events on an equal footing.

By summer 2004, local community organizations and individual residents had already organized themselves into the Sara D. Roosevelt Coalition and were committed to having a greater role in the design of the new playground. We worked closely with the Coalition and NYC Parks to shape a design process that would be inclusive, accessible, and engaging for all the members of the community. Since young children, recent Chinese immigrants, seniors, and teenagers were all using the playground in different ways and at different times, our challenge was to create a series of design-led workshops that would effectively and playfully unearth, visualize, and channel everyone's aspirations for the park.

Our work at the Hester Street Playground in Sara D. Roosevelt Park led to similar local park-related projects at the Allen and Pike Street Pedestrian Malls, on the East River Waterfront, and in Luther Gulick Park. At the Allen and Pike Street Malls, we experimented with creating a large-scale, temporary installation entitled the "Avenue of the Immigrants" (Figures 5.1 and 5.2). Residents nominated people and places significant for the history of the area, and also for the current immigrant communities living in the Lower East Side. It was conceived of and made with our community partners and students from M.S. 131. The installation mapped community history and identity onto a public space and helped our coalition draw attention to the larger capital-improvement goals for the site. As we became involved in more parks capital-improvement projects, we found ourselves struggling to design a consistent protocol for the community engagement process. While NYC Parks and the local Community Board 3 had official touch points for community input, we saw the potential for a more in-depth civic and community engagement process which could have a meaningful impact on the redesign of the park. Encountering similar challenges across several projects and sites helped us to identify a systemic need to increase both transparency and access to the capital process. With the Partnerships for Parks, we formed an initiative called People Make Parks to develop and implement a toolkit for participation in the NYC Parks' capital process (Figure 5.3). People Make Parks is a set of tools and a timeline that builds capacity for community engagement within NYC Parks' official capital process while also ensuring that community needs are being authentically met. Through the process of developing People Make Parks, we learned that in order to be effective we needed to bring stakeholders and decision-makers together, and we needed to understand how

◀ Figure 5.1

Avenue of the Immigrants
© HSC archives.

▶ Figure 5.2

Avenue of the Immigrants
© HSC archives.

▼ Figure 5.3

People Make Parks Toolkit
© HSC archives.

CHAPTER 5 Hester Street Collaborative   65

to navigate the official decision-making protocols. In 2008, we began to formalize our model of inclusive participatory design and advocate for it citywide.

Over the course of working on the above projects, a distinct approach, a set of tools and a new methodology have emerged. We found that the deeper hands-on engagement was often difficult to secure approvals for and that there was still a need to reach a broader set of constituents than NYC Parks had the capacity to engage. Also, it was important to create more opportunities for gathering input, and to work with NYC Parks to make the existing channels for input more inclusive. By creating tools for engaging youth and recent immigrants and translating materials into Spanish and Chinese, we could reach more people. By partnering with local organizations, we could bring their constituents to the table. In addition to the more traditional feedback meetings, we organized engaging events in parks slated for capital projects in order to bring the process closer to the community and meet people where they gather, play, and relax. This model of bringing our design-led process into informal urban spaces of community gathering became a key strategy for our work.

In 2007, The Lower East Side Waterfront Alliance[3] was organized to address concerns about the city's proposal for development at the East River Waterfront. The original coalition members[4] focused on the section of the East River Waterfront below the East River Park and above the South Street Seaport. We focused our attention on formerly industrial piers 35, 36, and 42, where the bulk of the open space on this section of the waterfront is located. The original East River Waterfront development proposal included luxury housing and a high-end retail development adjacent to one of the largest swaths of public housing in Manhattan. Many residents were concerned that the proposed development would further exacerbate the gentrification of the neighborhood and that the renovated waterfront would not serve the needs of the largely low-income communities that live in the public housing nearby. In a meeting with two Alliance members (CAAAV and GOLES), after one contentious community board meeting, we were invited by those organizations to work with the Alliance to develop an alternative and more responsive plan. Our partners in the Alliance mobilized their members and constituencies to voice their concerns about the proposal, and we worked with them to envision an alternative set of recommendations. We conducted research about the history of the waterfront and organized participatory charrettes and visioning sessions. In our research, we highlighted the history of land use decision-making at the waterfront, to help community members understand how the often opaque city processes had shaped their waterfront to date. We worked with membership-based organizations in the coalition to create multilingual input-gathering sessions tailored to their members and constituencies. The result was a report entitled the People's Plan for the East River Waterfront,[5] which encapsulated the local communities' concerns and aspirations for the waterfront (Figure 5.4).

As we had learned from our other park-related work, creating a set of recommendations was not enough. In order to sustain a community-driven capital campaign we needed to support the grassroots efforts to translate our findings and recommendations into a tangible reality (Figure 5.5). Because there was no capital funding in place for the recommendations, it was necessary for community

▲ Figure 5.4

People's Plan for the East River Waterfront © HSC archives.

▲ Figure 5.5

Socio-demographic map of the East River Waterfront © HSC archives.

CHAPTER 5 Hester Street Collaborative

◀ Figure 5.6

People's Plan poster campaign
© HSC archives.

members to stay focused on this site. To advocate for the recommendations in the People's Plan, we developed a neighborhood-wide poster campaign: We photographed residents from the surrounding communities on the existing waterfront line and created posters illustrating their aspirations for the waterfront (Figures 5.6, 5.7 and 5.8). In addition to creating a poster campaign to advocate for the recommendations in the People's Plan, we identified the need to further articulate design recommendations for Pier 42, the largest undeveloped section of the piers. The recommendations in the People's Plan laid out an overall site strategy for the broader waterfront site, but had not developed a propcsal for Pier 42 in greater detail. By liaising with our elected officials, NYC Parks, and

▶ Figure 5.7

People's Plan poster campaign
© HSC archives.

the local Community Board 3, we began to develop a strategy that would both advocate for funding for the capital improvement of Pier 42 and further articulate design recommendations. We created a traveling model of the waterfront called the Waterfront on Wheels (Figures 5.9 and 5.10). The Waterfront on Wheels was attached to the back of a bike trailer and traveled to parks, community meetings, schools, and other venues to bring a participatory design process for Pier 42 out into the communities implicated in this development project. The Waterfront on Wheels was used to visualize and discuss the waterfront, and to create a site in which to set alternative, community-built models of Pier 42. Because the Pier 42 section of the model was removable, community-designed models were

CHAPTER 5 Hester Street Collaborative

69

◀ Figure 5.8

People's Plan poster campaign © HSC archives.

inserted into the larger model to be viewed in context. We analyzed the community-built models to identify programmatic ideas for the site, which we then shared with NYC Parks.

Building on these advocacy efforts, our local elected officials were successful in allocating US$14 million in capital funds for the first phase of the improvements to Pier 42. However, NYC Parks has estimated that the full renovation will require between US$40-US$60 million. Our Alliance decided that it was important in the interim to be able to reclaim this site as a resource for the community, to continue to provide a place for residents to access the waterfront, and also to continue to draw attention to the site and advocate for

▶ Figure 5.9

Waterfront on Wheels © HSC archives.

▼ Figure 5.10

Waterfront on Wheels © HSC archives.

the full capital improvement. The site presented an ideal opportunity to do the kind of community-built intervention that we had employed in ENY and at other park sites; however, it also presented a much more complex environment than we had ever worked on before. The challenge was to build the capacity to develop a larger site with a small leading team, very limited resources, and a largely volunteer staff.

In 2012, we worked with our Alliance partners to develop Paths to Pier 42, a program for activating a section of that pier (Figure 5.11). We partnered with the Lower Manhattan Cultural Council to create the temporary park at Pier 42. In the process of developing this interim site we worked closely with NYC Parks to secure approvals and scrutinize our proposals, and we also brought along Leroy Street Studio and dlandstudio to develop an overall site strategy and landscape approach. Five site-specific art and design installations were commissioned for the site in the summer of 2013, and we also developed public programming for the new park. An advisory committee composed of local residents, tenant leaders, public art administrators, NYC Parks representatives, and many others was convened to help oversee the entire Paths to Pier 42

▼ **Figure 5.11**

Paths to Pier 42 development over the summer of 2013
© HSC archives.

process. The team of artists and designers was asked to develop a process for engaging community members in the creation of their art and design installations. Over the course of installing their work, a series of community-build days was integrated into the construction schedule (Figures 5.12, 5.13, and 5.14).

The work on Pier 42 in many ways is a return to the roots of HSC: Because the project is outside of an official capital process, we have the ability to foster the type of hands-on creative engagement that was so successful in all of our projects. At Pier 42, we have also learned that working on a larger scale requires additional partners with specific expertise and capacity to execute the project

▼ Figure 5.12

Paths to Pier 42 © HSC archives.

▶ Figure 5.13

Paths to Pier 42 © HSC archives.

CHAPTER 5 Hester Street Collaborative

◀ Figure 5.14

Paths to Pier 42 © HSC archives.

successfully. Many artists and designers are looking for opportunities to do truly engaging and critical community-based work, but often lack the relationships or experience of working with grassroots organizations. In working closely with community-based organizations in New York City, we have built meaningful relationships between local organizations and public agencies, partnered with artists and designers who brought their knowledge to address community-based initiatives, and created design processes through which all of them can be engaged. We see our role as a bridge builder, facilitator, and critical instigator channeling the talents of artists and designers to effectively address community identified needs, working alongside communities to visualize and articulate their self-identified needs for public spaces, integrate more opportunities for youth and community participation, and leverage urban redevelopment as a catalyst for building deeper community connections.

Notes

1. For reference see: www.nycgo.com/articles/nyc-statistics-page (Last accessed on February 15, 2015).
2. For reference see: www.nycgovparks.org/about (Last accessed on February 15, 2015).
3. The Lower East Side Waterfront Alliance was formerly the O.U.R. Waterfront Coalition.
4. The original coalition members included: CAAAV: Organizing Asian Communities, Good Old Lower East Side (GOLES), Public Housing Residents of the Lower East Side (PHROLES), Two Bridges Neighborhood Council (TBNC), the Lower East Side Ecology Center, Urban Justice Center/Community Development Project, University Settlement, Jews for Racial and Economic Justice, and Hester Street Collaborative.
5. The document can be downloaded from: www.urbanjustice.org/pdf/publications/peoples_plan.pdf (Last accessed on February 15, 2015).

Chapter 6

Images of the City: The Work of the Center for Urban Pedagogy

Christine Gaspar

The Center for Urban Pedagogy (CUP) is a nonprofit organization based in New York City and committed to the role design can play in making public policy and urban planning accessible to the residents they impact. Every day, the staff of CUP and our collaborators translate hard-to-understand public policy into visual explanations that help the average person understand the complicated systems and forces that shape their communities. Each project is produced and distributed in the context of grassroots community organizing and advocacy, thus laying the foundation for more effective democratic participation, particularly among historically underrepresented communities.

The group that would eventually become CUP was initially formed in 1997 as a collective of recent college graduates with backgrounds in architecture, graphic design, government, art, and public policy.[1] The first projects were personally driven investigations into different aspects of how the city works. Some of the group's projects resulted in exhibitions and publications, such as the 2001 *Building Codes: The Programmable City* exhibition held at The Storefront for Art and Architecture. The *Building Codes* exhibit focused on the history of New York City's building regulations, and in some ways marked an important turning point for CUP's work. The exhibit contained many clues about the way CUP's working methods would evolve in the coming years as the organization matured and developed consistent programs and program areas. The reliance on extensive, multidisciplinary collaborations, including with young people and community organizers; the use of techniques like interviews to reflect multiple perspectives; and the incorporation of visual and hands-on educational materials would all continue to form the core of CUP's work. However, as the organization began to shape ongoing programs and new projects, it would focus more on how to make the projects useful to communities who could benefit from the information, and use it in their own organizing work. In the last seven years, the focus on social justice became more explicit, and what began in the realm of art with political content would move more clearly towards popular education.

Today, CUP's mission is to use the power of design and art to increase meaningful civic engagement, particularly among historically underrepresented communities. To that end, CUP's work comprises two program areas: Youth

Education, in which we work with New York City public high school students in low-income communities; and Community Education, in which we work with grassroots organizations in many of the same communities. Though the two program areas are distinct, they intersect often and are unified by the collaborations that shape them and the projects they produce. This chapter will focus more closely on one aspect of the Community Education programs, namely on the Envisioning Development Toolkits (Table 6.1) that organizers use to train their constituents about urban development issues. For example, the toolkit *What Is Affordable Housing?*, described in detail in what follows, has helped a number of urban communities understand the complex technical aspects of current housing policies.

In 2005, CUP began to work with an informal advisory board of grassroots organizations to produce what would become the Envisioning Development Toolkit series (Figures 6.1 and 6.2). The idea was to create hands-on, visual, and tactile workshop tools that community organizers could use to educate their constituents. The information would be easier to understand, easier to remember, and would increase the impact and effectiveness of organizing work. The advisory board originally identified three perennial and challenging topics for the toolkits: affordable housing policy, zoning law, and the land use review process in New York City.

Many use the term "affordable housing" informally, but it means different things to different people. In fact, the federal government provides its own definition, which is adopted into state and local laws, and determines what kind of housing gets built and who gets to live in it. The federal government's definition of affordability has two parts, both of which are shown on the felt chart that is the central component of CUP's first toolkit, *What Is Affordable Housing?* (Figure 6.3). The first part is that housing costs are considered affordable if they make up less than thirty percent of household income. The colored bar

▼ Table 6.1 An overview of CUP's programs.

YOUTH EDUCATION	COMMUNITY EDUCATION
Urban Investigations are semester-long intensive research projects in which students ask a question about how the city works, interview key stakeholders, and work with a teaching artist to produce an educational tool that makes that issue accessible. For example, in *Share, Where?* students from the South Bronx created an illustrated guide to New York City's Fair Share policy, how it works, and where it has failed.	Making Policy Public is CUP's poster series, in which grassroots groups propose a complex policy issue that their community is struggling with, and CUP collaborates with them and a designer to break the topic down into a graphically-based fold-out poster. For example, *What's in the Water?* explains how hydraulic fracturing works and its potential impacts on NYC's drinking water.
City Studies are shorter projects that use research and design to look at a current social justice or civics issue. For example, in Voters Rule, students who are recent immigrants made a pamphlet about voter eligibility rules.	Public Access Design also breaks down issues into visuals in partnership with a community organization and a designer, but is helps Spanish-speaking day laborers avoid wage theft.
Teacher Trainings are professional development sessions in which we train educators to use our project-based learning methods in their own classrooms.	Envisioning Development is a series of hands-on workshop tools that organizers can use to train their constituents about development issues. For example, *What Is Affordable Housing?* helps communities understand the technical aspects of housing policies.
Curriculum Development is production of curriculum guides to help educators use CUP projects in their own classroom settings.	Technical Assistance projects are custom tools that CUP develops on a fee-for-service basis with organizing and advocacy groups.

◀ Figure 6.1

What is Zoning toolkit © CUP archives.

◀ Figure 6.2

What is Zoning toolkit © CUP archives.

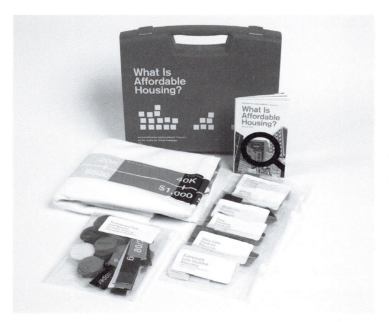

◀ Figure 6.3

What is Affordable Housing toolkit © CUP archives.

in the center of the chart shows annual household income on the top line, with the corresponding affordable monthly housing costs on the bottom line. Workshop participants are often familiar with this definition, but the chart reinforces the visual link between income and expense. The second part of the definition is more complicated. The U.S. Department of Housing and Urban Development (HUD) organizes families into different income ranges, which are later used to define affordability levels for different affordability programs. The chart shows these categories in the form of colored bands along the rent/income bar. The categories range from "Extremely Low Income" to "High Income." Because income levels and housing costs range considerably across the country, HUD tries to define the ranges of these income categories in relation to the local economy. It does so by calculating a regional income level that marks the centerline in the income distribution. The income categories are then calculated as percentages of that income level.

More specifically, HUD calculates the median family income (MFI) for a family of four in a metropolitan area, and then calls all of the incomes below thirty percent of the MFI "Extremely Low Income," incomes from thirty to fifty percent "Very Low Income," and so forth, across the full spectrum of income levels. In New York City, the current median family income for a family of four is $83,900.[2] The chart makes all of these calculations visible, so that workshop participants do not need to memorize the figures and ranges, but rather can see how they play out visually. This helps them build a mental map of how the policy works, on which they can draw later from memory (Figures 6.4—6.8).

Once participants understand income and rent costs, the workshop facilitator helps them look at what this means in their own neighborhood. The toolkit includes a table showing the number of families of four in each of the income categories, in each neighborhood in New York City, as well as each borough, and the city as a whole (Figure 6.9).[3] Workshop leaders use that data to help participants build a histogram of neighborhood income demographics by placing colored felt squares on the chart that corresponds with the number of families in each category (1 square = 1,000 families of four). This process always generates extensive discussions of how the chart reflects individuals' perception of the neighborhood (Figures 6.10 and 6.11).

To address the cost side of the affordability equation, facilitators ask participants how much it costs to rent an apartment in the neighborhood: first a 1-bedroom, then a 2-bedroom, and finally a 3-bedroom. This allows participants to draw on their own knowledge of the area, and also gives them a chance to discuss a range of perspectives to come up with an agreed upon number. Once rent is placed on the board, a large disparity is revealed between the number of people living in the neighborhood in the low-income levels and the cost of even a 1-bedroom unit (Figure 6.7). Participants are asked to explain what is happening, and usually manage to come up with several factors. The commonly identified reasons are: Some residents live in old or substandard units that charge below market rate; some live in units with grandfathered rents that have not gone up; some live in subsidized units of various sorts; some residents double up (while this is true, this would not be reflected in the numbers since only families of four are counted); and, many residents live in units that are

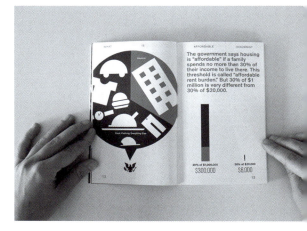

◀ Figure 6.4

What is Affordable Housing booklet © CUP archives.

▲ Figure 6.5

What is Affordable Housing booklet © CUP archives.

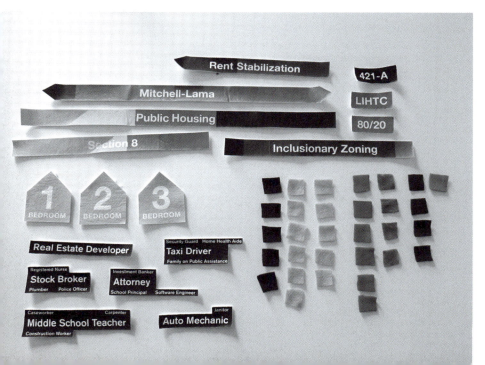

◀ Figure 6.6

What is Affordable Housing kit components © CUP archives.

▲ Figure 6.7

What Is Affordable Housing kit components © CUP archives.

◀ Figure 6.8

What Is Affordable Housing workshop run by a community organizer © CUP archives.

▼ Figure 6.9

What Is Affordable Housing workshop © CUP archives.

◀ Figure 6.10

What Is Affordable Housing workshop © CUP archives.

simply unaffordable by HUD's definition. In NYC, more than half of renters pay over thirty percent of their income in rent. One of the ways people are able to stay in a neighborhood they cannot afford is through affordable housing programs.

The next step in the workshop is to look at different affordability programs available and see how they correspond to the different populations and income levels. Facilitators ask residents to name programs, and then what they know about them. Public housing and Section 8 are the most familiar, and eventually more contemporary, market-based programs like tax credits and inclusionary zoning are addressed.[4] The overall dynamic one sees is that older programs tended to make housing available to lower-income residents more than current programs do, and that many of the city's older programs are expiring and losing units quickly. Participants discuss the trade-offs in these programs and begin to understand the importance of asking for affordability in specific income ranges

◀ Figure 6.11

What Is Affordable Housing workshop © CUP archives.

and for permanent affordability. Much of the workshop takes the form of discussions among participants and it is clear in every workshop that individuals come away with a deep understanding of housing policy and its manifestations in their neighborhoods and everyday lives.

Process and Methodology

Each CUP project begins with the team of collaborators—consisting of CUP staff, designers, and community organizers or advocates—working to understand the policy issue raised by the community partner. All CUP projects are produced through collaborations with three sets of participants: local communities, visual thinkers, and CUP staff.[5] Together, we work to understand the information and to develop a product that uses visuals to explain that issue in an accessible way, and that will ultimately be distributed to the community members who need that information. These products range from posters, booklets, and pamphlets to short documentaries, animations, web sites, interactive graphics, and hands-on workshop tools. We select the medium based on what is most appropriate for each topic, context, and audience. The methods CUP has developed over time place a strong emphasis on ensuring that every project in which we invest resources has a real impact. We do this, first, by collaborating directly with community organizations on topics that are important to them, which ensures that our collaboration will be relevant and useful to their communities. We also work directly with these constituents throughout the design process to ensure that the work responds to their specific needs, that the information conveyed is clear, and that the design resonates with them.

In the Youth Education programs, the goal is for young people in communities impacted by social injustice to understand that their community's problems are not naturally occurring, but are the products of decision-making. They learn that they can hold decision makers accountable. The experience helps reframe their perception of the city, helping them find pathways to civic engagement, while also giving them hard skills in interviewing, research, art-making, and collaboration. Most importantly, the projects take the natural cynicism of young people and develop it into critical thinking. In our Community Education programs, we focus on creating educational tools that increase the capacity of community organizers and advocates to do their work. The tools educate constituents using accessible, easy to understand graphics and text, and empower them to advocate for their own community needs. Through these programs, we work to increase the number of people in historically under-represented communities who are able to influence the decision-making that impacts their lives, in the moments that matter most to them.

CUP's projects range from four months of development, as with our Public Access Design programs, to three years of development, as with the workshop tools in our Envisioning Development Toolkit series. For those toolkits—like *What Is Affordable Housing?*—we divide the three years into roughly three phases: research, workshop development and testing, and design and production. We begin by conducting research into the policy, trends, and impacts and then turn that information into a rough visual translation in the form of a slide presentation, which we test with target audiences to get feedback on what type of information is useful, confusing, or missing. As we fill in the information gaps, we introduce tactile elements to our presentation, allowing the audience to interact directly with the tools. This process is messy, awkward, and benefits from quick iteration. We conduct dozens of test workshops over a period of a few months to develop the workshop mechanics.

In the next phase, we collaborate with a design team to develop the mechanics of the workshop and the visuals that guide and underlie them. In this stage, the design and content push each other as the tool becomes clearer. At the same time, we write the text and develop preliminary diagrams for the booklet that accompanies the toolkit, which is then further developed by the design team. Finally, the toolkit is packaged and produced, comprising a branded toolbox, a set of tactile components, and a guidebook with policy information and detailed workshop instructions.

We launched *What Is Affordable Housing?* with four days of workshops for community organizers, community board members, and walk-ins to announce its availability and to train potential toolkit users to run the workshop. Since the launch of *What Is Affordable Housing?* in 2010, CUP has distributed over eighty toolkits to organizations throughout New York City (and a handful outside of the city), which are regularly used for workshops, and we continue to provide workshops directly to several hundred individuals each year. *What Is Affordable Housing?* was also launched with a digital version of the tool,[6] because organizers asked for a version they could use outside of workshops to show elected officials and others how this issue impacts their communities (Figure 6.12). We are

◀ **Figure 6.12**

What Is Affordable Housing online interface © CUP archives.

currently in the process of creating an affordable housing toolkit for Chicago, and testing the feasibility of making it adaptable for other cities. In November 2013, we also launched *What Is Zoning?* and are in the process of developing *What Is ULURP?*[7] to be launched in 2015.

Response to the toolkit has been overwhelmingly positive. CUP conducts an annual evaluation with the groups that have toolkits, and we have consistently found that they continue to run workshops regularly on their own. Some organizations use the tools to train new staff members, others use it as a way to train their members about their organizing agenda, while yet others use it to work with members to develop that agenda. We have also found unexpected uses. For example, organizers at the Urban Homesteading Assistance Board use it in workshops to help low- to moderate-income tenants organize to convert their rental buildings to coops.[8]

In CUP's early projects, we worked with an intuitive understanding that visual tools made good popular education materials. Inspired by traditions like the work of civil rights leader Septima Clark and the Highlander Folk School (Clark and Brown 1990), and the visual work of people from Sister Mary Corita Kent to Richard Scarry (Scarry 1980), CUP's work fused accessible images with the belief that complex processes could be understood, and that the understanding could lead to powerful social change. In recent years, more and more research has emerged to support the impact that visual and tactile information can have on deepening learning and on making information significantly easier to recall (Brady et al. 2008). CUP's work, in some ways, uses design to make some of the thorniest social justice issues "imageable" to the population most impacted by them.[9] The tools CUP creates provide mental maps of complex information. If we build those maps successfully, workshop participants and others who use our tools will be able to return to those maps over and over again, as needed, whether in an organizing meeting or in a public hearing. As a result, they can more effectively advocate for their community needs.

Notes

1. The group included Damon Rich (now Chief Urban Designer for the City of Newark), Jason Anderson (now an architect at SOM), Josh Breitbart (Director of Field Operations at Open Technology Institute), Stella Bugbee (Editorial Director, *The Cut*), Sarah Dadush (Assistant Professor, Rutgers Law School), AJ Blandford (artist), and Althea Wasow (filmmaker), and was joined in 2001 by Rosten Woo (designer and educator).
2. For HUD, MFI is two times the "Low Income Limit" or 50 percent of the MFI. See Income Levels Documentation System, available at: www.huduser.org/portal/datasets/il/il2014/2014summary.odn (Last accessed on February 15, 2015).
3. Families of four are used because 1) that's how HUD does its basic calculation and 2) to simplify the number of variables present in the workshop. The accompanying guidebook shows how to adjust the numbers for other family sizes. "Neighborhoods" are based on "Sub-borough areas," a geography that closely parallels Community Board districts and that the city government often uses in administering its own programs. Among other advantages, using this geography allowed us to sidestep arguments about where the boundaries of particular neighborhoods are located.

4. Public housing is a federal program that technically ended in 1974, through which local entities like New York City Housing Authority built, owned, and maintained housing, which was made available to low-income tenants at the price of 30 percent of their monthly income. Section 8 is made up of two different rent voucher programs in which tenants who are admitted into the program pay 30 percent of their income in rent and the government provides a subsidy that covers the cost between that amount of money and the market rate.
5. **Local communities**. Each project begins with a social justice issue that negatively impacts a community and with grassroots collaborators who are struggling to understand that issue. In our Youth Education programs, the local partner is a group of students, while in our Community Education programs, it is a community organizing or advocacy group. **Visual thinkers**. CUP engages designers, artists, teaching artists, animators, illustrators, programmers and other visual thinkers to translate complex information into clear visuals. **CUP Staff**. Observers of CUP's work sometimes describe our programs as "pairing up" designers with organizers, or teaching artists with students. In fact, our staff are integral to the projects. CUP staff shape and facilitate the collaborations, art direct, play a key role in breaking down the policy information, conduct research, and oversee production, among other roles. We also help to make sure that everyone on the project is working to understand the information and contributing collaboratively to creating a clear visual explanation.
6. For reference see: www.welcometocup.org/Projects/EnvisioningDevelopment/ (Last accessed on February 15, 2015).
7. Uniform Land Use Review Procedure (ULURP) is a standardized procedure whereby applications affecting the land use of the city would be publicly reviewed. For further reference see: www.nyc.gov/html/dcp/html/ap/step5_ulurp.shtml (Last accessed on February 15, 2015).
8. For reference see: www.uhab.org/ (Last accessed on February 15, 2015).
9. In *The Image of the City*, Kevin Lynch analyzes urban form through its imageability, that is, by the extent to which the city's inhabitants can form and retain an accurate mental map of the city. See Lynch (1960).

Bibliography

Brady, T. F., Konkle, T., Alvarez, G. A. and Oliva, A. (2008) Visual Long-Term Memory Has a Massive Storage Capacity for Object Details. *Proceedings of the National Academy of Sciences of the United States*. PNAS, 105 (38), pp. 14325–14329. Available online at: www.pnas.org/content/105/38/14325.full (Last accessed on February 15, 2015).

Clark, S. P. and Brown, C. S. (1990) *Ready from Within: Septima Clark & the Civil Rights Movement, a First Person Narrative*, Brown, C. S. (Ed.). Africa World Press.

Klanten, R., Ehmann, S. and Schulze, F. (2011) *Visual Storytelling: Inspiring a New Visual Language*. Gestalten.

Lynch, K. (1960) *The Image of the City*. MIT Press.

Neurath, O. (2010) *From Hieroglyphics to Isotype: A Visual Autobiography*. University of Reading Press.

Nonko, E. (August 29, 2013) "How Bloomberg Changed New York Real Estate." NewYork.com. Available online at: www.newyork.com/articles/real-estate/how-bloomberg-changed-new-york-real-estate-99465/ (Last accessed on February 15, 2015).

Scarry, R. (1980) *Richard Scarry's Best Word Book Ever*. Golden Books.

Tufte, E. (1983) *The Visual Display of Quantitative Information*. Graphics Press.

Vossoughian, N. (2011) *Otto Neurath: The Language of the Global Polis*. Distributed Art.

Chapter 7

Citizen Collectives, Co-Design and the Unforeseen Future(s) of the Post-Socialist City

Ivan Kucina

I write this chapter from the perspective of an educator, architect, urbanist and design activist working in the city of Belgrade, Serbia. I am a professor of architecture teaching at the School of Architecture, University of Belgrade. Most of my urban research and projects involve close collaboration with my students, as I refuse to recognize the walls of the academic studio as the boundaries of the educational world I simultaneously produce for and inhabit.

Working in Belgrade, one of the most challenging of the post-socialist cities, has been both a complex task and an incredible learning experience. Since the mid-1990s, the city has developed by following the radical shock therapy prescribed by neoliberal economists (Harvey 2007): The market has been deregulated, state-owned enterprises as well as public-sector property and the commons have been rapidly privatized,[1] and globalization has become synonymous with the expectation of limitless improvements in quality of life for all. Shaped also by private developers' financial agenda—to maximize returns on investment in land, construction, and real estate—this welfare city has been transformed into a Hobbesian field of endless business opportunities. Uneven development policies now favor the sites that have commercial potential to such an extent that public funds, when available, are diverted to the urban infrastructure that is expected to increase the number of development opportunities offered subsequently to private developers. These investments in urban infrastructure have created a mechanism for transferring public funds into private companies controlled by members of the ruling political coalitions and their business partners. In this way, an informal system of public–private partnership has been established. The most direct and obvious features of this system are, on the one hand, the rise of authoritarian power mechanisms and political structures that guard it and, on the other, the exclusion of citizens from decision-making processes at large. During Serbia's socialist period (1945–1990), citizen involvement in the urban planning and design processes in Belgrade was by-and-large structured through public hearings in Municipal Board meetings.

Even though such opportunities were often extended as mere formalities, they did give citizens a platform to voice their opinions in public. In the 1990s, however, political instruments for public engagement simply vanished. As a result, citizens were rendered politically powerless, and the alliance between corrupt public institutions and private urban developers continued unchallenged.

Wild City—the Self-Organized Urban Development

Pushed to the social margins by the unfair distribution of wealth and political power, many citizens chose to self-organize and produce their own places of living or exchange in the city. Between 1993–2009, triggered by the blast of the gray economy and living in an indistinctive blend of nonregulated and regulated environments, citizens began to produce innovative ideas in domains as varied as informal commerce, housing and services alike. There was no overarching strategy or idea that united these citizens into groups; on the contrary, they were tactically-minded, self-interested urban practitioners who acted out of a desire to survive. Informal structures occupied all available urban spaces. This fast and dynamic process created an emergent system in which self-organized citizens played a major role. Their potential for small-scale innovations and unpredictable distribution of programs all over the city appeared to be essential for the massive, yet informal, urban transformations.

In the early 2000s, we studied the internal logic of these transformations and investigated how to describe seemingly chaotic events in systemic and process-oriented ways. In our subsequently published findings (Džokić et al. 2005), we argued that such rapidly adapting social and human organizations are achieved through iterative daily interactions, and often conflicts, between public authorities and citizens (Figure 7.1). In what was for us a surprising turn, we found that the organizational capacity of public authorities weakened significantly when citizens' initiatives strengthened and evolved towards new organizational typologies and solidification of emergent practices. By unearthing and organizing the logic of these processes of urban transformation, we identified a wide array of innovative bottom-up activities that were subsequently used as a source for creating algorithmic, alternative concepts for post-socialist urban futures. Among our findings is that individual citizens, when not organized, tend to be tactically-minded and driven only by self-interest, just like small, private developers (Figure 7.2). In that sense, urban public space was the first to be overtaken and transformed to serve individual ambitions in an emerging Hobbesian battle in which everyone was fighting against everyone else.

▶ Figure 7.1

Organizational typologies of emergent practices © Stealth group.

▶ Figure 7.2

Organizational typologies and subject relations © Stealth group.

The Fifth Park—the Participatory Project for The Public Space

In 2009, my design studio at the Faculty of Architecture, University of Belgrade, began to study and then take part in the most promising urban uprising Belgrade

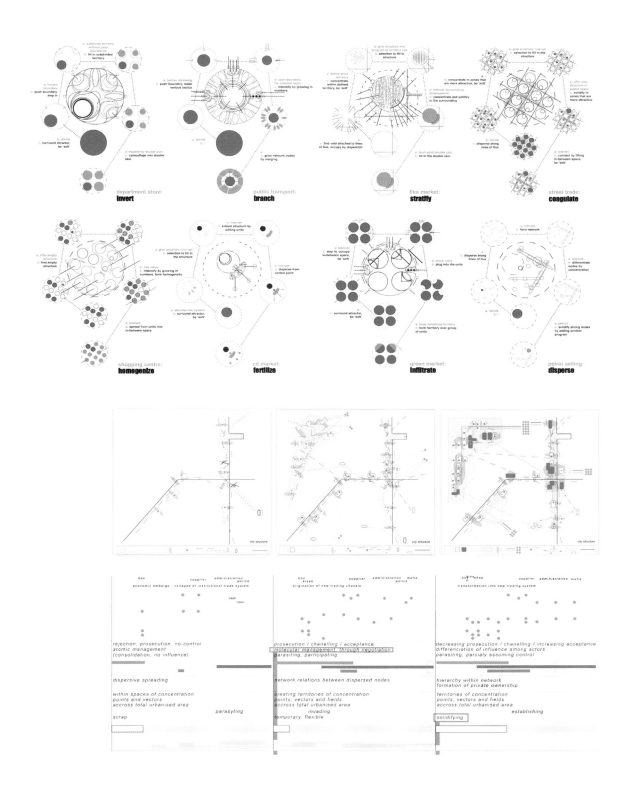

CHAPTER 7 Citizen Collectives

had seen since the collapse of the socialist state. The defence of the Fifth Park in Belgrade was triggered by the revolt of the citizens who had been violently denied access to the public park after it was taken over by a private developer who was supported by public authorities. The park worked as an entryway into their public housing complex, the basketball court that was part of the public park, and the playground. This three-year citizens' struggle that followed was the first public act of urban resistance against the corrupt urban development practices of post-socialist Belgrade. The park became a symbol of civic responsibility and proof that self-organization has the power not only to work for the benefits of individual communities, but also to defend public interest at large.

The Fifth Park is a 3,000 square meter (0.75 acres) neighborhood park located in the old city, three kilometres southeast of the city center. It stretches along one of Belgrade's most important traffic arteries, the King Alexander Boulevard (Bulevar Kralja Aleksandra). From the early twentieth century until the 1960s, the area consisted of a mix of the neoclassical single-story revival buildings with courtyards in the back. In 1963, a new urban redevelopment plan was created for the construction of a public sector housing scheme imagined as a modern urban residential ensemble with six five-story buildings and five ten-story towers. The ensemble included some five hundred apartments together with comprehensive community services comprised of a primary school, a kindergarten, a supermarket, coffee shops, small variety stores, and the local community center. Also, the spaces between these concrete housing blocks was designed as a sequence of green spaces called parks. The Fifth Park was the last in the sequence of green spaces extending through this urban ensemble.

Following the issuing of building permits, the construction began in earnest in 1965. However, land expropriation was not completed in a timely manner because occupants of the old one-story houses refused to leave. As a result, the area around the fifth housing tower remained only partly cleared for construction. By the early 1980s, most of the ensemble was already built and occupied, and the last standing houses were finally demolished, clearing the way for the completion of the urban block surrounding the fifth tower. At that time, however, the political and economic situation in Yugoslavia (and in Belgrade) changed radically, and the ideas that drove the development of large urban ensembles and mega-blocks were abandoned. Hence, after demolition of the old buildings was completed, the city government opted to expand the Fifth Park over the newly-cleared lot instead of building the last housing tower and the public parking space. The city's Parks Department continued to manage the Fifth Park, now double its original size. During the 1990s, a basketball court and a new playground were added together with benches, trash bins, and lighting posts. In the meantime, local chapters of the ruling political parties *de facto* privatized all communal and collective gathering spaces in the surrounding buildings, thus turning the parks into the only publicly accessible space and therefore the locus of community life.

The official urban plans continued to demarcate this territory as slated for construction of a mixed-use building of two thousand square meters. On Sunday morning June 11, 2005, The Parks Department cut down twenty-seven mature pine trees and began to clear the site for new construction. Through an unclear and obviously corrupt process, the city government together with the local municipality leased the land of the Fifth Park to a large local developer who also obtained a building permit for the construction of a six-thousand-square-meter residential and office building with shops and a garage space, *de facto* replacing the park in its entirety. The scheduled start of construction in 2005 met with resistance from the residents of the nearby buildings, who organized the civic defence of the park led by the newly founded Citizen's Coalition (Figures 7.3 and 7.4). The momentum building up around the aggressive privatization of public resources led by the government had inspired a public outcry, but it was not until the Fifth Park case that public opinion began to solidify and citizens to self-organize. It was no longer about individual and fragmented cases of privatization of public land and the commons; it was now about a collective struggle for the right to public space and the right to the city (Belaćević 2012). Despite the uprising, the developer managed to clear the park and remove the playground and basketball court (Figure 7.5). An enormous media interest followed these events, and many public personalities joined the fight for the park. The most popular hip-hop group in Serbia, The Belgrade Union (Beogradski Sindikat), created a highly politically-charged song called "The Fifth Park" ("Peti Parkić"), in which politicians and developers were accused of bribery, political and financial wrongdoing, and the manipulation of public interest. They held a public concert in the park on February 17, 2007 to much media attention and

▶ Figure 7.3

Citizen protest in Peti Park, Belgrade © Studio Peti Park, Faculty of Architecture University of Belgrade.

CHAPTER 7 Citizen Collectives

▶ Figure 7.4

Citizen protest in Peti Park, Belgrade © Studio Peti Park, Faculty of Architecture University of Belgrade.

▼ Figure 7.5

Demolition of Peti Park, Belgrade © Studio Peti Park, Faculty of Architecture University of Belgrade.

in front of the delighted members of the Citizen's Coalition and the general public.[2] Finally, on October 8, 2008, after three years of self-organized struggle, the newly elected mayor, Dragan Djilas, decided to permanently stop construction, offer an alternative site to the developer, and return this city-owned land to the citizens. That day, newspaper headlines read, "The Fifth Park Has Won!"[3]

The Fifth Park looked like a deserted battlefield when our team[4] started work on a participatory project with the Citizen's Coalition in order to help reimagine alternative programs (Figure 7.6). The Citizen's Association never became a legal entity, and continued to exist as an informal organization of local residents. With no park and no communal spaces available to them, local residents had no meeting place. As a result, a space for gathering and a clear leadership structure were missing, and the objectives for moving forward could not be easily agreed upon. The emerging question was: "Can a self-organized group of citizens, fighting to defend their living environment as well as public interest, continue to bring about a significant change in social and political life, at least at the local level?"[5] We quickly learned that the transition from the process of resistance (so obviously based in solidarity), to the process of the creation of new values (where differences and self-interest began to emerge) was to mark the second phase of this citizens' movement. At this stage the introduction of design-led processes of cocreation and participation could make a qualitative difference. We operated with two main ideas: first, we would treat the Fifth Park as commons and insist on identifying and ultimately removing all manifestations of socio-spatial exclusion; and, second, we would isolate and define a set of strategies, actions, and tools in order to transfer them to new sites of struggle and to involve residents in the next phase of the project. At this stage, our team decided to

▶ Figure 7.6

Design team at work in Peti Park, Belgrade © School of Urban Practices & Studio Peti Park, Faculty of Architecture University of Belgrade.

CHAPTER 7 Citizen Collectives

93

work with residents to build a participatory platform, to manage discussions and hands-on workshops until agreements were reached, and to translate the emerging collective imagination into a new socio-spatial system.

The participatory platform brought together local residents and representatives of local authorities and other urban organizations as well as members of our team. The platform combined parallel and successive levels of decision-making so that the next level always verifies the decisions made at the previous one. Although the design of such a small park would conventionally seem to be a relatively simple task, our mission was made complex by the range of different inputs that needed to be reconciled. At the beginning of the participatory process, four separate working groups were formed in order to generate design options that were as divergent as possible. Groups were composed of up to four students and thirty residents. We used a blend of methods derived generally from design user-centered research (Laurel 2004), participatory action research, and particularly, use of sociograms (Buckles and Chevalier 2013). For us, the local residents were a "unit of identity," and we argued that they were in the best position to address, research, analyze, and respond to the situation as it unfolded. In the language of participatory action research, they are the "bearers of knowledge." Using prepared questionnaires, the students began to work with the residents in order to create group profiles, affinities, and affiliations. Questionnaires were designed as instruments for detecting residents' motivations, daily practices, the symbolic capital of the community, and other variables. The profiles of the groups did not constitute a simple sum of the attributes of those observed, but rather a complex value that bears the most vital and often contradictory attributes that the interpreter considers important for defining the elements of the project. We proceeded to create graphic representations, sociograms, and stakeholder maps of the community's social network and power structure. Within the community, we recognized and categorized distinct types of actors and intra-community relationships between actors, identifying both obstacles and opportunities. Our aim was to dismantle internalized social hierarchies and provide the community with a map of their socio-spatial territory so that they could continue to act collectively.

In the following stage, based on four group and actor profiles and their relationships, we began to map out what spatial, programmatic, social, and functional properties the park needed to assume in order to begin to serve this community once again—this time, however, without the imminent threat. Our team members led hands-on workshops and initiated the community into the process of codesigning by collectively making maps, drawings, and prototypes of the park. These prototypes were suggestive of the general scope of the project at hand and its constitutive spatial elements, but not deterministic or prescriptive in closing the process too early, or proposing final outcomes. The prototypes served as catalysts for further work and debate on important social and community issues in spatial terms. Working together for weeks, the members of the Citizen's Coalition in their four groups worked with four working models, physically manipulating prototype elements and discussing options. This process created the contours of the project that we processed and defined after the workshops were over (Figures 7.7–7.10).

▶ Figure 7.7

Design team at work in Peti Park, Belgrade © School of Urban Practices & Studio Peti Park, Faculty of Architecture, University of Belgrade

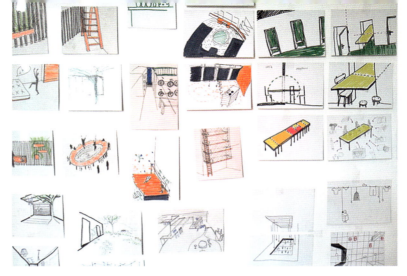

▲ Figure 7.8

Working sessions with the Citizen's Coalition © Studio Peti Park, Faculty of Architecture, University of Belgrade.

▲ Figure 7.9

Working sessions with the Citizen's Coalition © Studio Peti Park, Faculty of Architecture, University of Belgrade.

▶ Figure 7.10

Working sessions with the Citizen's Coalition © Studio Peti Park, Faculty of Architecture, University of Belgrade.

Based on the information gathered and knowledge accumulated, and enriched with the experience of cocreation, our team designed four scenarios for the Fifth Park, and subsequently presented them to the residents. Through a vigorous public debate that followed, the most promising actionable insights from the four scenarios were identified and used to create the communal design proposal everyone agreed upon. After this was accomplished, instead of creating conventional plans, sections, and final models, we created a life-sized schematic drawing on the ground of the Fifth Park (Figures 7.11 and 7.12). This enabled residents to comprehend spatial dimensions of the shared ideas and to imagine the eventual "feel" of the park. Another public debate followed for the citizens to better comprehend the advantages and shortcomings of the new design and to agree on the final features of the proposal that was then presented, in the required technical form, to the Parks Department.

This project has shown that this group of self-organized citizens was indeed capable of continuing to work together after the imminent threat of privatization was over. However, it is also clear that design acted here as the connective tissue, as a vehicle for cooperation and co-imaging of social collectives that have internal spatial coherence, and thus, as a powerful agent of progressive urban transformation. Interestingly enough, nominally speaking, the elements of the new proposal do not deviate much from what was previously destroyed in the park. Those are standard elements of public space in Belgrade's residential areas: trees and bushes, grass fields, a basketball court, benches, safe and sustainable playground equipment, parking spaces along the surrounding streets, trash receptacles, and discreet lighting. Citizens do not expect their park to stand out

◀ **Figure 7.11**

Students and residents inscribing the outlines of the proposal in the actual scale © Studio Peti Park, Faculty of Architecture University of Belgrade.

▶ Figure 7.12

Students and residents inscribing the outlines of the proposal in the actual scale © Studio Peti Park, Faculty of Architecture University of Belgrade.

from similar urban parks; indeed, it is precisely its conventional aspects that make the Fifth Park a part of everyday urbanism, *a priori* resisting adversities and differentiation.

The Fifth Park demonstrates the power of participatory projects to transform imposed autocratic processes into platforms for debates between citizens, urbanists, architects, public authorities, and private developers. The conceptualization, cocreation, and shared maintenance of such platforms is critical in the context of neoliberal regimes for the production of urban space. Active citizen participation in the processes of decision-making is the only way to challenge established urban hierarchies and the overconfidence of the institutions of political power. It is through the process of collaboration, cooperation, coproduction, and knowledge-sharing that citizens generate opportunities for improving their urban habitat. As this example shows, design is a powerful vehicle for achieving just that.

Notes

1. These are the forms of property developed under Yugoslav self-management system in the 1970s and 1980s. For reference see: Zukin (1975); Bartlett (2007); Stanilov (2007).
2. For reference see: www.pressonline.rs/info/beograd/4364/sindikalci-brane-pet-park.html (Last accessed on February 15, 2015).
3. For reference see: www.novosti.rs/vesti/beograd.74.html:224340-Peti-park-pobedio (Last accessed on February 15, 2015).
4. Out team included graduate students from my design studio at the Faculty of Architecture, University of Belgrade.
5. Srdjan Prodanović quoted in Belaćević (2012: 7).

Bibliography

Bartlett, W. (2007) *Economic Reconstruction in the Balkans: Economic Development, Institutional Reform, and Social Welfare in the Western Balkans*. Routledge, p. 158.
Belaćević, B. et al. (2012) *Struggle for the Everyday: The Example of the Fifth Park*. Kontekst.
Buckles, D. J. and Chevalier, J. M. (Eds.) (2013) *Participatory Action Research: Theory and Methods for Engaged Inquiry*. Routledge.
Džokić, A., Topalović, M., Kucina, I. and Neelen, M. (2005) Belgrade: Evolution in an Urban Jungle. Read, S., Rosemann, J. and Van Eldijk, J. (Eds.) *Future City*. Spon Press.
Harvey, D. (2007) *A Brief History of Neoliberalism*. Oxford University Press.
Laurel, B. (Ed.) (2004) *Design Research: Methods and Perspectives*. MIT Press.
Stanilov, K. (2007) Democracy, Markets, and Public Space in the Transitional Societies of Central and Eastern Europe. Stanilov, K. (Ed.) *The Post-Socialist City*. Springer, pp. 269–283.
Zukin, S. (1975) *Beyond Marx and Tito: Theory and Practice in Yugoslav Socialism*. Cambridge University Press.

Chapter 8

Cohabitation Strategies: Socio-Spatial Approaches, Practices, and Pedagogies with a Dialectical Perspective

Gabriela Rendón

In the midst of the ongoing worldwide recession, grassroots groups have strengthened existing, and created new, local alliances and movements advocating for urban, social, and economic justice across the world. These mobilizations prompted the first urban uprisings in the beginning of the new century which have since rapidly spread and intensified. Cohabitation Strategies' practice emerged during this period as citizens' discontent rose in neighborhoods and communities due to the consequences of the advanced neoliberal urbanization. Partly in response to the acute world-wide financial crisis but also to the prolonged uneven distribution of wealth and development, the benefits of public policy, programs, and funds were increasingly diverted from urban communities in need and funneled toward urban development projects favoring private investors and financial institutions. This process resulted in further marginalization of underprivileged citizens and urban communities. Cohabitation Strategies started as a project intended to bring together a cohort of local groups, activists, artists, and academics involved in responding to the outcomes of the urban crisis in the Netherlands and envisioning alternative approaches to understand and change cities. It was cofounded as an international nonprofit cooperative focused on socio-spatial research, design, and development in the city of Rotterdam. Since its inception, the cofounders[1] have been actively engaged in working toward overcoming the traditional divisions of research, planning, and development by working with a wide range of transdisciplinary collaborators and citizens engaged in the social and spatial production of the city.

A Nonhierarchical and Transdisciplinary Working Model with a Dialectical Perspective

Cohabitation Strategies is a cooperative primarily concerned with socio-spatial investigations leading to transformative projects and actions. The aim of the cooperative is three-fold: first, facilitating the production and exchange of scientific and popular knowledge through innovative research methods; second, understanding and disseminating complex urban processes through participatory practices and pedagogical instruments; and finally, responding to the conditions of urban decline, inequality, and segregation via the design of strategic processes and interventions.

The cooperative's cofounders hold expertise in architectural design, urban theory, spatial planning and strategy, curatorial practice, and cultural and art production. This core team expands to include collaborators with knowledge in other fields such as political economy, geography, anthropology, sociology, environmental sciences, and other areas when a project demands additional perspectives. Cohabitation Strategies' operations constantly change because its research and working structures are participatory. The cooperative usually establishes a working space in the investigation area to work collaboratively with residents and public and private institutions involved in the social, economic, and physical development of the area. The cooperative has collaborated with municipalities, non-profit organizations, art and cultural institutions, and non-profit foundations throughout Europe and the Americas.

The cooperative's investigative framework seeks an understanding of urban dynamics at macro- and microscales through scientific and action research. These mutually supporting research components take various forms depending on the nature of each project. The first approach centers on scientific knowledge and academic understanding produced through transdisciplinary research using quantitative and qualitative methods. The second focuses on popular knowledge and wisdom belonging to the citizens as well as local grassroots organizations and collected through local initiatives and projects using innovative participatory research tools. These instruments have evolved through the cooperative praxis and observation. For instance, when the traditional quantitative and qualitative perspectives on social and urban research prove limited, a more diversified approach is sought. This search has led the cooperative to a dialectical perspective that has generated the richer social and spatial understanding needed to forge transformative interventions. Exploring and learning from other disciplines and dialectical research methods, such as participatory action research[2] and socio-praxis,[3] have strengthened the two-fold research approach with unorthodox fieldwork instruments and creative tools for disseminating the work of the cooperative. Participatory action research is an experimental and innovative approach to economic, social, and political change which actively engages people in generating knowledge about their own living conditions in order to produce fundamental reorganization of urban socioeconomic systems and relations of power. Similarly, socio praxis offers participatory mechanisms and methodologies that go beyond merely describing social and urban reality. Both methods recognize the importance of knowledge oriented toward transforming situations of inequality while recognizing the people as protagonists in the research and intervention processes.

The urban practice envisioned by Cohabitation Strategies seeks to be flexible and dynamic while remaining rooted in the dialectical perspectives on urban research (Fals-Borda and Rahman 1991; Lara 2012; Pereda et al. 2003; Villasante 2006). This vision is enacted in five ways. First, we seek to eliminate the asymmetry implicit in subject–object relationships—professionals/researchers versus the people/locals—by constructing subject–subject (i.e., researchers–community members) associations to generate authentic participation in the urban research and design processes. This symmetry encourages people to become active in their communities, self-conscious of their own knowledge and assets, and involved in the decision making process. Second, we strive to produce knowledge for and with people; namely, it is not enough to democratize access to scientific knowledge as knowledge must be produced by people according to their needs and interests. The combination of scientific and popular knowledge without hierarchy defines the problems to be addressed, priorities to be considered, and suitable strategies to be proposed. This is important in redistributing control in the production of the city because power is exercised through access to and control of knowledge. Third, we acknowledge that all of the groups involved in the research and design development must assume a symmetrical position in the analysis process, including identification of problems and necessities as well as setting priorities and directions by taking into account local capacities and agency. Fourth, we pursue fusing reflection and action: avoiding theory without praxis and practice without reflection. And, finally, we aim to facilitate self-organization, autonomy, and the emancipation of people and local groups to be protagonists in the formulation and implementation of local plans—in other words, in urban processes aimed at transforming their very reality.

In the practice of Cohabitation Strategies, planning and design are always the products of both scientific and action research processes. Taking into account the most pressing problems, as well as local priorities, demands, and resources, a number of strategies and actions are usually proposed to catalyze grassroots-led transformations that could influence different levels of urban governance. The strategies and actions vary in format and scale depending on the nature and duration of the project and the type of impact or transformation needed. Long-term projects tend to benefit from strategies and actions designed to be led by residents with the assistance of community leaders and activists, members of the cooperative, and/or local experts in relevant fields. Over time, such initiatives are taken over by local grassroots groups and community organizations. Examples of such actions include: participatory planning at the neighborhood level; proposing new legislation or making current legislation accessible; neighborhood-based initiatives to develop or improve local services, housing, and/or facilities; and urban interventions in public spaces and underutilized sites leading to permanent occupations. Short-term projects usually comprise small-scale actions and target more specific issues. Urban campaigns and art-based projects that lead to comprehensive and transformative action plans could exemplify these activities, as well as multilevel platforms that strengthen communication between diverse power structures and interests.

A key objective of Cohabitation Strategies has been to conduct outreach and mediate between different levels of urban governance in the intervention area, including residents, community leaders, nonprofit organizations, public and private institutions, and developers and planning institutions as well as ocal representatives and politicians. Cohabitation Strategies proposes a strategic combination of written, oral, and visual presentations during the research and design process to support across-the-board communication and collaboration.

Unfolding the Urban Practice

The three projects outlined in what follows reflect some of the propositions of the cooperative projects. *The Other City: Exposing Tarwewijk* was initiated as part of the "Urban Segregation" cluster of the 2009 4th International Architecture Biennale Rotterdam, *Open City: Designing Coexistence*. The project was developed in Tarwewijk, a district recently ranked as one of the most problematic in Rotterdam and in The Netherlands as a whole. It aimed to expose the socio-spatial decline and restructuring of low-income districts in Rotterdam while stressing the outcomes produced by the ongoing neoliberal housing and urban policies in the Netherlands. Pressing issues in this urban district were known to Cohabitation Strategies' members who had worked previously in the area in an art-based project that helped to establish strong connections with local groups and residents. *The Other City: Exposing Tarwewijk* included research, community meetings, district excursions, public assemblies, publications, and an exhibition (Figures 8.1–8.4). Soon after the biennial events, the initial short-term research evolved into a thorough participatory action research. The project was funded by the Netherlands Architecture Fund, and a number of local groups, academic institutions, and art organizations became active collaborators. The two-fold research method of the cooperative emerged as the initial means to building and organizing a neighborhood-based research, community and learning hub. This entity was conceived to have the agency to organize, mobilize, and plan according to local problems, capacities, and priorities. An "Urban Union" was envisioned based on the model of a traditional labor union to improve the area's political, social, economic, and physical condition. We formed a strategic research unit (SRU) to manage and make scientific knowledge accessible, and an action research unit (ACT) to collect and share local knowledge. The units would exchange information and assist in the coordination of programs and activities at the local level. Committees addressing various local affairs were conceived as part of the "Urban Union". Each committee would organize and lead neighborhood initiatives to identify local concerns and resources to collectively propose transformative action plans. Some of the initiatives included: *Pension Tarwewijk*, a local housing cooperative planning and organizing the occupation of vacant housing units for short-term stay (Figure 8.5); *Craft-Work*, a project-based research initiative addressing local economies and labor relationships; and *Consortium for Useful Knowledge*, a neighborhood hub with a number of pedagogical programs addressing public policy, legal assistance, urban and tenant rights, and other issues related to housing and social justice.

▶ Figure 8.1

The Other City: Exposing Tarwewijk, Research Diagram. Hand made collage © Cohabitation Strategies.

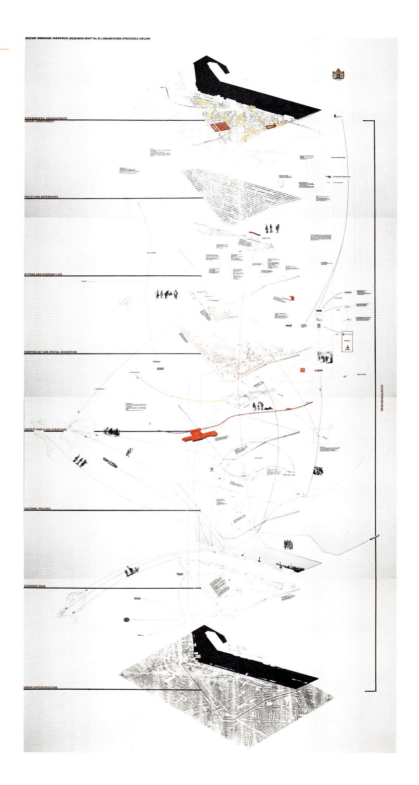

CHAPTER 8 Cohabitation Strategies

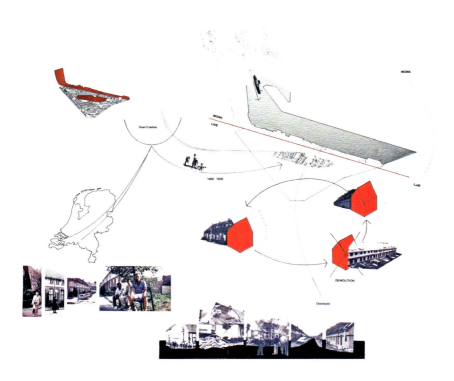

◀ Figure 8.2

The Other City: Exposing Tarwewijk, Tarwewbuurt Fragment: Social and spatial changes. Hand made collage © Cohabitation Strategies.

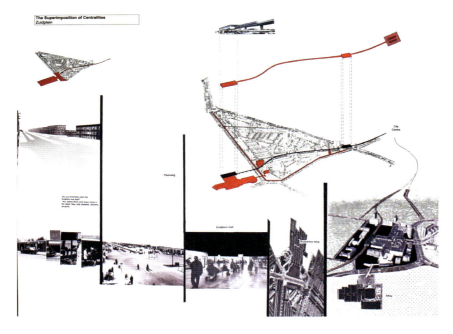

◀ Figure 8.3

The Other City: Exposing Tarwewijk, Zuidplein Fragment: Zuidplein mall and the decline of local economies. Hand made collage © Cohabitation Strategies.

▶ Figure 8.4

The Other City: Exposing Tarwewijk, Katendrechtse Lagedijk Fragment: Housing Renewal. Hand made collage © Cohabitation Strategies.

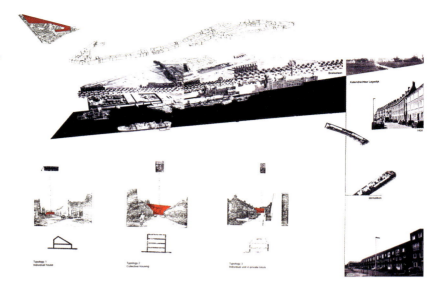

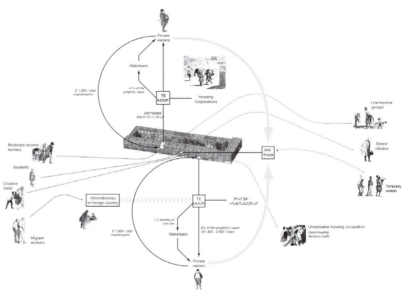

▶ Figure 8.5

Urban Union: *Pension Tarwewijk* © Cohabitation Strategies.

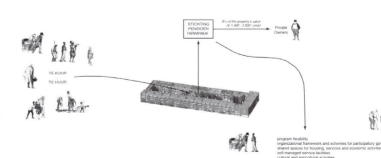

The urban and social realities exposed during the development of this project and its initiatives encouraged discussion among residents, local organizations, and city officials. Ongoing urban visions and housing renewal plans led mostly by public–private partnerships in the area were questioned: such plans had mostly offered physical solutions to social problems and had led to the perceived supremacy of public–private partnership schemes that caused replacement of low-income by middle-income households. In contrast, our work proposed that urban and housing renewal through displacement was not the only means to improving the current situation of inner city districts of Rotterdam. The community-based approaches proposed by our cooperative provided a viable alternative to the schemes currently in place. Indeed, the potential of the project to formulate alternative strategies and improve local conditions without displacement disqualified the project from further funding because of the conflicting interests between the ongoing plans led by the city and the participatory process initiated by the cooperative. Nevertheless, some local initiatives continued to work along the lines codesigned in this project, and have prompted interaction with local communities and more participatory approaches working with tenants and owners associations.

The *Bordeaux Report* was part of *Evento Bordeaux: Art for an Urban Re-Evolution* in 2011. Cohabitation Strategies was invited by Michelangelo Pistoletto, the principal curator of this cultural biennial, to frame the *problematique* of the city and potential areas of intervention; local partners, artists, and designers were also to take part in the event. The biennial's aim was to employ art as a vehicle of social transformation, to transform Bordeaux into an experimental platform for social and cultural innovation, and to create alternative models for "everyday life," thereby generating an "urban re-evolution" for tomorrow's cities. In addition to these objectives, Cohabitation Strategies sought to employ this project to empower local citizens as subjects of urban knowledge in the processes of urban transformation.

The development of a city-wide research project was proposed for two reasons: First, to map current urban policies, visions, and trends while identifying new centralities and peripheries, or in other words, current areas of investment and disinvestment in the city (Figure 8.6). Second, to identify and select districts that manifest rapid changes in the city, and at the same time act as prolific platforms for long-term community-based initiatives that could be initiated by socially and politically engaged artistic practices. The districts of Saint-Michel and Grand Parc, both vulnerable and segregated neighborhoods in the left bank of Bordeaux, were selected for different reasons and investigated. The first one was experiencing gentrification and displacement due to municipal development and investment, whereas the second one experienced decline due to municipal abandonment and disinvestment. The research process was conducted by a transdisciplinary team comprised of local urban researchers. Scientific and popular knowledge were, once again, produced through various methods. Ethnographic research was fundamental in getting to know the citizens in each district; so were the associations and institutions as potential partners in creating the conditions for engagement. Discovering forgotten and hidden urban narratives

▶ Figure 8.6

Bordeaux Report: Introduction to Territory © Cohabitation Strategies.

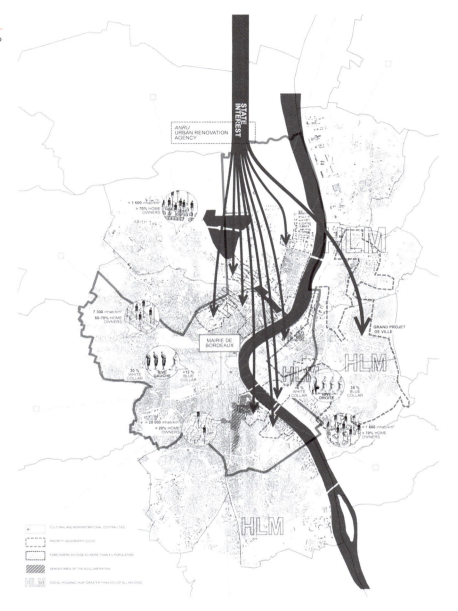

and anecdotal references through personal encounters and interviews was part of the research process. These interactions were essential for infiltrating the districts and constructing local alliances. Members of the research team, including an anthropologist and a sociologist, worked with residents to gain a perspective on their experiences in inhabiting these neighborhoods. The stories depicting urban, economic, and social processes and issues affecting citizens' daily environment were intertwined with scientific research, constructing a complex narrative of the city's urban policy, development, and transformations (Figure 8.7). The research was published in The *Bordeaux Report*, a document providing a thorough view of the city and its people. It served as the initial document employed by artists and designers to propose transformative long-term interventions, and by the citizens and local groups to find points of engagement within the biennial's projects and beyond. The report also included a guide to the two aforementioned districts, including the location and contacts of educational, cultural, sport, religious and social facilities, and civic associations as well as public and social-housing services (Figure 8.8—8.10). A number of long-term urban projects were developed with the assistance of the report. One of the most successful projects was "The Great Unpacking of Associative Life" by Dutch artist Jeanne van Heeswijk. Hidden relationships between associations active in the neighborhood of Saint-Michel were "unpacked" for the first time by van Heeswijk through a number of gestures and activities that took place at the Marche des Douves, an abandoned old market.

The *Bordeaux Report* brought to light urban realities that the city had not addressed in its ongoing urban policy and existing urban plans; a number of city districts were affected by the plans as conceived, while other urban territories

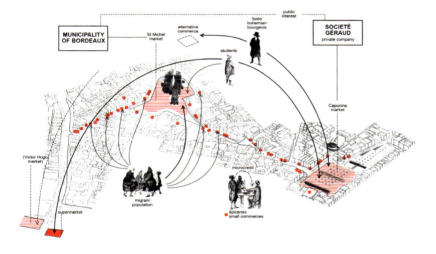

◀ **Figure 8.7**

Saint Michel Report: Commercial activities and local markets
© Cohabitation Strategies.

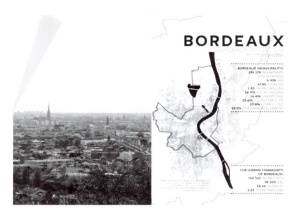

▲ Figure 8.8

Bordeaux Report Cover © Cohabitation Strategies.

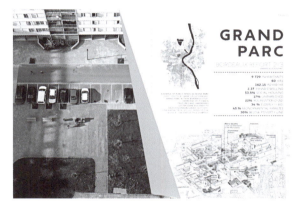

▲ Figure 8.9

Grand Parc Report Cover © Cohabitation Strategies.

▲ Figure 8.10

Saint Michel Report Cover © Cohabitation Strategies.

were excluded for political reasons. For instance, the lack of city investment in Grand Parc—as well as its exclusion from the biennial activities—became evident during the research process and was exposed in the report. This heavily immigrant-populated neighborhood was clearly an area of disinvestment and the site of socio-spatial segregation. Because the report prompted discussion and mobilizations among residents in the neighborhood and across the city, it was eventually censored by the municipality. Soon after, several groups from the Grand Parc area organized themselves and demanded inclusion in the biennial. They proposed an alternative plan for their participation in the city's cultural activities. Additionally, a local committee became actively engaged in the neighborhood and started negotiations with the city around a long-term vacant building, Salle de Fetes; they proposed plans for investment and communal management that would make the building accessible for neighborhood events. Furthermore, the *Bordeaux Report* encouraged a number of other artistic interventions in both districts and across the city.

The *Guelph-Wellington Rural-Urban Program* was commissioned in 2012 by the Musagetes Foundation, an international organization that promotes the arts and artistic creativity as a tool for social transformation. This project was conceived as an instrument to delineate a strategic plan for artistic and transdisciplinary interventions for the coming years in the City of Guelph, Canada, where Musagetes Foundation is based. The program aims to raise crucial questions about the city's urban, economic, social, and artistic development in order to stimulate local debate and generate knowledge. At the same time, it seeks to produce a cultural development agenda and establish new connections among artists, designers, groups of citizens, inhabitants, and cultural, educational, and social institutions. Cohabitation Strategies collaborated with local and international researchers to build up a local network for the furthering of the program's vision by using traditional as well as participatory action research methods. A number of activities aimed at unearthing local knowledge were organized with citizens from various social, economic, and political strata. In these sessions, innovative research methods and tools were used, such as: discourse production and analysis that introduced local images and quotes acquired through interviews as catalysts for opening up the discussion; social maps (sociograms) that revealed power relationships between local residents, immigrant groups, civic associations, grassroots groups, community organizations, public services, corporations, and politicians; periodic community workshops; and participant observation in community and public meetings. The knowledge produced during these sessions was disseminated city-wide in a periodic publication, the GWRUP Gazette, with the intention of engaging and mobilizing the general public (Figure 8.11).

The research process and the localized urban knowledge produced will be published by a local publishing company, to assist the community to generate a critical understanding of the issues, struggles, and potential of Guelph and its immediate assets, while exposing the current social and labor

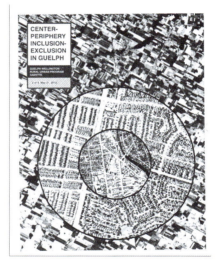

◀ Figure 8.11

Guelph-Wellington Rural-Urban Program: GWRUP Gazettes © Cohabitation Strategies.

relationships and possible points of collaboration (Figure 8.12). Making this knowledge accessible to the citizens of Guelph is the ultimate objective of this program—thus a virtual format has been proposed to continuously trace future investigations and interventions, providing new understanding of the city's evolution. The research process revealed visible and invisible spaces within the city and the divergent collective perspectives of the two citizen groups residing in these areas, which hardly meet and interact. On the one hand, there are what we called "the connected citizens," middle-class families rooted in the territory. On the other hand, there are "the unconnected citizens," a volatile working-class mostly comprised of recent immigrants. Our research and the process of mapping these realities revealed labor and housing issues previously unknown to many citizens. In addition, the project opened a discussion and initiated

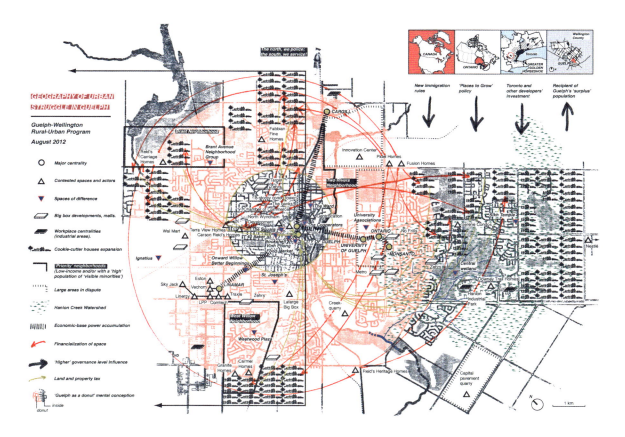

▶ Figure 8.12

Guelph-Wellington Rural-Urban Program: Geography of Urban Struggle in Guelph © Cohabitation Strategies.

cooperation among local groups working on urban issues. Some community outreach projects, mainly in marginalized neighborhoods, were launched during the research phase, aiming to exchange knowledge with locals and test small-scale actions around relevant local issues, such as food accessibility. Since this is an ongoing project, various future initiatives have been envisioned by Cohabitation Strategies that will address alternative housing models, cooperative economies, food access systems, and public platforms to make public policy accessible and transparent to citizens.

In the last two years, the cooperative has expanded its work to challenge the traditional conception of property through art and community-based projects, as well as through projects commissioned by public institutions. Envisioning alternative and nonspeculative property and housing models has been a constant effort throughout the cooperative trajectory, and particularly in the ongoing projects.

Designing Pedagogies

The work produced in Cohabitation Strategies has inspired us to explore alternative pedagogies in academia. Members of the cooperative have been active in academic work and most of our pedagogical projects have involved extensive fieldwork and hands-on learning that scrutinizes pressing and complex urban and social issues. Contributing to the construction of the nonhierarchical and transdisciplinary urban practice we have envisioned in the cooperative has been fundamental for our pedagogy.

Urban projects with strong and deliberate social impact have been at the core of our academic work. Such projects have been developed by intersecting and interweaving various disciplines. Among the core topics for our pedagogical work have been the socio-spatial implications of urban decline, inequality, and segregation as well as the formulation of alternative property and housing models with a social justice approach. The academic work is always produced in cooperation with engaged external partners and collaborators including local experts, citizens, grassroots groups, civic associations, community organizations, community leaders, and urban activists. Some of the experimental projects have assisted in the development of actual projects undertaken by communities and neighborhood groups.

Reflecting on our academic work, it is crucial to point out that academic projects require a coalition of popular and academic knowledge to codesign innovative strategic projects. In academia, participatory research and planning can be taught but not always practiced due to time constraints and the commitment that those processes demand. Nevertheless, it is critical to acknowledge the potential, value, and implications of these approaches. Furthermore, in the context of design education, it is also critical to avoid working exclusively with designers: innovative and transformative projects are always achieved through collaboration among people with diversified expertise. Finally, urban learning in the context of strictly fragmented knowledge among the academic disciplines is not suitable for urban praxis. Dialectical urban pedagogies aimed at constructing urban practices with the agency and tools to understand urban complexities and to achieve systematic transformations must be formulated using dialectical and subversive research and planning approaches.

Notes

1. Cohabitation Strategies cofounders are Lucia Babina, Emiliano Gandolfi, Gabriela Rendón, and Miguel Robles-Durán.
2. Participatory Action Research is a dialectical perspective on social research cofounded by researcher and sociologist Orlando Fals-Borda. See Fals-Borda and Rahman (1991).
3. Socio-praxis is a dialectical perspective on social research founded by sociologist Thomas Rodriguez Villasante. See Villasante (2006).

Bibliography

Fals-Borda, O., and Rahman, M. A. (1991) *Action and Knowledge: Breaking the Monopoly with Participatory Action-Research*. New York: The Apex Press.

Lara, A. L. (2012) "What Is Socio-Praxis? A Dialectical Perspective in Social Research." Lecture at The School of Environmental Design and Rural Development, University of Guelph, Canada. March 19, 2012.

Pereda, C., Prada de M. A., and Actis, W. (2003) *Investigacien Acción Participativa: Propuesta Para un Ejercicio Activo de la Ciudadania*. Madrid: Colectivo Ioé.

Villasante, T. R. (2006) *Desbordes Creativos: Estilos y Estrategias para la Transformacion Social*. Madrid: La Catarata.

Chapter 9

Citizenship by Design

Kadambari Baxi and Irene Cheng

Today, traditional definitions of citizenship based on place of birth (*jus scli*) and blood (*jus sanguinis*) have been eroded by the increasing mobility of individuals, capital, and national borders. Although historically citizenship was conceived as a singular status, today, many individuals acquire multiple citizenships through family ties or naturalization. Countless others are stateless or in between states, including refugees of war, guest workers, and inhabitants of occupied lands. Contemporary transnational citizens include a spectrum of identities, from undocumented immigrants, barred by their extralegal status from participating politically in their communities, to globetrotting citizens in search of tax havens. A Vietnamese laborer working in a British-owned factory in the Mariana Islands and a Latvian-born investor with dual citizenship in Russia and Canada exist on opposite ends of a continuum of privilege and opportunity. Yet both individuals can claim multiple national affiliations through ties of location, family, labor, and investment. Examples of nonstandard or "flexible" citizenship—increasingly more typical than anomalous—raise the question: How should citizenship be defined today?[1] Citizenship is both an abstract idea and a legal category that produces concrete effects in the lives of individuals, regulating where one can live, vote, work, and travel. Citizenship is also materialized and made visible in the form of official procedures and documents—such as the passport—that link the individual to the state, the personal to the political, and the private to the public.

Citizenship by Design[2] raises critical questions about the nature of contemporary political identities by focusing on an object whose design is often taken for granted—the passport. The project asks how passports might be redesigned to reflect new forms of "nonstandard" citizenship in a world marked by increasingly fluid and contentious national borders.

The Passport as an Object of Design

Whereas the primary purpose of the modern passport is to certify the identity and nationality of its bearer, early modern passports were essentially semi-formalized letters of recommendation issued by a king or noble person asking foreign entities to allow the bearer safe passage. Almost all modern passports bear the vestiges of these origins by including a formulaic ceremonial phrase that varies only slightly from the wording of an 1860 passport:

> We, Charles, Augustus Lord Howard de Walden and Seaford, a Peer of the United Kingdom of Great Britain and Ireland [. . .] request and require all those whom it may concern to allow Dr. Loney, British subject and officer going to Germany to pass freely without let or hindrance, and to afford him every assistance and protection of which he may stand in need.[3]

The contemporary passport, like many bureaucratic documents, operates under a guise of neutrality and artlessness. We imagine its birthplace to be a shadowy government printing office, its features the result of default settings determined by anonymous officials. Passports are designed, however. Attributes like color, cover image, and interior content signify more than we think; together, they comprise an object that determines its bearer's freedom of movement across borders, and that embodies the very terms of sovereignty—an imaginary relationship between a nation-state and an individual. Interrogating the design of the passport therefore can open up inquiry into the conditions of contemporary national citizenship and governmentality.

The project consists of several parts. First, we researched several key attributes of the passport—such as color, symbolism, language, security printing, and biometric identification techniques—as a way to denaturalize the object, and to uncover some of the ideological content hidden within the aesthetics of contemporary passports. Following the analyses of passport design, we explored the rights and responsibilities of contemporary citizens, with a special focus on the asymmetries in the freedom of movement enjoyed by holders of different nations' passports. We created semi-fictional accounts of eight nonstandard citizens and diagrammed their personal geographies. Lastly, we conducted a series of "Inconclusive Surveys" at street fairs and in gallery exhibitions, asking visitors to tell us their views on contemporary citizenship. By honing in on the aesthetic qualities of the passport and telescoping out to examine the effects of passports on individuals around the world, *Citizenship by Design* asks how the passport—and the relationships embedded within it—can be redesigned to reflect a contemporary reality in which many individuals have heterogeneous national affiliations, virtual identities, and multinational rights and responsibilities.

The Form of the Passport

Through our research into the aesthetic properties of the passport, we discovered that seemingly insignificant attributes such as color, herald, and page texture could be interpreted as metonyms for issues of national identity, political subjectivity, postcolonial nationhood, security, and unequal citizen status. Color is one of the most conspicuous and ostensibly innocuous attributes of a passport, with red, green, and blue the most common hues. Yet the shade of the passport can signify discord as well as unity, and can mislead as well as clarify, as several examples evince (Figure 9.1). Many nations have multiple passport colors, each designated for a different class of citizen. In the United States, regular passports are blue, official passports are maroon, and diplomatic passports are black. In Switzerland, the government's corporate design guide in 2007 designated

◀ Figure 9.1

Examples of international passports arranged by color © Baxi and Cheng.

Pantone PMS 485 as the official shade of red for the Swiss passport. The Chinese government has recently hired Roger Pfund, the designer of the most recent Swiss passport, to consult on the design of its new passports. Although members of the European Union have agreed upon a standard burgundy red passport cover, individual nations' symbols, fonts, and layouts vary. Continental unity—and uniformity—must be balanced against distinct national typographic expression.

The visual symbols on passport covers also hold more significance than one might imagine. A special case is the World Passport: the symbol gracing its cover is a homalographic projection map of the globe. Homalographic projections, also known as Mollweide or Babinet projections, were popularized beginning in 1857. They forego accuracy of angle and shape in favor of a truthful representation of area. The World Passport is a 30-page machine-readable document issued by an organization called the World Service Authority. The document was created in 1953 by peace activist Garry Davis, who argued for a world government composed of world citizens in place of the existing system of nation-states. World Passports have purportedly been accepted on a case-by-case basis by over 150 countries, and have even received *de jure* or official recognition by such nations as Ecuador, Zambia, and Togo.[4]

Security printing techniques like intaglio and holograms do more than prevent counterfeiting, they can convey subtle aesthetic effects and political messages. A close examination of passport security printing techniques— responsible for the appealing moiré textures found in the backgrounds of many passport pages—reveals the occasional use of these surfaces as canvases for patriotic inculcation. In 2007, for example, the United States redesigned its passport according to the theme "American Icon." Visual emblems printed onto the pages include a bald eagle, sheaves of wheat, the flag, a clipper ship, Mount Rushmore, and a long-horn cattle drive. The images are accompanied by snippets of patriotic texts such as the national anthem lyrics, the opening lines of the Constitution, a Mohawk Thanksgiving speech, and inspirational quotes from former presidents. Since the terrorist attacks on September 11, 2001, increased attention has been paid to biometrics—methods for recognizing humans based upon one or more unique and intrinsic physical traits. Currently, face, fingerprint, and iris scans are the standard biometric measures used in passports. Some countries have begun collecting DNA information from selected citizens, giving rise to heated debates about the expansion and limits of governments' access to individuals' biological information. The United States, European Union, and numerous other countries now require electronic passports in which biometric information is embedded in a contactless RFID chip. The RFID chip has raised security concerns from those who fear that information can be scanned and stolen from a distance. Currently, the International Civil Aviation Organization, which regulates passport standards, stipulates that an RFID chip can only contain information that is also printed in the passport itself—in other words, only information available to the naked eye.

Polymorphous Citizens

Although a passport typically promises passage "without delay or hindrance" to its bearer, some passports offer more mobility than others (Figure 9.2). The Henley Visa Restrictions Index is a global ranking of countries according to the freedom of travel enjoyed by their citizens. According to this index, holders of a Danish passport enjoy the greatest freedom of movement, since they can obtain visa-free access to 157 other countries. Afghan citizens have the least freedom of movement, with only 22 visa-free destinations available to them. The ranking was produced by Henley & Partners, a law firm specializing in "citizenship planning." As the firm suggests, "today, a person of talent and means need not limit his or her life and citizenship to only one country. Making an active decision with regard to your citizenship gives you more personal freedom, privacy and security."[5] While some individuals have multiple passports, others cannot obtain one due to political obstacles. The conditions of contemporary migration and movement are glaringly unequal. Many kinds of polymorphous citizens fall between or outside officially recognized categories. On one end of the spectrum are undocumented immigrants whose views are often "not counted" in the public sphere. On the other end are "discounted" citizens who seek the shelter of tax havens.

As part of the project, we created semi-fictional accounts of several polymorphous citizens, culled from news reports and other media sources. We then produced maps diagramming the individuals' multiple national affiliations. Each person is treated as a network, located somewhere but connected to many places at once through ties of blood, money, and law. These individuals are deemed to fall into four categories: the Not Counted, the Undercounted, the Overcounted, and the Discounted (Figures 9.3–9.10).

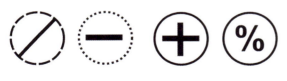

▲ Figure 9.2

Today many kinds of polymorphous citizens fall between or outside officially recognized categories. On one end of the spectrum are undocumented immigrants whose views are often "not counted" in the public sphere; on the other end are "discounted" citizens who seek the shelter of tax havens © Baxi and Cheng.

▲ Figure 9.3

Not Counted: Undocumented workers and refugees are Not Counted, not only in the sense that their exact number is unknown, but also because their status and views are insufficiently accounted for in the public sphere.

Not Counted: Maria. Maria was born in Mexico City and immigrated illegally to San Diego. She has two children: one was born and lives with Maria in the United States, while the other remains in Mexico. Maria sends part of her paycheck back to Mexico each month © Baxi and Cheng.

▲ Figure 9.4

Not Counted: Gideon. Gideon was born in Harare, Zimbabwe. His parents moved to Zimbabwe from Malawi; thus Gideon holds a passport from Malawi. Because Zimbabwe does not allow dual citizenship, he is not able to obtain a Zimbabwean passport. He recently fled Zimbabwe's political persecution and failing economy, crossing the Limpopo River to South Africa in search of safety and farm work. He was deported back to Zimbabwe, but soon found his way back to South Africa © Baxi and Cheng.

▲ Figure 9.5

Undercounted: The Undercounted include guest workers and permanent residents. They are legally permitted, and even required or encouraged, to live and pay taxes in a country, but are not entitled to the same political and social rights as citizens.

Undercounted: Ali. Ali was born in Turkey and holds citizenship there. He immigrated to Germany in the 1960s under the country's guest worker program. He is now retired and receives social benefits from the German government. Ali is reluctant to give up his Turkish nationality and therefore has not attempted to obtain German citizenship. His two children were born in Berlin and are dual German and Turkish citizens; they will have to choose between the two nationalities when they reach age 23 © Baxi and Cheng.

▲ Figure 9.6

Undercounted: Rafael. Rafael was born in the Philippines. He worked for some time on a U.S. naval base in Luzon; however when the Philippine government refused to renew the lease on the base, Rafael lost his job. He immigrated to Bahrain and found employment as a construction worker. After a few months, he returned to the Philippines. Today he lives and works in Singapore, as part of the country's guest worker program. His children still live in the Philippines, and he sends money home to them each month © Baxi and Cheng.

▲ Figure 9.7

Overcounted: Mobile by choice rather than by need, the Overcounted are entitled to work and to receive social and political benefits from multiple nations, but they are not necessarily politically active in all of their "homelands."

Overcounted: Emile. Emile was born in and is a citizen of the United States. His mother was British by birth, so he also has U.K. citizenship. His father was French and therefore he also has French citizenship. None of these countries prohibits multiple citizenship, so he holds passports from all three. Emile divides his time between London and New York, and pays taxes and votes in both the U.K. and the U.S. © Baxi and Cheng.

▲ Figure 9.8

Overcounted: Sofia. Sofia's mother is Brazilian (ethnically Italian and Brazilian) and her father is Portuguese. She has dual nationality, and holds Brazilian and Portuguese passports as well as European Union citizenship. After she lost her job in Brazil, Sofia moved to Lisbon to work in a textile factory for four months. Because she is a dual citizen, she did not have to apply for a work permit. After several months she found a job through an agency in a food processing factory in Edinburgh, where she now resides © Baxi and Cheng.

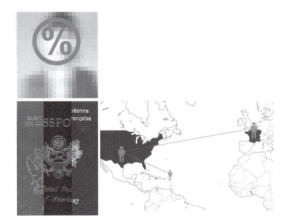

▲ Figure 9.9

Discounted: Discounted citizens roam the world in search of tax havens and minimal state interference in their private affairs. They take what benefits they can from each country in their passport portfolios but contribute as little as possible in return.

Discounted: Roger. Roger was born in Houston, Texas. His work as an investor frequently takes him to Germany, France, Hong Kong, and the United States. He now lives in France, but recently renounced his citizenship in the United States, which taxes citizens regardless of their place of residence, and acquired economic citizenship in St. Kitts and Nevis, which does not tax income. Roger's assets are distributed in numerous foreign bank accounts in Switzerland, Andorra, and Monaco © Baxi and Cheng.

▲ Figure 9.10

Discounted: Nadia

Nadia was born in Latvia, then part of the USSR. She now lives in Russia, where she is the president of a trading company. Concerns about the stability of the Russian government and economy led Nadia to begin developing a "passport portfolio" with the assistance of a professional adviser. She has since acquired citizenships in Cyprus, Canada, and Latvia. Each of these citizenships affords her specific benefits: tax shelter, access to good educational opportunities for her children, and ease of travel © Baxi and Cheng.

Inconclusive Surveys

Citizenship by Design has been exhibited in several settings, including street fairs and art and architecture galleries (Figure 9.11). At each venue, we sought to engage the broader public in a critical discussion and debate over the terms of contemporary citizenship by creating a series of questionnaires (Figure 9.12). Although surveys are typically taken with the aim of measuring public opinion

◀ Figure 9.11

Citizenship by Design exhibition at Van Alen Institute, New York, 2009 © Baxi and Cheng.

▲ Figure 9.12

Examples of questionnaires and surveys from *Citizenship by Design* exhibitions © Baxi and Cheng.

objectively and empirically, our questions were designed to provoke uncertainty, and to open up new lines of interrogation.

One of these public installations took place in 2008 at the Chinatown Summer Street Festival in Columbus Park, New York City, in partnership with Asian Americans for Equality (AAFE). We set up a station with bilingual questionnaires and a color-coded display that made the "voting results" instantly visible. New York's Chinatown is one of the largest and oldest ethnic Chinese enclaves outside of China, and it continues to be home to both new immigrants and Chinese Americans whose families have resided in the U.S. for four, five, and six generations. The Chinatown residents and visitors who participated in our installation were intimately familiar with the experience of inhabiting multiple and overlapping ethnic, national, and geographic spaces. The open-ended nature of the questionnaires invited respondents not only to register their votes but also to reflect on their own histories in relation to these multiple affiliations (Figures 9.13 and 9.14).

In some of the other surveys we conducted, we asked respondents both to identify a citizenship profile that best described their own status, and to select another that stood in stark contrast to their own—that is, to imagine a radically different political subjectivity. We also asked visitors to consider the meaning of passport design elements, such as color and symbol, as well as the terms under which individuals may be identified and screened—for example, what kind of information a state should be able to collect about individuals passing through its borders. The responses—by turns thoughtful, generic, humorous, and unexpected—manifested what were hopefully only the beginnings of a larger debate over contemporary citizenship and political sovereignty.

▲ Figure 9.13

Citizenship by Design public installation in Chinatown Summer Street Festival in Columbus Park, New York City © Baxi and Cheng.

▼ Figure 9.14

Citizenship by Design public installation in Chinatown Summer Street Festival in Columbus Park, New York City © Baxi and Cheng.

CHAPTER 9 Kadambari Baxi and Irene Cheng

Notes

1. On "flexible" citizenship, see Ong (1999). Ong defines flexible citizenship as the "cultural logics of capitalist accumulation, travel, and displacement that induce subjects to respond fluidly and opportunistically to changing political–economic conditions."
2. Project Team included Christina Yang, Daniella Zalcman, Christian Ruud, Marcella Del-Signore, and Rodrigo Zamora. This project was funded by IFG-Ulm (International Design Foundation, Ulm), Germany and by the Barnard College Research Fund.
3. For reference see: http://home.wxs.nl/~pdavis/Passport_B.htm (Last accessed February 15, 2015).
4. For reference see: www.worldservice.org/visas.html (Last accessed February 15, 2015).
5. For reference see: www.henleyglobal.com/citizenship-planning/ (Last accessed February 15, 2015).

Bibliography

Ong, A. (1999) *Flexible Citizenship: The Cultural Logics of Transnationality.* Duke University Press.

Chapter 10

Urban Method Acting

Tobias Armborst

> Rather than urban design, urban planning, urban studies, urban theory, or other specialized terms, urbanism identifies a broad discursive arena that combines all of these disciplines as well as others into a multidimensional consideration of the city. Cities are inexhaustible and contain so many overlapping and contradictory meanings—aesthetic, intellectual, physical, social, political, economic, and experiential—that they can never be reconciled into a single understanding. Urbanism is thus inherently a contested field.
>
> Crawford (2008)

> In the last fifteen years, urban theory has moved a considerable way towards recognizing the varied and plural nature of urban life. Most of the major contemporary urbanists [. . .] acknowledge the inadequacy of one positionality on the city. They note the juxtaposition of high-value added activities with new kinds of informed activity, the co-presence of different classes, social groups, ethnicities and cultures, the stark contrast between riches and creativity and abject poverty, and the multiple temporalities and spatialities of different urban livelihoods.
>
> Amin and Thrift (2002)

Over the last decade or so, a number of practitioners around the world—many of them represented in this book—have developed architecture, planning, and urbanist and public art practices that not only take the inexhaustibility and contentiousness of the city into account, but make them the source of a reimagined urbanism. When Georgeen Theodore, Daniel D'Oca, and I started Interboro Partners[1] in 2002, after having graduated from programs in urban planning and design, we did so out of dissatisfaction with the then existing professional options for young urbanists in the United States. In the field, we found a strange disconnect between the exciting, surprising, and inexhaustible complexity of the city and the complete predictability of the urban planning and design professions' responses, which ranged from the deployment of trite formulas such as "mixed-use" and "walkability" to the spicing-up of large development schemes with spectacular forms and images. In distinction to the existing professional models, we intended to develop an urban practice that would engage the city by identifying innovative socio-spatial practices and by working with them to blur the boundary between observing the city and transforming it through design. The projects we have developed in the ten years since have dealt with the question of how we act as urbanists vis-à-vis the specific circumstances of a place: How do we define our practice beyond the traditional client-based models? Are there multiple possible clients with different agendas? Whose side do we pick in the conflict that every urban project necessarily entails? While we define the way we act specifically in relation to the actors and forces in each situation, there are some recurring roles that we define as *Ghostwriter, Matchmaker and Detective.*

Ghostwriter

As keen observers of cities and the built environment, we are fascinated by how people use everyday urban places and transform them over time.[2] A big part of our work at Interboro consists in naming, describing, and drawing forms of everyday urbanism in order to render them visible and thereby negotiable. In 2005, we spent an extended period of time studying Detroit, and by living in the city we noticed an interesting unidentified phenomenon: namely, homeowners were taking over, borrowing, or buying one or more vacant lots adjacent to theirs and thereby expanding their properties via incremental acquisitions. We termed the expanded parcels that resulted from these *blots*, a neologism we used to describe such newly formed "blocks" of "lots"[3] (Figure 10.1). Victor Toral's property at 4930 Wesson Street is an exemplary blot (Figure 10.2): ten years ago, Victor owned one house on a 30' x 135' lot. The house, like most Detroit bungalows, was oriented front to back. Victor later bought the vacant lot next to his property and erected two additions, reorienting the house in a direction parallel to the street. A few years later, he built a fence around his newly expanded property as well as the city-owned lot next door, turning his property into a courtyard house (Figure 10.3). He has since added a tree-house and swing-set for his children in the courtyard. The blot enclosed by the fence currently measures 90' x 135' (Figure 10.4).

Researching cadastral maps and property records, and comparing them with the observations, maps, and photographs from our journey through the city, we found countless blots across the city of Detroit. We found that the bottom-up tactics of individual actors such as Victor were *de facto* changing the genetic code of the entire city by creating new ownership patterns. To us, these tactical, small-scale practices of self-interested individual homeowners were significant in two ways: Fisrt, if properly recorded and institutionalized, they pointed toward the possibility of an incremental approach to urban redevelopment that could restore property to the city's tax rolls and thus contribute much needed property tax revenue; second, they challenged the conventional reading of Detroit as being abandoned due to the combination of industrial restructuring, anti-urban federal policies, and racism. At the time, Detroit still had about 800,000 residents who were curiously absent from the stories and photographs capturing abandonment. Blotting pointed to the fact that remaining urban residents were still actively involved in configuring their environment, but also

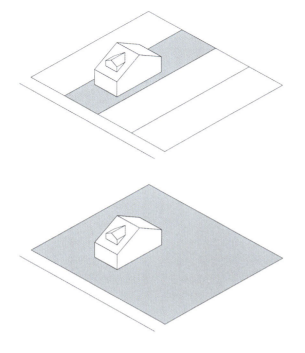

▲ Figure 10.1

What is a blot? *blot* (n.) from block and lot, i.e. a block of lots. When a homeowner takes, borrows, or buys one or more adjacent lots, the connected lots form a "blot" © Interboro Partners.

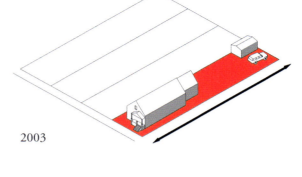

2003

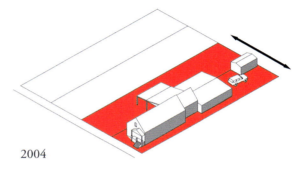

2004

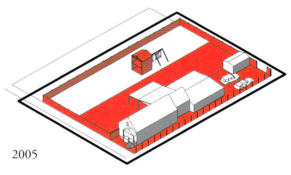

2005

▲ Figure 10.2

Over a period of ten years, Victor Toral created a three-lot-blot and turned his bungalow into a courtyard house © Interboro Partners.

that they were pragmatically taking advantage of the city's shrinkage to do so.

For Interboro Partners, naming, describing, drawing and mapping the practices of individual blotters was a way to retroactively give a coherent and compelling story to these unsung heroes of urban redevelopment and their everyday spatial tactics. While it set the stage for a number of innovative interventions aimed at organizing and scaling up the blotting practice, this form of ghostwriting also in itself became an urban intervention. Since blots were the results of tactical, self-interested efforts by individual homeowners, there was no formal organization of blotters, there wasn't even a name around which these unique urban practitioners would create a community of practice. Ghostwriting became de facto a way to bring blotters together and advocate for what they were doing. While traditional advocacy planning requires the existence of some sort of organized community group as the advocacy planner's client,[4] here "the client" actually was rendered through the act of ghostwriting, pointing towards a new kind of advocacy that emphasizes the importance of identifying, documenting,

▶ **Figure 10.3**

Victor Toral's blot © Interboro Partners.

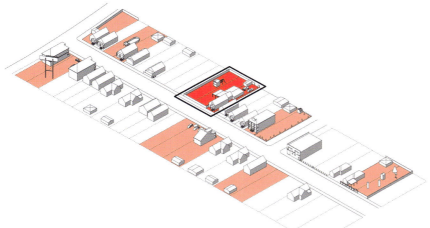

◀ **Figure 10.4**

There are many blots on Victor's block. Some are evident through physical signs such as the use of fencing, while others are identifiable only through cadastral maps © Interboro Partners.

and scaling up existing, innovative socio-spatial practices that have little to no self-awareness and legitimacy. Our belief is that the practices of blotters represent an important incremental approach to urban redevelopment, in Detroit and beyond, and could be turned into a model of tactical urban work, acknowledging simultaneously that Detroit metro region certainly also needs decisive regional planning to redistribute risks and opportunities within the region.[5]

Matchmaker

Ghostwriting of ongoing urban transformations can also lead to the identification of new projects that can range from small-scale architectural tasks to long-term plans. Given that they are the outcome of investigation rather than commission, these projects typically lack clearly defined budgets, programs, or funding sources. Developing such projects is therefore as much about design as it is about identifying and connecting with constituents, initiatives, funding streams, and material sources. In our recent project *Rest Stop*, we worked with a number of Lower East Side community organizations to build a temporary grove on the East River waterfront[6] (Figure 10.5). As the budget was very small, we exclusively used free, recycled materials from a variety of sources, such as mulch from the New York City Department of Parks and Recreation and discarded scaffolding lumber from Build It Green NYC.[7] To provide immediate shade and green we also "borrowed" plant material by diverting about twenty five trees on their way to housing projects in Lower Manhattan. After Hurricane Sandy had uprooted a great number of trees in October 2012, the housing authority of New York City commissioned the New York Restoration Project (NYRP) to replant trees at public housing sites the following year. We were able to convince NYRP to store the trees at *Rest Stop* for the summer instead of keeping them at the nursery, before planting them during tree-planting season in the late fall. Over the summer, the Lower East Side Ecology Center's Summer Street tree interns watered and cared for the temporary tree grove. The point of the *Rest Stop* was to gain short-term use-value by temporarily diverting an existing material and funding stream.

By contrast, in the project titled *Holding Pattern*, we turned existing funding for a temporary project into more sustained, long-term use-value, by matching the needs of an art institution together with over fifty surrounding community organizations and individuals (Figure 10.6). The project began as a winning

◀ Figure 10.5

Rest Stop (2013), a temporary waterfront park on the Lower East Side had an immediate need for shade and green, we borrowed twenty NYCHA-bound trees to be held here instead of the nursery until tree-planting season in the late fall
© Interboro Partners.

▶ Figure 10.6

MoMA PS1's 2011 Holding Pattern installation © Interboro Partners.

submission to MoMA PS1's annual Young Architects' Prize. Every year, the Museum of Modern Art commissions an architecture office to design and build a temporary setting for the "warm-up concert series." Warm-up takes place in the courtyard of MoMA PS1 during the summer months, attracting about six thousand visitors to the museum in Long Island City on Saturdays from July to September. We approached the project with two simple goals: first, to extend the lifespan of the temporary project beyond the three summer months; and, second, to make the project useful to the surrounding communities beyond the walls of the museum. Accordingly, we started the design process by asking the museum's Long Island City neighbors if there was something they needed that we could design, use in the museum courtyard during the summer, and then hand over to them at the end of the summer. We talked to taxi management companies, public libraries, high schools, senior and daycare centers, community gardens, a post office, and dozens of other Long Island City-based institutions, trying to make matches between the devices and tools they needed, and those we could employ in the MoMA PS1's courtyard. The result was an eclectic collection of objects, including mirrors, ping pong tables, a lifeguard chair, a rock-climbing wall, and eighty four trees (Figures 10.7—10.9). Before these objects and trees were delivered to their new owners in the fall, they were stored in the museum courtyard during the summer, and created the setting for a temporary public space for a diverse range of people (Figures 10.10 and 10.11).

Many of the museum's neighbors—including those who don't typically enter a museum of contemporary art—came to visit and attend one of many events we organized in collaboration with our community partners. These events included b-boy workshops with the 5 Pointz Aerosol Art Center, a ballet

CHAPTER 10 Urban Method Acting

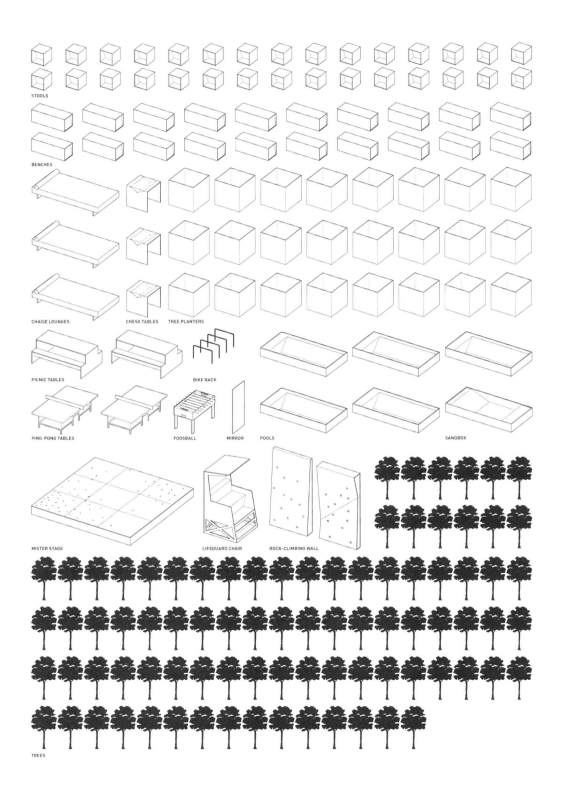

◀ Figure 10.7

An eclectic collection of objects and eighty-four trees © Interboro Partners.

▶ Figure 10.8

When *Holding Pattern* was de-installed in the fall, we delivered the objects and trees to more than fifty organizations in Long Island City and beyond. This map shows their final destinations © Interboro Partners.

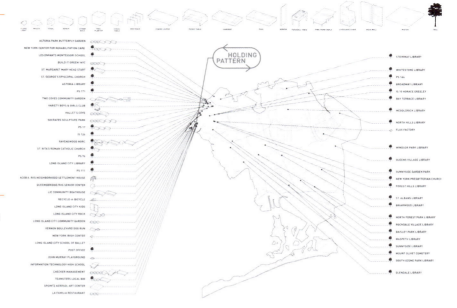

▲ Figure 10.9

Map showing final destinations of objects and trees © Interboro Partners.

CHAPTER 10 Urban Method Acting

131

▲ Figure 10.10

Labels and brands were placed on each object. Labels indicated community-based organizations for which the objects were held © Interboro Partners.

◀ Figure 10.11

Sixty red-oak trees were held in the Tree Room. With the help of New York Restoration Project, we planted these trees around the neighborhood when Holding Pattern was de-installed in the fall © Interboro Partners.

▼ Figure 10.12

The ping pong table and outdoor furniture installed across the street from MoMA PS1 upon closing of the *Holding Pattern* © Interboro Partners.

performance with the Long Island City School of Ballet, a "Family Summer Reading Celebration" with the Queens Library, a quilting workshop with the New York Irish Center, bike workshops with Recycle-A-Bicycle, and composting and rain barrel workshops with Western Queens Compost Initiative. We also invited our partner organizations to nominate books for the museum store. During the lifespan of the *Holding Pattern* installation, MoMA PS1 sold books that are not typically found in a contemporary art museum bookstore, but that gave a snapshot of the activities, ideas, and ideals in the museum's neighborhood. While this project began with a clearly defined site, schedule, client, and budget, we expanded the site beyond the walls of the museum and the schedule beyond the summer. We also redefined the notion of "client" while diverting an existing institutional funding stream to meet the needs of diverse community groups (Figure 10.12).

Detective

The third role we frequently assume in our work is the role of the *detective*. For us, design begins with the earnest attempt to understand the forces and actors at play. By looking for clues, following traces, talking to people, and listening carefully, we try to suspend our judgment as long as possible. *The Arsenal of Exclusion and Inclusion* is an ongoing project, in which detective work figures not as the first step of a design process, but as a method of reading the city. When we were invited to curate the American section of the 2009 International Architecture Biennale Rotterdam (IABR), we decided not to present a collection of architectural projects or urban case studies, but instead to focus on a set of tools and technologies for city-making. Specifically, we wanted to assemble urban tools, widely conceived, that were invented to either keep people apart or to bring them together—tools that architects, planners, policy-makers, developers, real estate brokers, community activists, and individuals have used to increase or decrease spatial segregation in American cities. We have since identified over two hundred such tools and have collected them into a volume titled *The Arsenal of Inclusion and Exclusion* (Armborst et al. 2014).

The exclusionary tools in the arsenal range from micro tactics of demarcation to regulatory tools that selectively block people from accessing urban space (Figure 10.13). They represent a range of artifacts such as: armrests on public benches that keep the homeless from sleeping; fire hydrants that keep people from parking near beach access points; outdoor speakers designed to frighten off skateboarders by playing classical music; and many others, including zoning codes, residential parking permits, loitering ordinances, and "no cruising" zones. Most of the explicitly exclusionary tools in the arsenal have fortuitously been outlawed, such as the rules and restrictions that prohibit nonwhites from buying or renting homes in "white" neighborhoods. Others have been replaced by subtler, more indirect tools of exclusion: An example of such a tool is what the legal scholar Lior Jacob Strahilevitz has identified as the "exclusionary amenity."[8] Thanks to the Fair Housing Act of 1968, it is illegal to develop a community explicitly for one race, ethnicity, or religion. However, it is not illegal

◀ Figure 10.13

The Arsenal of Exclusion and Inclusion is a collection of tools that architects, planners, policy-makers, developers, real estate brokers, community activists, and individuals have used (or are still using) to increase or decrease spatial segregation in American cities and suburbs. Illustration by Lesser Gonzalez Alvarez © Interboro Partners.

for a developer to implicitly discourage members of a race, ethnicity, or religion from moving into a community by offering the so-called "shared amenities." Such shared amenities are a typical feature of Common Interest Developments, the most prevalent housing developments in the United States today.[9] While the homes in these developments are individually owned, shared amenities such as golf courses, tennis courts, and swimming pools are held in communal ownership by all residents, and managed by the Homeowners' Asscciation. Home owners pay for the maintenance and management of the amenities through monthly fees to the Homeowners' Association. It is precisely through such fees, Strahilevitz argues, that shared amenities turn into exclusionary amenities: Despite the reasonable price for the home, potential residents who do not play golf or tennis will not be interested in paying high monthly fees in addition to their mortgage, and will thus not be inclined to move into such a community. Given the fact that through the 1980s and 1990s only about three percent of American golfers were African American, the golf course became an effective proxy for all-white communities. As Strahilevitz argues, "an exclusionary amenity is a collective good that is paid for by all members of a community because willingness to pay for that good is an effective proxy for other desired membership characteristics" (Strahilevitz 2014), such as race or religion.

A powerful example of such an exclusionary amenity is an imposing structure of a Catholic church at the center of Ave Maria, a master-planned, Catholic-themed community near Naples, in Southwest Florida. This town for 25,000 inhabitants that opened in 2007 was built by the billionaire Tom Monaghan as a community that would reflect traditional Catholic values. While it is *de jure* illegal to exclude non–Catholics from settling in the community, the church makes the community *de facto* undesirable for those not willing to pay a high monthly fee for the maintenance of the church building, be they Catholic or not. Understanding how protocols, practices, and specific artifacts have been used to keep people apart is the first step to appropriating, inverting, or neutering such exclusionary tools. Our assumption behind *The Arsenal of Exclusion and Inclusion* has been that we can indeed subvert existing exclusionary tools, or invent new inclusionary ones, to redefine urbanist practice across the United States. *The Arsenal* includes a number of legal tools that increase access to socio-spatial justice and the right to the city, such as the Fair Housing Act, inclusionary zoning, and the Americans with Disabilities Act as well as newer, inventive tools such as the 2008 Los Angeles Urban Rangers' map of Malibu beaches.[10] For decades, wealthy Malibu homeowners posted illegal "private property" and "no trespassing" signs in addition to bulldozing the beach, establishing toll roads, and hiring private security that prevented the public from reaching the public beach.[11] In many ways, they have attempted and nearly succeeded in privatizing the public beach by limiting access. Activists in the Malibu area have organized public hearings, publications, and media campaigns, public outreach, as well as resource and capacity building in order to maintain some free access to the coastline. In that sense, Los Angeles Urban Rangers' map explains the public's basic rights to the beach, and it informs the public how and when to gain access to the public beaches. Often, the only way to get to the beach is by walking through shallow waters or by swimming around fenced private properties.

While the Rangers' map is a way of spatializing and visualizing access routes, it is also a form of engaged public advocacy because it presents a sociospatial strategy for reclaiming the coast as a public good. It does so by prescribing a complex web of routes and tactical moves that have the capacity to scale up individual actions and thus reimagine and remap the urban territory by opening it up to reappropriation, reclaiming, and reenvisioning of public life. In a word, mapmaking, along with other tools in the repertoire of the reimagined urbanist practice, indicates yet another desired positionality in the contested field of urbanism today and proposes a new urban ecology in the making.

Notes

1. For reference see: www.interboropartners.net/ (Last Accessed on February 15, 2015).
2. This interest in the potential of everyday practices to transform the meaning and the form of the built environment is obviously heavily influenced by Michel de Certeau (1984), and the work of such different scholars as Margaret Crawford (2008), John Brinckerhoff Jackson (1970, 1984, 1994) and Henri Lefebvre (1991, 2004).
3. Blots (along with technical terms such as blotters, blotting analysis, "de-facto blots" and "de-jure blots") have by now entered planning language. See for example: Herscher (2012); Lepeska (2011); Davidson (2011); "Blotting Analysis" (2012); and for a more in-depth discussion Armborst et al. (2008).
4. I am referring here to the definition of advocacy planning in Paul Davidoff's influential essay "Advocacy and Pluralism in Planning" (1965).
5. The obvious risk of this type of project is that it can be seen as romanticizing bottom-up practices, as Brent Ryan asserted in his *Design After Decline* (2012).
6. The project was part of the Paths to Pier 42 temporary waterfront park, launched in 2012 by the Lower Manhattan Cultural Council, Hester Street Collaborative, Good Old Lower East Side (GOLES), Committee Against Anti-Asian Violence (CAAAV), Lower East Side Ecology Center and the Two Bridges Housing Council.

7. Build It Green NYC is New York City's only non-profit retail outlet for salvaged and surplus building materials. For reference see: www.bignyc.org/what-we-do (Last accessed on February 15, 2015).
8. Strahilevitz, L. J. (2015) Exclusionary Amenity. Armborst, T., D'Oca, D. and Theodore, G. (Eds.) (2015) *The Arsenal of Inclusion and Exclusion*. Actar.
9. Common Interest Developments (CID) are private master planned communities governed by a Homeowners' Association on the basis of incorporated Covenants, Conditions, and Restrictions (CC&Rs). According to Evan McKenzie (McKenzie 1994), over half of the new homes in the United States in the 1990s were part of CIDs. While the nomenclature is slightly different, the Foundation for Community Association Research puts the number of all homes in the US that were part of CIDs in 2012 at 24 percent. For reference see: Foundation for Community Association Research (Statistical Review 2012) at www.cairf.org/foundationstatsbrochure.pdf (Last accessed on February 15, 2015).
10. Malibu Public Beaches, at: www.coastal.ca.gov/access/MalibuGuide2010.pdf (Last accessed on February 15, 2015).
11. The City Project: Equal Justice, Democracy, and Livability for all, at: www.cityprojectca.org/ourwork/beachaccess.html (Last accessed on February 15, 2015).

Bibliography

Amin, A. and Thrift, N. (2002) *Cities: Reimagining the Urban*. Polity Press.
Armborst, T., D'Oca, D. and Theodore, G. (2008) Improve Your Lot! Rugare, S. and Schwarz, T. (Eds.) *Cities Growing Smaller*. Cleveland Urban Design Collaborative at Kent State University.
Armborst, T., D'Oca, D. and Theodore, G. (Eds.) (2015) *The Arsenal of Inclusion and Exclusion*. Actar.
"Blotting Analysis." (January 2012) *Reinventing Detroit's Lower East Side: A Summary Report of the Lower Eastside Action Plan—Phase I*.
Brinckerhoff, J. (1984) *Discovering the Vernacular Landscape*. Yale University Press.
Brinckerhoff, J. (1994) *A Sense of Place, a Sense of Time*. Yale University Press.
Brinckerhoff, J. and Zube, E. (Eds.) (1970) *Landscapes: Selected Writings of J. B. Jackson*. University of Massachusetts Press.
Crawford, M. (2008) Introduction. Chase, J., Crawford, M. and Kaliski, J. (Eds.) *Everyday Urbanism*. Monacelli Press.
Davidoff, P. (1965) "Advocacy and Pluralism in Planning." In: *Journal of the American Institute of Planners*, Vol. 31, No. 4, pp. 331–338.
Davidson, K. (December 5, 2011) "Blotting—Not Squatting—In Detroit Neighborhoods." NPR All Things Considered.
De Certeau, M. (1984) *The Practice of Everyday Life*. University of California Press.
Herscher, A. (2012) *The Unreal Estate Guide to Detroit*. The University of Michigan Press.
Lefebvre, H. (1991) *The Production of Space*. Blackwell.
Lefebvre, H. (2004) *Rhythmanalysis: Space, Time, and Everyday Life*. Continuum.
Lepeska, D. (November 10, 2011) "Is Blotting the Best Solution for Shrinking Cities?" Available online at: www.citylab.com/housing/2011/11/blotting-good-or-bad-shrinking-cities/470/ (Last accessed on February 15, 2015).
McKenzie, E. (1994) *Privatopia: Homeowner Associations and the Rise of Residential Private Governments*. Yale University Press.
Rugare, S. and Schwarz, T. (Eds.) (2008) *Cities Growing Smaller*. Cleveland Urban Design Collaborative at Kent State University.

Ryan, B. (2012) *Design After Decline: How America Rebuilds Shrinking Cities.* University of Pennsylvania Press.

Strahilevitz, L. J. (2015) Exclusionary Amenity. Armborst, T., D'Oca, D. and Theodore, G. (Eds.) *The Arsenal of Inclusion and Exclusion.* Actar.

Conversations 3

RAO: A thread which comes across is the question of the public. I think that all of the projects are acts of design at another level insofar as they're acts of rendering a public, they're acts of designers' rendering. If you think about design strictly as a form-giving practice, then what they remind us is that the public is not just there as the normative abstract concept that people in social sciences are used to thinking with, but something that always has to be rendered and brought into being. And it also suggests to me that what is innovative about the projects is that you are harnessing an idea not only of rendering a public, but also of rendering that public through the lens of the counter-public, like Michael Warner has done: so a public that is always in opposition to what is, that is always struggling to bring something else into being. I think it is incredibly interesting how the different projects were mobilizing this idea of the space in between a public and a counter-public, a public that we can all understand and share with, and then this other public which is there but invisible, not quite realized yet. It seems to me that the power of the counter-public resides in harnessing of other temporality as the emergent temporality.

That said, the thing that also seems so interesting in your harnessing of the idea of meta-topics: for instance, the idea that "service" in Lara Penin's work is something that gets blurred when a giver and a receiver are both the same, or in the idea of the "blotting" in Triboro's work where what lies underneath the normative framework is still visible, but it's simultaneously being erased and it's coming into being.

LARA PENIN: It is essential for us to have the perspective of discovering through research what's there, but I think this thing of going and seeing what is already there is design. It's really a part of design, it's not like you're going to do research and then you're going to propose something. We are in a comfortable position because we are doing our work from a research lab in a university, it's not that we have a client to which I have to respond. So it's a comfortable position for a researcher to be in. So, nobody gave us a brief and defining the brief, or the problem-finding aspect of it, for me is design. It's in the DNA of designing.

GABRIELA RENDON: When I started my practice as an urbanist, I moved from Monterrey, a city in the north of Mexico, to the Netherlands, one the most planned countries in the world. We started our cooperative with people who are from other places, none of us were Dutch and we didn't speak the language. When we started the projects in the neighborhoods in Rotterdam, it was really amazing to discover that many of the same conditions we encountered there were happening in other places too. Particularly, doing the work in the neighborhoods inhabited by immigrant communities and building close working relationships with local organizations were interesting ways of discovering that we had many things in common, partly because we were all from abroad. Officials in the local municipality were impressed by how effectively we could relate to the local people, specifically with a lot of illegal immigrants in this area. Local immigrant communities in Rotterdam were hurt by many urban policies that were implemented with no connection at all to the practice of everyday life in these areas. We were aware that doing research with this public is really sensitive because they have been put through so many programs that have failed and that ended up displacing them. With that experience in mind, we are trying to design projects where we can involve the inhabitants but clearly in different ways than the municipalities of Rotterdam usually do. You need to have a transdisciplinary approach in order to properly tackle issues and really work in the city.

TOBIAS ARMBORST: Our practice is very much New York-based, and we're very much based here because our work method requires being in a place for a really long time, otherwise it's very inefficient to look very closely at what's already there. Also, I would say that it's actually not that typical in the conventional design and urban planning practice. I know it's changing, but urban planning has historically not been a practice of looking very, very closely at what's already there. In our project in Detroit we saw local residents making all sorts of things with their land, and recoding and making sense of all the stuff that's going on out there has been fascinating, but again I don't think that has been traditionally the role that planning plays.

RAO: What I was trying to say is that this particular aspect of your work is where innovation occurs. To the contrary, planning has been based on the premise of an erasure of the present, of imagining something new but not really taking into account what is already there. Moving from what is to what could be without actually presuming that in order to innovate you have to be in a particular position, a part of a critical, creative population and yet not be part of those who participate in a particular kind of strategy of urban renewal, that is, gentrification.

PENIN: In terms of mapping creative and innovative urban practices, it was interesting to compare Lower East Side with Williamsburg because Williamsburg seems to be the Lower East Side of 20 years ago. Sometimes we tend to look at places and we assume that there is a conflict between the gentrifiers and the traditional population, but often we discovered that there wasn't a conflict, and that the quality of the urban experience relies precisely on the dialogue between those different historic layers and populations. We realized that the Polish community likes the hipster bar next door, not everything about it, but there are also positive aspects.

BRIAN McGRATH: Some of the interesting things in this discussion are the different research and operational tactics all of you employ. Given that you are all foreigners in cities where you work, I wonder how difficult is it within your practices to engage all these different people, communities, and organizations? Vyjayanthi, from your disciplinary position, can you put on your anthropologist hat and critique the terms of designers' delving into ethnography?

RAO: I think that the tactics of making these incredibly detailed maps and lists and observations all our colleagues presented are incredibly rich, and what you have to know is when to deploy which tactic and under what circumstances. From that point of view, all of the speakers gave us a very different palette, and it all hinged upon what is the problematique at hand. Is it about time? Is it about suggesting that research itself is an act of design? Is it about making an intervention that can actually reclaim a certain aspect of urban life that has been really disavowed? After all, it's taking a point of departure which is theoretical and then trying to reclaim or re-script it. I would say that one is always re-scripting: the ethnographer is rescripting by performing a particular locality, having observed enough and having socialized that observation. But then so are you all.

In relation to the observation that was made earlier about the structure that the researcher creates by his or her presence: If you extend that to saying that structure always leaves a trace, but that structure is also a trace of the kinds of institutional forces that go into recognizing the slum condition and as a problem to be solved, and by identifying the actors who will be solving those problems. If you combine that with an earlier discussion of removing or reserving the question of the problematic nature of the object of research, then I think there might be a space for thinking more productively of where the research and the researchers sit vis-a-vis the potential for solution, right? Potential for solution and in that sense, I guess, potential for design, and also potential for a solution that's not necessarily simply functional but it also could be speculative, which I think was what Ivan Kucina was suggesting. So it may or may not involve the community, and I think we have to be open to that.

Chapter 11

Building Community Capacities through Design: Amplify New York

Lara Penin and Eduardo Stasowski

Amplifying Creative Communities in New York City (Amplify) is a project carried out by Parsons Design for Social Innovation and Sustainability (DES S) Lab between 2009 and 2012.[1] Parsons DESIS Lab is a research laboratory at Parsons School for Design, The New School. A significant part of our work involves faculty colleagues, fellow researchers, and our students, as much of the research, ideation, and prototyping occur as part of the course-work in different programs across The New School. We are also a member of the DESIS Network—a network of design labs, based in design schools and design-oriented universities, actively involved in promoting and supporting sustainable change.[2] Parsons DESIS Lab explores the relationship between design and social change, bringing nuanced approaches drawn from integrated design practices to communities of all kinds. In Parsons DESIS Lab, service design is considered an advanced design approach, one integrating many design disciplines[3] essential in a complex world facing numerous systemic challenges. This is an important disciplinary clarification since the service design approach differs from more traditional fields centered in the urban sphere such as urbanism, as the Amplify projects will demonstrate in what follows.

There are two premises that are foundational to our approach: the first is that of *creative communities* (Meroni 2007), and the second is of *collaborative services* (Jégou and Manzini 2008). Both originated in the research project titled Emerging User Demands for Sustainable Solutions (EMUDE)[4] led by the research team at the Politecnico di Milano in Italy, and initially involving a number of other European design institutions and schools. The work subsequently expanded geographically to Brazil, India, China, and South Africa, and eventually the network was formalized into DESIS. The definition of *creative communities* overlaps with that of *social innovation* in that "creative communities" are deeply rooted in places, they make the most innovative use of available local resources, they promote new forms of social exchange and cooperation, and they align individually-minded solutions with shared social and environmental goals (Manzini 2007: 14). By definition, they lead the community-based social innovation that redefines "creativity" as a collective social praxis oriented toward creating a common good. Not surprisingly, such communities tend to be created in complex and challenging urban environments where citizens cooperate, self-organize, and create innovative ideas in neighborhoods that lack municipal support, and are entrepreneurial out of necessity.

While "creative communities" defines a type of communal organization of citizens, the term "collaborative services" defines a type of social practice. Collaborative service is a type of service based on collaboration within a creative community. EMUDE—the research project from which DESIS emerged—studied and documented hundreds of cases of creative communities and collaborative services from around the world. Collaborative services include cohousing solutions, food coops, senior self-help groups, neighborhood care groups, community-based care groups, and time banks, among many others. Even though analogous models were found in different geocultural contexts, each case was unique and responded to different kinds of social and economic pressures. It is worth noting that when this series of projects first started, these ideas and service schemes were quite new forms of social enterprise. Now, 10 years later, that might still be the case for some; however, many collaborative services have evolved into successful business models and become accepted and valued by the general public. Car sharing businesses have prospered across cities and regions around the world, as have models based on optimizing idle infrastructure, such as AirBnB and several other models of sharing (Botsman and Rogers 2010). The collaborative consumption models mapped by Botsman are characterized both by cultural innovation and their business and income generation possibilities. Some of them have the distinct social qualities of the initiatives covered by EMUDE, and later by Amplify. As design researchers studying innovative services, we focused on the relational aspects and social mechanics of collaboration. These appeared to us as key qualities in the definition of a sustainable conviviality[5] in the city and, moreover, represented a critical aspect in approaching the services we studied as transferable models.

Services are commonly defined by the interaction between a service provider and a service user; a typical example of such an interaction is the bank teller. At the moment when service happens, the quality of interaction can be empirically measured. In contrast, what happens in collaborative services is that those involved are simultaneously performing the roles of "service users" and "service providers," blurring the traditional binary distinction. When that happens, existing social norms often give way to new types of social interaction based on equality and reciprocity. Collaborative services are often demanding and time-consuming, and based on social relationships. Individuals are involved as volunteers benefiting from the social interactions produced in collaborative services. In this process, design is understood as social praxis, and as "an activity that aims to make social innovation practical and desirable" (Jégou and Manzini 2008).

With the Amplify project in New York, we were interested in understanding what kinds of collaborative services have been practiced in the city. In the process of sampling from specific neighborhoods in the city, we formed partnerships with organizations that were essential for the development of Amplify. These organizations included the Green Map System, a sustainability-focused mapping system and platform, and the Lower East Side Ecology Center

(LESEC), a not-for-profit organization carrying out a myriad of community initiatives around environmental issues. LESEC's standing in the Lower East Side (LES), and the trust they had built over thirty years, made our work in the community possible. Our design partner was IDEO, the well-established design consultancy and innovation company, whose capacity to do complex work was an incredible asset to us, given our limited human and financial resources. We also established a special partnership with In Your Own Backyards (ioby), a crowd-funding platform for micro community-based environmental projects.

The Amplify project proposed an original perspective on how design-based action could help urban communities promote sustainable lifestyles. The trigger point for the project was that urban communities could no longer afford to wait for municipal governments to take action and resolve the challenges of everyday life. Many had self-organized, reorganized local resources, and promoted communal initiatives that, in aggregate, could be understood as new models for defining more sustainable urban living. Our focus was on how we as designers could facilitate the process of identifying such social practices; provide spatial logic to them; disseminate knowledge and promote a structured social discourse around them; and advance the conversation around amplifying sustainable lifestyles in communities across the city. On the one hand, our goal was to advance the design capacity of urban communities by modeling emerging collaborative service ideas, and on the other, to define a new domain of professional design practice.

In the first two years of the project, we conducted what we call "amplification processes" in two neighborhoods of New York City: the Lower East Side of Manhattan and in North Brooklyn (Figure 11.1). Working in these different neighborhoods and with very different communities allowed for the productive parallels and comparisons that drove the research aspect of this project. The process of amplification started with unearthing hidden examples of social innovation in the above neighborhoods: cases of individuals who had organized themselves resourcefully and who had promoted radically more sustainable ways of urban living. Then we showcased these practices. Our process included design-led field research, the production of short films, and exhibitions where discovered and framed stories of local social innovation were shown and debated. One of the main questions driving our work was: How can these situated models of social innovation be transferred to other communities across the city? One kind of outcome we produced consisted in making models of creative communities and communal services through manuals and toolkits. Paramount to our approach was to capture the voice of the community in order to build a positive approach toward sustainability and *amplify* positive change.

In 2010, we initiated our research in the Lower East Side—a unique urban place based on wave upon wave of immigration, starting with Europeans who inhabited tenement houses in the nineteenth and early twentieth centuries, through more recent immigrant groups from Latin America in the 1970s, and to the expansion of Chinatown in the 1980s (Figure 11.2). Because of its unique ethnic diversity, the Lower East Side's cultural life has been extraordinarily rich. With the transition from a manufacturing-based to a service-based economy in the mid-twentieth century, and later, with the city's fiscal and economic crisis

▶ Figure 11.1

Amplify project map © Parsons DESIS Lab.

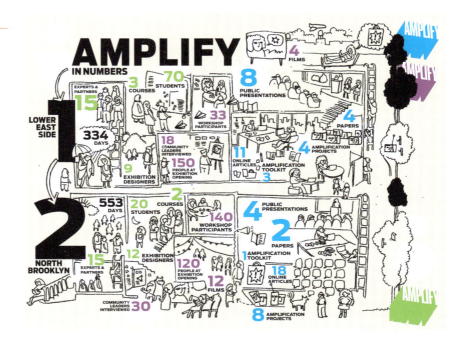

▲ Figure 11.2

Lowe East Side, corner of Rivington and Clinton Streets, 2010 © Parsons DESIS Lab.

CHAPTER 11 Building Community through Design

in the 1980s, the tenement buildings became economically obsolete and much of the building stock in the area decayed or was demolished. As a result, the 1970s and 1980s saw the emergence of numerous vacant urban lots that became dead spots in the urban fabric of the area. The then-affordable rents were attractive to recent immigrants, emerging artists, and numerous creative individuals committed to communal living and working. Many vacant spaces, thanks to the community's self-organization, were incrementally transformed into the current community gardens (Figure 11.3). With an initial historical analysis of the area and later interviews with residents and urban activists in the neighborhood, our hypothesis was that these once vacant urban lots transformed into community gardens embodied the know-how of the local social innovation practices in the LES, and they consequently became the main focus of our research into the situated creative communities of the LES.

In our research we learned that the individuals involved in the community gardens already partake in collaborative service schemes; for example, these community gardens are based on a membership model that grants access to those who participate in garden maintenance. Together with our students, we

▼ Figure 11.3

Community Garden on Avenue B and 6th Street, 2010 © Parsons DESIS Lab.

approached gardeners in eighteen different communities in order to map out the collaborative modalities and potentially hidden social practices that occur inside their gardens. Focusing on the gardens' activities, services, and overall sets of values, we began to better understand the social innovation agendas and modalities in the area. We learned that each community garden is unique in terms of history and personal investment of residents and users. Some function as the backyards of residential buildings and expand neighborhood relationships. In other cases, the ethnic background of the community is the key aspect of the garden, functioning as an informal social center for a cultural group. This is true of many gardens with a "casita" (little house) used to shelter players of the domino game, popular within Puerto Rican and other Central American communities.

Some gardens have invested in urban agriculture (Figure 11.4), where users can have plots to grow herbs, tomatoes, and other crops for their own consumption. Typically these gardens are open to the general public during the day (in the warm months) and groups of residents are the guardians and have the keys. There is support from the NYC Parks Department (through the Green Thumb program), but to gain privileged access residents must carry the responsibility of taking care of the gardens on a daily basis. This semi-public, and, in some cases, fluctuating use of the community gardens can result in gardeners complaining about things such as missing tomatoes. In practice,

▼ Figure 11.4

Community Garden on Avenue B and 6th Street, 2010 © Parsons DESIS Lab.

gardens function more as a social recreation practice than a steady source of produce. Talking to the gardeners, however, revealed a high sense of pride and responsibility for the gardens. This sense of ownership contributes to the viability of community gardens, which depend on committed individuals who invest time and effort in their upkeep.

After interviews and data collection done by our team, we analyzed the modes and functioning of a sample of the gardens, identifying four main areas of interest that synthesized the social innovation agenda in the LES (Figure 11.5). The first of these areas is *cultural diversity*, framed by the question: How can rich cultural heritage translate into a social asset? The second is *senior care*, which, with the recent withdrawal of public investment in local senior centers and the significant senior population of the LES, became a priority in the local social agenda. The third area of interest is *housing*, particularly significant given the increasing pressures of gentrification, where communities struggle to learn how social capital and traditional neighborhood practices can act as references for resistance. Finally, the fourth area is *food*: with crescent interest in alternative and healthy food provisions such as urban agriculture and food coops, how to

▼ Figure 11.5

Analytical graph visualizing the main social innovation typologies occurring in selected LES community gardens © Parsons DESIS Lab.

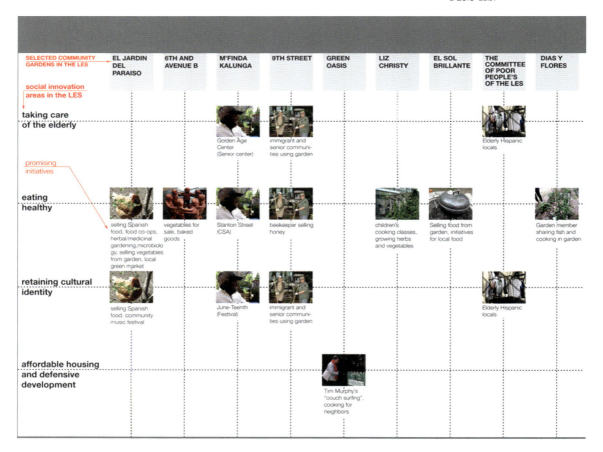

promote these in an accessible way so that they become inclusive models for the entire LES population?

The findings/questions above guided the following actions dedicated to the design of new scenarios. The four "themes" (cultural diversity, senior care, housing, and food) were articulated as four design briefs proposed to our students in a summer course at Parsons (Figure 11.6). Our students worked with IDEO designers to design scenarios and concepts of new services responding to the four questions/themes. The resulting projects included a proposal for a community supported agriculture scheme within residential buildings, a peer-to-peer recreation service for seniors, and a skill-share program in a residential building. The projects reconfigured existing models into different scales and connection modalities. These projects/scenarios were publicly shown in an early development phase in Amplify's first public exhibition, got feedback from residents and design experts, and were later reworked into a series of *instructables*, available on the project website.

Abrons Art Center in the Henry Street Settlement hosted the Amplify Lower East Side exhibition in August 2010. The exhibition was instrumental to our research strategy (Figure 11.7), aiming at sharing insights, collecting data, and promoting collective debate about local issues. It was conceived partly as a showcase of research findings (regarding the local collaborative practices, including the community gardens), and partly as a public consultation and

▶ Figure 11.6

Table with four main themes and corresponding design briefs © Parsons DESIS Lab.

Theme	Design brief
Theme 1: Amplifying Healthy and Local Food Initiatives Access to fresh, locally produced, and chemical-free food is becoming a priority for many families. There are many interesting sustainable food initiatives in the North Brooklyn neighborhood: a thriving farmers market, cooking clubs, community supported agriculture group, community gardens, composting initiatives, restaurants sourcing local and organic produce.	How can these initiatives inspire us and help us amplify the access to healthy and local food in North Brooklyn?
Theme 2: Amplifying Sharing Economies Sharing is about optimizing the use of existing resources. It is a phenomenon that is quickly spreading throughout Williamsburg and Greenpoint. It is challenging and transforming the way people live, work and consume. Not only do sharing initiatives reduce environmental impact but they also strengthen social ties within the community. North Brooklynites share spaces for living and working as well as sharing their skills and resources to save money and the environment.	How can we amplify the idea of sharing so that more people can benefit from it and improve the quality of their lives and the neighborhood as a whole?
Theme 3: Amplifying Environmental Well-being North Brooklyn is a place in transformation. This once industrial and manufacturing powerhouse is quickly becoming predominantly residential. However, the legacy of its industrial past still lingers with both positive and negative implications. Urban activists in the community are fighting for more open and green spaces, proposing solutions for vacant lots and dilapidated structures; and, advocating for the revitalization of the waterfront.	How can we amplify our capacity to influence the transformation of the city and give the community the tools to voice their opinions and concerns?
Theme 4: Amplifying Alternative Transportation With a growing population and saturated public transportation services, people are looking for alternative modes of transportation that keep our streets clean, calm and safe. North Brooklyn has a bicycle culture of its own that manifests across different cultures, whether they are Latino, orthodox Jewish or hipster. There are bike clubs, bike repair classes, bike racks, bike rentals and even vending machines for bike parts. These initiatives demonstrate how the neighborhood is open to embrace smarter solutions.	How can we amplify and diversify sustainable modes of transportation?

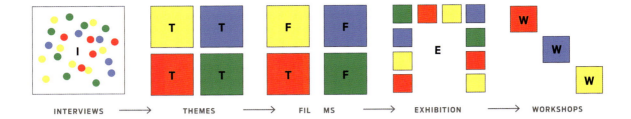

▲ Figure 11.7

Synthesis of the Amplification Process © Parsons DESIS Lab.

research device with interactive installations. One such installation was a large tabletop map of the LES where the public was asked to flag anecdotes and narratives of social innovation using prompt cards (Figure 11.8). In another installation we showed international cases of creative communities and asked the public to imagine if such a practice would work in the Lower East Side—in other words, if it was transferable as a model or not. We gathered a significant amount of data through the interactions that occurred during the exhibition (Figure 11.9).

▶ Figure 11.8

Table installation in Abrons Gallery © Parsons DESIS Lab.

▶ Figure 11.9

View of installations in Abrons Gallery © Parsons DESIS Lab.

The impact of the project actions on the LES was in part measured through the great turnout at the exhibition as well as the vigor and quality of the discussions and debates that happened during the events (pre-opening event, opening, and workshops). Luring busy residents into participating in workshops and debates is often challenging, especially when it involves people who are particularly active in their own initiatives, such as community gardens. The events and debates were nevertheless rich and critical. The main topics of public discussions revolved around the ongoing real-estate pressures and the rampaging gentrification that has engulfed this area of the city, and its effects in the LES. Even though the current neighborhood income levels are still low when compared to the city's average,[6] the picture today is quite different from the images of the past, and the need for creative communities and collaborative services has never been greater than it is today.

The results of Amplify LES can be measured therefore not only in terms of outcomes, but also as a process. The articulation of the four themes through mini-documentaries and scenarios/concepts proposed by our students proved to be a valid approach and helped feed the residents' conversation about their own priorities. As part of social design practices, DiSalvo et al. (2011) define the *collective articulation of issues* as a "practice of social design and social innovation by which designers and participants work together to reveal the factors, relations and consequences of an issue" (Figures 11.10 and 11.11). Through the use of "staged events, objects and settings to elicit concepts for products and services," our project helped answer the question around the possible roles a designer can play in the collaborative process of social innovation (Margolin and Margolin 2002: 28; DiSalvo et al. 2011: 196).

In 2011, the second year of the project, we worked in the North Brooklyn area (Williamsburg and Greenpoint). With a strong industrial background, Williamsburg also has a history of urban decay that is comparable to that of the Lower East Side. After the Bloomberg administration-led 2005 re-zoning of the neighborhood, based largely on the repurposing of the old industrial warehouses

CHAPTER 11 Building Community through Design

◀ **Figure 11.10**

Workshops with residents and experts during , St Nick's Allience Gallery in North Brooklyn © Parsons DESIS Lab.

▼ **Figure 11.11**

Workshop with the MFA Transdisciplinary Design students and the IDEO team at St. Nick's Alliance Gallery © Parsons DESIS Lab.

and factories (such as the old Domino Sugar factory) into high-end residential and mixed-use buildings, rapid urban transformation has been in progress. Many residents are being forced out, and the ongoing process of gentrification is considerably affecting the social dynamic of the neighborhood. These changes affect particularly the more traditional urban populations who have inhabited the area for a long time, such as the Polish, Hasidic Jewish, Puerto Rican, and African American communities.

Our design and research approach, in this second iteration of the Amplify project, built upon the learning outcomes of the LES research. First, we enhanced the research action, this time guided by an ethnographer, who helped structure the thirty interviews with local social innovators. In Williamsburg there is no comparable urban situation to the community gardens of the LES, and therefore there is less clarity regarding the drives and priorities of local social innovation. The research analysis was essential to helping our team define the themes/topics that were the most critical for local residents. We identified the following topics: *occupation of the waterfront* now that the area was leaving behind its industrial character; *transportation alternatives*, since the neighborhood was becoming more and more integrated in the fabric of New York City, and bicycles were beginning to be incorporated into the urban transportation and mobility infrastructure; *access to fresh, healthy food*, where a local farmers market offered a good starting point for better food provisions; and, *the boom of a local sharing economy*, in which young residents interested in exploring new forms of resourcing their everyday lives have turned to cohousing schemes, coworking spaces and skill sharing organizations.

Based on interviews and field research, we collaborated with filmmakers to produce short documentaries about these innovators and their stories. These were first shown in May 2011 in the exhibition we set up at the St. Nick's Alliance (a local not for profit organization) arts space. Expanding on the LES experience, the Brooklyn exhibition was proposed as an events space where a series of workshops involving different groups of stakeholders were carried out for two weeks (Figures 11.12 and 11.13).

The Amplify project is a design-based contribution to the production of complex urban conditions; our perspective and approach are defined by focusing on the urban experience of creative communities in New York City and their struggles to improve the sustainability and resilience of their life in the city by resorting to socially-innovative practices that include the design of groundbreaking communal service schemes. Service design is important to us here because our focus is on the space of human and social interaction, not urban forms, be they gardens or buildings. Service design looks at how human interactions can be designed, over time, through different material channels that include urban space; however, in parallel, we also consider other subjective perceptions that define the urban experience, especially relational and social. Even though space and urban morphology are important to determine the quality of urban experiences, in our practice we are focused on designing services and suggesting models of social interaction, thus contributing to the understanding and practice of designing the so-called "soft" dimensions of urban systems and urban infrastructures that are equally important to the quality

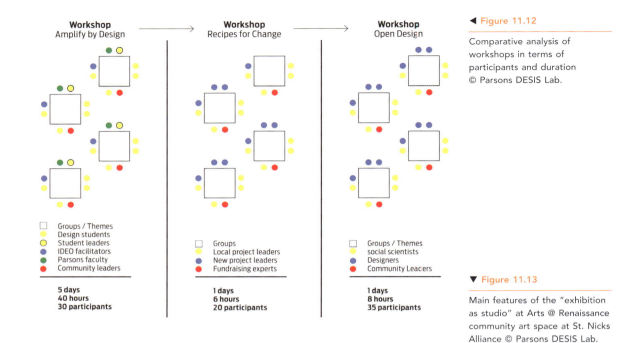

◀ Figure 11.12

Comparative analysis of workshops in terms of participants and duration © Parsons DESIS Lab.

▼ Figure 11.13

Main features of the "exhibition as studio" at Arts @ Renaissance community art space at St. Nicks Alliance © Parsons DESIS Lab.

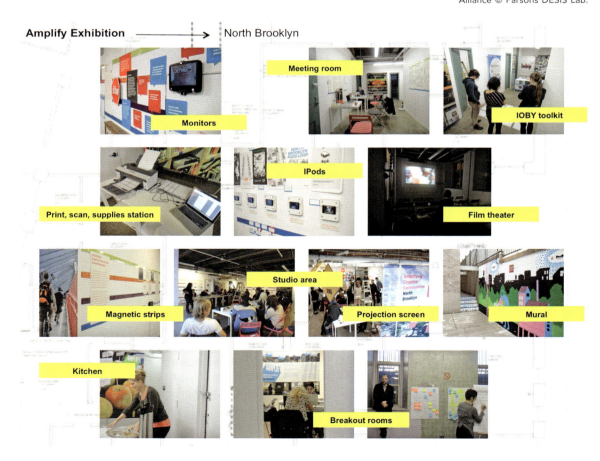

of everyday life. We maintain that this is a dimension that can be activated by design, which can help by creating new circuits for public engagement and participation.

The contribution of the Amplify project toward a new vision of urbanity is partly methodological, partly epistemological, and partly political. Service Design is defined as essentially a human-centric design, where understanding and learning from people "is not optional" (Manzini 2011) but a fundamental part of a research practice based on ethnography as well as on participatory methods such as workshops and probes. These and other "orchestrated" events aim at unlocking the understanding of communities regarding their own values and aspirations, as well as codeveloping and debating potential solutions and ideas for change. It contributes to the "articulation of issues" (DiSalvo et al. 2011) on a local scale as a strategy to promote positive change. Our aspiration is that this approach supports the development and diffusion of new, democratic urban governing practices. Through a model such as Amplify, we see a way to reconnect citizens to the production of their own convivial spaces where industrial tools (Illich 1973; Sanders and Stappers 2012) as well as governmental bureaucracies have failed. In his 1973 book *Tools for Conviviality*, Ivan Illich called for setting limits to the industrial approach to society, where mass production (applied to both products and services) turns "people into the accessories of bureaucracies and machines," undermines "the texture of community" and estranges people from the power of producing and controlling their own physical and social spaces. By bringing this kind of human-centric approach into the realm of the urban, we hope to contribute to the recuperation of people's right to determine their own meanings and attributes of the urban environment in which they live.

Notes

1. Amplify was made possible by a grant from the 2009 Rockefeller Foundation's New York City Cultural Innovation Fund, which focused on New York-specific initiatives. The project aimed at identifying and highlighting communities in NYC neighborhoods who promote sustainable social innovations and use service design to make them more robust.
2. For reference see: www.desis-network.org/ (Last Accessed on February 15, 2015).
3. Parsons DESIS Lab Vision as stated on its website, www.newschool.edu/desis/ (Last accessed on February 15, 2015).
4. EMUDE (2004–06) was a Specific Support Action financed by the European Commission Directorate:

    > The project started by observing a phenomenon of social innovation: the emergence in Europe of groups of active, enterprising people inventing and putting into practice original ways of dealing with everyday problems, ways that can be considered promising in terms of sustainability. Taking these cases as a base, the research outlines a comprehensive map of emerging sustainable user demands and generates a set of qualitative scenarios of how these demands, and the consequent product-service innovation, may co-evolve.
    >
    > (Manzini and Meroni 2007)

5. The term "conviviality" is used by Ivan Illich to describe a society "in which modern technologies serve politically interrelated individuals rather than managers" (Illich 1973),

articulating a relationship between persons, tools, and a new collectivity. Illich questions the industrial system on which the power of technology and technology-based systems end up reducing the role of individuals into mere consumers, removed from decision making. In this sense, conviviality evokes individual freedom, personal agency and creativity as well as personal interdependency. A convivial society "would be the result of social arrangements that guarantee for each member the most ample and free access to the tools of the community and limits this freedom only in favor of another member's equal freedom."
6. The Lower East Side's income is nearly half of the average of all of Manhattan, according to the NYC Income Map (2009).

Bibliography

Botsman, R. and Rogers, R. (2010) *What's Mine Is Yours: The Rise of Collaborative Consumption*. HarperBusiness.

DiSalvo, C., Lodato, T., Fries, L., Schechter, B. and Barnwell, T. (2011) "The Collective Articulation of Issues as Design Practice." *CoDesign: International Journal of CoCreation in Design and the Arts*, Vol. 7, No. 3/4. Special Issue: Socially Responsive Design. Taylor & Francis.

Illich, I. (1974) *Tools for Conviviality*. Marion Boyars Publishers.

Jégou, F. and Manzini, E (2008) *Collaborative Services: Social Innovation and Design for Sustainability*. Edizioni Polidesign.

Manzini, E. (2007) A Laboratory of Ideas: Diffused Creativity and New Ways of Doing. Meroni, A. (Ed.) *Creative Communities: People Inventing Sustainable Ways of Living*. Polidesign, pp. 13–15.

Manzini, E. (Spring 2010) "Small, Local, Open, and Connected: Design for Social Innovation and Sustainability." *The Journal of Design Strategies: Change Design*. No. 1, pp. 8–11.

Manzini, E. (2011) Introduction. Meroni, A. and Sangiorgi, D. (Eds.) *Design for Services*. Gower.

Manzini, E. and Meroni, A. (2007) Emerging User Demands for Sustainable Solutions, EMUDE. Ralf, M. (Ed.) *Design Research Now*. Birkhäuser, pp. 157–179.

Margolin, V. and Margolin, S. (2002) "A Social Model of Design: Issues of Practice and Research." *Design Issues*, Vol. 18, No. 4, pp. 24–30.

Mendelsohn, J. (2009) *The Lower East Side Remembered and Revisited: History and Guide to a Legendary Neighborhood*. Columbia University Press.

Meroni, A. (2007) *Creative Communities: People Inventing Sustainable Ways of Living*. Polidesign.

Mulgan, G., Tucker, S., Ali, R. and Sanders, B. (2007) *Social Innovation: What It Is, Why It Matters and How It Can Be Accelerated*. The Young Foundation, Skoll Centre for Social Entrepreneurship, Oxford Said Business School.

Murray, R., Caulier-Grice, J. and Mulgan, G. (2010) *The Open Book of Social Innovation*. The Young Foundation/Nesta.

New York City Department of City Planning. (2012) Manhattan Community District 3 Profile. Available online at: www.nyc.gov/html/dcp/pdf/lucds/mn3profile.pdf (Last accessed on February 15, 2015).

NYC Income Map. (2012) The Envisioning Development Toolkit. Center for Urban Pedagogy, Pratt Center for Community Development, and the Fifth Avenue Committee. Available online at: http://envisioningdevelopment.net/map (Last accessed on February 15, 2015).

Sanders, E. B. and Stappers, P. J. (2012) *Convivial Toolbox: Generative Research for the Front End of Design*. BIS.

Chapter 12

Design Action

Deborah Gans

In 2007–08, I worked with the curators Aaron Levy and Bill Menking to conceptualize the exhibition *Into the Open: Positioning Practice*[1] that debuted as the official United States entry in the 2008 Venice Architecture Biennale. The Biennale's 11th International Architecture Exhibition, titled *Out There: Architecture Beyond Building*, was directed by Aaron Betsky and presented an excellent context for the new and emerging American sensibility in that it challenged exhibitors to face critical social themes in curating architecture. For those who were already familiar with the long-standing urban and architectural practices selected for the exhibition, the show might not have seemed very radical. However, for the State Department of the George W. Bush administration —which officially promoted the pavilion—the idea of a national exhibition devoted to design-led social practice was radically innovative. The very staging of such an exhibition in the American national pavilion in Venice was meant to send a global message of the general repositioning of American social values. As straightforward as the front-stage message repositioning of "design by the people and for the people" was, the behind-the-scenes discourse was much more complex and nuanced.

In arriving at the final selection of projects, we focused on two critical issues: first, the distinction between architecture produced through social processes rather than autonomous formal explorations; and second, the distinction between top-down and bottom-up social processes. Clearly, the exhibition's message foregrounded the bottom-up processes and social and civic engagement; but our internal decision-making regarding the projects was marked by hard negotiations over these terms. For instance, the curatorial team had ongoing arguments about separating the power of form from the power of social processes. The iconic buildings of the Rural Studio were admired for their formal properties, and as such were to be included in the exhibition, even though it was unclear how potent such one-off rural structures built without significant code regulations were as a generalizable social practice. On the other hand, when presented with Ted Smith's alternative sweat equity-based development process in the highly regulated context of San Francisco—where Smith and Others Architects designed a series of cooperative, experimental urban housing prototypes—the curators regretted that Smith's building forms were not equally radical. The pitfalls of the curatorial devotion to the bottom-up process became seriously challenged in the discussion of the Floating Pool Lady, a floating pool built on a barge designed by Jonathan Kirschenfeld Architects because it was the brainchild of a socialite and managed by the top-down bureaucracy of the New York City Department of Parks and Recreation. Additionally, its carefully detailed rationalist aesthetic lacked the messy playfulness commonly associated with an "architecture of the people." Only after the pool was indeed included in the Biennale did its importance as a social project emerge. During the summer of 2008, the actual traveling pool was docked in the Barretto Point Park in the South Bronx (SoBro), where the community had to cross highways, train tracks, and garbage dumps to reach the park. The difficult walk to the pool galvanized the community to self-organize vis-a-vis environmental justice issues and approach city officials demanding the brownfields they crossed be cleaned. The protest received wide media coverage while the Venice Biennale was in progress.

The strength of *Into the Open* resided in the way the exhibit transgressed initial categorical distinctions between socially and formally determined work, bottom-up and top-down processes as well as small individuated acts and large-scale projects. These dialectics can be disempowering to the people they supposedly serve, as evidenced in post-Katrina New Orleans. There, the city was paralyzed by its inability to negotiate between citizens' right to stay and the public administration's desire to increase wetlands. In New York City after Hurricane Sandy, and increasingly in the context of climate change, we will need to invent complex design processes that connect and mediate between large-scale coordinated environmental actions, community plans, and acts of individual citizens.

Gans Studio's first-hand experience in the power and limitation of bottom-up design began with a series of product design endeavors, in which product design worked as a model for scaling up and for social form-finding. At its best, product design directly engages the potential community of users throughout the design process, produces objects whose aesthetic is based in their performance, and achieves large-scale transformation of society incrementally, one individual at a time. The studio's first foray into the product design process was in 2002, when The New York City School Construction Authority (NYCSCA) approached us to prototype the school desk for the future that ultimately became The Workbox-Next Generation School Desk (Figure 12.1). Before beginning design, we first visited a variety of New York City public schools and learned that due to overcrowding, cafeterias and gymnasia were used as provisional classrooms. Some of the students who did not have classrooms at school came from homes where they did not have bedrooms. They needed a "home base" desk that *de facto* performed as a portable property.[2] We designed the Workbox as a two-foot cube that unfolds to become an individual private space and operates like an office system. It has a place for nametags, a graffiti surface for personal expression, a coat hook, a book bag shelf, and an oversized surface that holds a computer and drawing pad simultaneously. When deployed, it can also create social interactive groups and be clustered so that the students interact not just with their screens, but also with the peers around them. The Workbox was tested in the so-called inclusive classrooms that combined children with and without disabilities, where it succeeded in engaging students both individually and in groups.

▶ Figure 12.1

The Workbox-Next Generation School Desk © Gans Studio.

Project team: Deborah Gans and Matthew Jelacic.

We brought the product design approach to an architectural commission in 2003 when asked by the nonprofit housing developer, Common Ground Community,[3] to design their so-called First-Step housing prototype for homeless individuals and families just off the streets of New York. As in the case of the Workbox, we began by visiting existing conditions, in this case Flophouses. We interviewed potential residents and worked with them throughout the design process, and then built a prototype for them to scrutinize and test out. We designed bedrooms to be located within a larger shelter space as a "flat-pack" system of a cruciform aluminum extrusion that acts as the frame and a plywood panel that acts as the wall. The units can be assembled separately for single room occupancy or in suites. To comply with the Americans with Disabilities Act (ADA)[4] requirements, the rooms needed to be spacious. One resident commented it was large enough for him to start a business there. The exterior porch, which gives the resident a private threshold, is created by the back of the projecting of the armoire which holds all the individual property that in common shelters would have to be discarded. The façade has three sliding doors of different transparencies that allow residents to control degrees of privacy, giving residents control over a range of environmental variables (Figure 12.2).

We also incorporated product design strategies for engaging community through tactical "game-changers" in larger urban planning scenarios, specifically in New Orleans East. There we worked in the quasi-suburban setting of the Plum Orchard (Figure 12.3) community as the architects for the now defunct Association

◀ Figure 12.2

First-Step housing prototype
© Gans Studio. Project team:
Deborah Gans, Matthew Jelacic
and Marguerite McGoldrick.

◀ Figure 12.3

Plum Orchard, New Orleans East
© Gans Studio.

for Community Organizations for Reform Now (ACORN).[5] The conventional conflict between the top-down and bottom-up approaches had paralyzed communities in East New Orleans where residents wanted to rebuild their houses in the aftermath of Hurricane Katrina, while the City intended to sacrifice the neighborhood to wetlands. In response, we tried to empower the community through design approaches that adapted the city's top-down environmental planning to their own needs. We discovered a small game-changer when we learned from the federal Environmental Protection Agency (EPA) that individual wetlands could be as effective as a major marsh.[6] Our "Project Backyard: An Alternative to Mowing" (Figure 12.4) presented a strategy for planting private property as wetlands with the capacity to absorb the first ten percent of a 100-year flood. If implemented consistently across a neighborhood of twelve blocks, which was the area of the community we worked with, that would translate to 150,000 gallons of water. As calculated by the Rational Method,[7] to reach the ten percent mark the yards have to be planted consistently and perform collectively in relation to drainage swales and catchment basins. While individual homeowners controlled their own backyard, our strategy was premised on the idea that they would also have to cooperate across their property lines for the overall strategy to be effective (Figure 12.5). Prior to the storm, the extended families with multiple properties that populated Plum Orchard had cooperated over issues of property, often renting to each other in order to provide internal socio-economic support to their families and neighbors in the absence of support from the government. The concept of community as a governing structure for fielding larger aspirations and planning strategies emerged over time as a consequence of the visioning sessions to discuss Project Backyard and other ideas in local church meetings. Our accomplishment in this project was in catalyzing communal scales of governance and action that had previously been missing in New Orleans (Figure 12.6).

▼ Figure 12.4

Project Backyard: An Alternative to Mowing © Gans Studio.

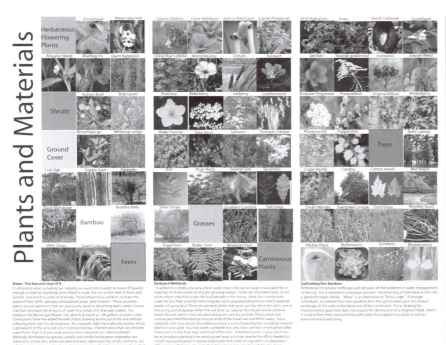

CHAPTER 12 Design Action

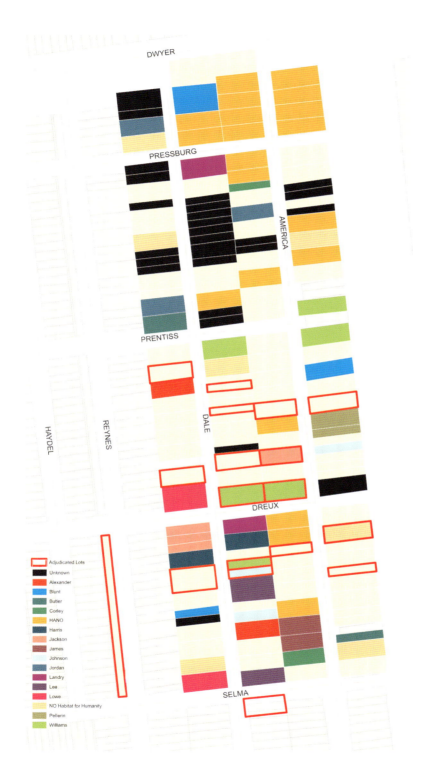

◀ Figure 12.5

Family networks, Plum Orchard,
Project team: Deborah Gans,
James Dart Architecture and
Justin Kray. © Gans Studio.

CHAPTER 12 Deborah Gans

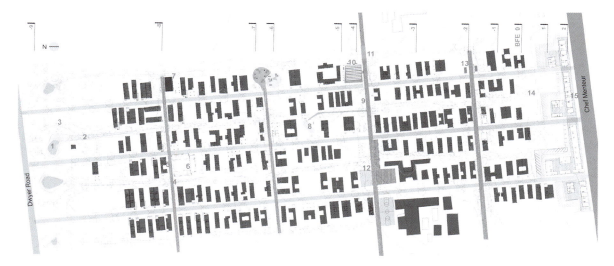

▲ Figure 12.6

Masterplan for Plum Orchard, New Orleans East © Gans Studio.

The ten percent goal depended on this social cooperation but also on the connection of the backyard infrastructure to larger scales of water management. In Plum Orchard, we were lucky to have had an exemplary situation in that the lower end of the site, where the backyard swales and retention ponds deliver the water, connected to a major pipeline under Dwyer Road that in turn connected to the adjacent Dwyer pumping station, which had been slated for improvement and increased capacity even before the storm. According to the calculations done by following the Rational Method, if all the proposed field conditions and instruments (including the Dwyer Road pump improvements) were implemented, the neighborhood would flood only at street level during a 100-year flood. It was the confluence of bottom-up and top-down strategies we had designed and instigated that gave the project its transformative capacity. It was also the inability of New Orleans to achieve that rapprochement of top-down and bottom-up on the political level as well as the demise of ACORN, that brought our project to a halt.

As an urban ecology, the dense settlement along the bayou of Lake Pontchartrain differs drastically form the ocean inlet of Sheepshead Bay in Brooklyn where we have been working since the super-storm Sandy in 2012. We likewise assumed the strategies for their post-flood futures would also differ. Yet, despite these environmental differences compounded by the difference in local cultures, a similar scale of urban operation and organization that is larger than a single block but smaller than a district has organically emerged. In New Orleans, this scale was the twelve blocks within natural and man-made boundaries of Plum Orchard. In Sheepshead Bay, it is a totality of six neighboring blocks called "courts" (Figure 12.7) that share an idiosyncratic structure of interior mews (Figure 12.8). Once again, as in New Orleans, this social and physical unit of urban planning has emerged as we have worked over an extended period with local residents: first, at the scale of the single property and then, as the neighbors have come together to leverage their efforts, at the scale of the block, community, and beyond.

CHAPTER 12 Design Action

Originally developed in the 1920s as bungalow settlements for seasonal usage on marshy infill, the courts now stand about four feet below street level in an area that was flooded to seven feet above street level by the super-storm Sandy. This sunken court structure is a consequence of the construction of the Coney Island Sewage Treatment Plant in the 1970s that entailed raising the streets but not the interior of the blocks. Consequently, the courts' water and power infrastructures are legally "off the city grid," and residents are responsible for all costs associated with upkeep and repair. The City contends that courts are private property because they do not connect to the network of public spaces and streets in spite of the fact that residents pay water, sewer, and property

▼ Figure 12.7

Stanton Court, Sheepshead Bay, New York © Gans Studio.

▶ Figure 12.8

Interior mews, Sheepshead Bay, New York © Gans Studio.

taxes, and the mews and street infrastructure ultimately connect. Because the mews flood with every storm, the cost of cleaning and draining the sewer lines is considerable.

The legally mandated and sustainable approach to reconstruction requires raising the houses to at least the insurable flood elevation, which in New York is two feet above the 100-year flood level, or as much as thirteen feet above the mews. The bungalows were originally not robustly built, and to make them insurable and structurally sound, truly weather-tight and systemically efficient by today's performance standards, means replacing rather than rebuilding. The residents have worked and deliberated collectively, and have embraced the idea of replacing all of their homes with raised, pre-fabricated "green" bungalows in order to take advantage of economies of scale, and also of the potential infrastructural benefits. Namely, if they raised their houses collectively, they could then raise the mews to street level and the drainage with it. The internal block drainage system would then become the city's responsibility. The created depth between old mews and the new street level would accommodate an arsenal of water management devices from subsurface drywells to separate sanitary and water lines, and their homes would be seven rather than thirteen feet off the ground (Figures 12.9 and 12.10).

The mews' residents understand that urban action at the scale of the court is effective in ways that city, state, and federal funding do not yet recognize. Namely, the current grants from the U.S. Department of Housing and Urban Development's (HUD) Community Development Block Grant Program (CDBG),[8] regionally available from New York City as the Build it Back[9] program and the Department of Housing Preservation and Development's (HPD) Houses Reconstruction program[10] are available only to individuals. The individual citizens meanwhile are calling for large-scale collective action, both in the form of major infrastructure for water mitigation and rebuilding initiatives at the scale of community. When we arrived with students and colleagues from Pratt Center for Community Development[11] in Sheepshead Bay in Spring 2013, this call for collective action had not yet taken concrete form. We encountered approximately one hundred and forty damaged homes, many inhabited by the descendants of the original occupants from the 1920s, bound together by familial and long-standing social connections but without a strong organizational structure.

CHAPTER 12 Design Action

◀ **Figure 12.9**

Option A: Proposed plan of the courts with new boardwalk. Sheepshead Bay, New York © Gans Studio.

▼ **Figure 12.10**

Option B (top) shows the mews at current level and individual houses raised to 11 feet. Option C (bottom) shows the mews raised to street level and the houses raised to 7 feet. Sheepshead Bay, New York © Gans Studio.

The noble role of the so-called "court captains" had revived during the emergency of the storm, but concerned itself only with the immediate needs and physical safety of the residents. The gap between the ability of public institutions and authorities to provide assistance, and the growing needs of the residents of Sheepshead Bay, was widening. To help bridge this gap in authority and decision-making, we initially extended open-calls for meetings at the Sheepshead Bay Yacht club and in the community room of the Sheepshead Nursing and Rehabilitation Facility, where we organized design charrettes and visioning sessions through which residents of each court reimagined their homes (Figure 12.11), community infrastructures, and their future including the existential question of would they stay or would they go in the face of climate change. As in New Orleans, a strong community has emerged out of this participatory communal practice enabled by the design process. Indeed, our greatest accomplishment has been to catalyze the formation of a more organized, more pro-active, and more politicized court collective (Figure 12.12).

The communities of Sheepshead Bay have a strong understanding of the challenges of water at scales larger than that of their own part of the coastline.

▶ Figure 12.11

Workshop with the residents, Sheepshead Bay, New York © Gans Studio.

◀ Figure 12.12

Proposed design for the raised mews and homes, Sheepshead Bay, New York © Gans Studio.

For example, they understand the limitations of the City's proposed beach replenishment along a coast that moves sand rapidly into their harbor, and the potential of a proposed levy system to exacerbate flooding if a drainage system is not built behind it. As in the case of New Orleans, the storm has served as a catalyst for communities to self-organize, and develop a collective voice, and for architects and urban planners to develop new and missing scales of design action. These new scales are the bridges across the gap between urban institutions of power and the spaces of engaged community and citizen action.

Notes

1. From the official promotional material:

    The exhibition *Into the Open* highlights America's rich history of architectural experimentation and explores the original ways architects today are working collaboratively to invigorate community activism and environmental policy In the absence of large-scale public infrastructure projects in the United States, local initiatives are becoming laboratories for generating new forms of sociability and civic engagement. These new community-minded architects are questioning traditional definitions of practice by conducting unique research into the socio-economic challenges and environmental rifts that define our times. They are going beyond building—defining architecture not just as a physical infrastructure, but also as a social relationship.

    For reference see: http://labiennale.us/ (Last accessed on February 15, 2015).
2. On December 9, 2013, a front page of *The New York Times* read: "Dasani's homeless life, revealed that for many the situation has not changed and "in the absence of a long awaited home, there is only school"." Elliot, A. (2013) "Invisible Child: Girl in the Shadows: Dasani's Homeless Life." In: *The New York Times*, December 9, 2013.
3. Common Ground's mission is to strengthen individuals, families and communities by developing and sustaining supportive and affordable housing and programs for homeless and other vulnerable New Yorkers. For reference see: www.commonground.org/mission-model#.UzSeTY2CKrY (Last accessed on February 15, 2015).
4. For the detailed ADA design standards, see: www.ada.gov/2010ADAstandards_index.htm (Last accessed on February 15, 2015).
5. ACORN was the largest community organization in the United States that brought together low and moderate-income families working toward social justice and building stronger communities. From 1970–2010, ACORN had grown to more than 175,000 member families, organized in 850 neighborhood chapters in 75 cities across the U.S. and beyond. For reference see: www.acorn.org/ (Last accessed on February 15, 2015).
6. For reference see: http://water.epa.gov/type/wetlands/marsh.cfm (Last accessed on February 15, 2015).
7. The Rational Method is the engineers' standard means of quantifying runoff as the inverse consequence of the ability of material or structure to absorb and hold water. The method is described in standard hydrology engineering textbooks. See: Viessman, W. and Lewis, G. L. (1995) *Introduction to Hydrology*. 4th ed., Section 15.2, pp. 311ff. Harper Collins.
8. The Community Development Block Grant program is a flexible program that provides communities with resources to address a wide range of unique community development needs since 1974. For reference see: http://portal.hud.gov/hudportal/HUD?src=/program_offices/comm_planning/communitydevelopment/programs (Last accessed on February 15, 2015).

9. NYC Build it Back is the City program designed to assist homeowners, landlords and tenants in the five boroughs whose primary residencies were damaged by Hurricane Sandy. For reference see: www.nyc.gov/html/recovery/html/homeowners/homeowners-renters.shtml (Last accessed on February 15, 2015).
10. This program is administered by New York City's Department of Housing Preservation and Development (HPD). For reference see: www.nyc.gov/html/hpd/html/home/home.shtml (Last accessed on February 15, 2015).
11. For more details see the Post-Sandy Resiliency Program at Pratt Center for Community Development www.prattcenter.net/projects/sustainable-community-development/climate-resiliency-planning-sheepshead-bay (Last accessed on February 15, 2015).

Bibliography

Elliot, A. (December 9, 2013) "Invisible Child: Girl in the Shadows: Dasani's Homeless Life." In: *The New York Times*.

Viessman, W. and Lewis, G. L. (1995) *Introduction to Hydrology*, 4th ed., Section 15.2, p. 311. Harper Collins.

Chapter 13

Handball Stadium: The Center for Recreation and New Media in Novi Sad

Srdjan Jovanović Weiss

> The near-decade-long civil war in the former Yugoslavia in the 1990s has left countries such as Serbia in a state of flux. As its cities emerge from the crisis and consider urban regeneration schemes, the focus has turned to the importance of creating new public spaces, cultural institutions, and recreational spaces for young people which can encourage social integration and exchange.
>
> Zoë Ryan (Ryan 2006)

Beginning in 2004, Normal Architecture Office (NAO)[1] began to work with the Center for New Media—kuda.org (Figure 13.1), based in Novi Sad, Serbia, on a proposal for a new Center for Recreation and New Media to be located in an abandoned handball stadium in Novi Sad.[2] The project objectives put forth by NAO about the upgrade of the stadium read:

> An exterior sports field will be upgraded. Existing concrete seating will receive better surface over the dilapidated concrete. The depressed floor below the inclined seating will be excavated even further to reach the bottom of the foundations. This will double the size of the interior below the seating in order to create info-lounge workshops as well as studios, a café, and a library. Two large holes will be cut through the existing inclined seating in order to visually connect the street to the handball field. A staircase will cut through the bleachers to connect the field with the upper level. The *elastic* auditorium space will occupy the inclination of the seating and it will adapt according to public needs. The upper level will include media libraries, wired public workspaces, audio-visual studios, control rooms, and open offices. The roof terrace will be used for artists' projects or leased for third-party events. The stadium will become a critical catalyst in Vojvodina, Serbia, and Southeast Europe.[3]

The history of late Yugoslav socialism is inextricably linked with the challenge faced by contemporary architecture and urbanism practice in rebuilding post-socialist cities in Southeast Europe. The value of the socialist heritage has

▶ Figure 13.1

kuda.org network. Image courtesy kuda.org

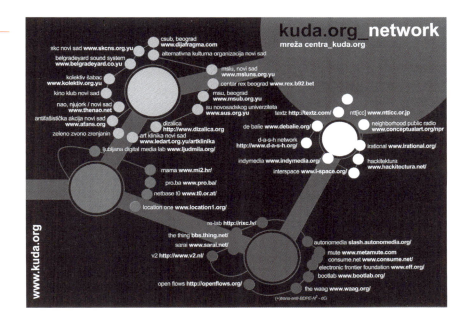

been debased across the former Yugoslavia thus making the socialist-era architecture a hindrance to current social progress. Public buildings and spaces which had been generously provided by socialist urbanism are now in danger of becoming balkanized,[4] privatized, and removed from the possibility of public use. In order to demonstrate the trend of transferring public land from collective to private property, this report will discuss a new role of architecture and design vis-a-vis emerging democracies: the project to preserve and adapt a handball stadium in Novi Sad is a case study for local urban activism as well as for relevant future projects aimed at creating new public spaces. The Stadium project in itself is a combination of research, design, and activism aimed to reclaim a former socialist public space in Novi Sad. Rather than being trapped by the traditional client-architect relationship, in NAO's practice the project emerges out of collaborative work with NGOs, rapidly changing governments, and a plethora of emerging commercial entities, companies, and entrepreneurs.

Novi Sad, the capital of the Autonomous Province of Vojvodina within Serbia, is a rare south eastern European city that grew in population during the 1990s. The city doubled from a quarter million to half a million inhabitants largely due to migration from the war-torn areas in former Yugoslavia.[5] While in existence (1943–1992), Socialist Yugoslavia was a multi-ethnic federal republic with one administrative capital city, Belgrade—also the capital of the Serbian state—as well as five additional states and their respective capital cities.[6] In addition, Yugoslavia also had two autonomous provinces, both administratively parts of Serbia: Kosovo and Vojvodina. Each had a capital city, Prishtina and Novi Sad respectively. As the main and largest capital city, Belgrade bore not only the legislative challenge of complex internal and embattled politics, but also the challenge of representing Yugoslav culture to the world. Though the country

CHAPTER 13 Center for Recreation and New Media

had already begun to balkanize into separate states in the 1970s, its decline into distinct ethnically-divided territories accelerated after President Josip Broz Tito's death in 1980. When the separation was finalized, all of the state capitals comprising the former Yugoslavia's complex political network gained independence from Belgrade, except the smallest of them all: Novi Sad, which I have proposed to call *The Ninth City* (Weiss 2010). In the aftermath of the Balkan crisis, Prishtina became partially recognized as a state capital, while Novi Sad, stripped of the key aspects of its political autonomy, developed as the regional cultural and economic capital. The refugees from Bosnia, Croatia, and Kosovo who migrated to Novi Sad during the 1990s brought along their ideas of urban living and continued to influence the urban scape of Novi Sad. New settlers have largely built their values into a new urban fabric by creating picturesque hybrids of urban and rural morphologies, known as *Turbo Architecture* (Weiss 2006).

In an expanded political context, since the beginning of the 20th century both Western and Russian building types were modified to create community athletic space for youth and workers of Novi Sad. Namely, Novi Sad inherited its institutional architecture from two former systems: the Kingdom of Yugoslavia (1918–1939) and the post-World War II Socialist Yugoslavia. The *Ninth City* inherited hardscape belonging to former administrations, bygone institutions, and erstwhile militaries. The city also inherited vast territories for urban recreation along the riverbanks of the Danube; there are sporting fields, handball stadia, and other recreation areas suited for a much bigger population than that of Novi Sad.

The stadium covered by the kuda.org-NAO proposal was built out of reinforced concrete in the mid-1930s by the Royal Railways in the former Kingdom of Yugoslavia. Originally meant as a sports field for the local workers and their families, the handball stadium saw a growth in attendance by workers from all over the region due to the location's proximity to the railway station (Figure 13.2). During the socialist period and under the rule of Tito, a number of institutions supporting youth culture were initiated. Accordingly, the handball stadium in Novi Sad, founded before World War II by the King's Yugoslav Railway, came into focus. As a form of "collective property" in socialism the stadium was owned by the local municipality and managed by the Yugoslav Railways after World War II.[7] By 1948, an inclined concrete seating area for eight hundred spectators was added, with spaces below equipped with changing rooms, showers, and club amenities. With the emergence of Yugoslav versions of Western Punk and New Wave music of the 1970s, the stadium took on a new cultural dimension. It became the most important venue for emerging Yugoslav punk and new wave music groups from Vojvodina as well as from Slovenia and Croatia.

At the time of Tito's death in 1980, Novi Sad had forty-eight state-supported youth organizations with robust sports and cultural programmes. In 2004, four years after the radical right-wing party took power in the city, there were only three kinds of youth organizations left operating. Those were the scouts, Christian Orthodox social centers, and nationalist initiatives. The declining number of youth organizations demonstrates a devastating damage for the

▶ Figure 13.2

Aerial map of the location of the proposed handball stadium © NAO.

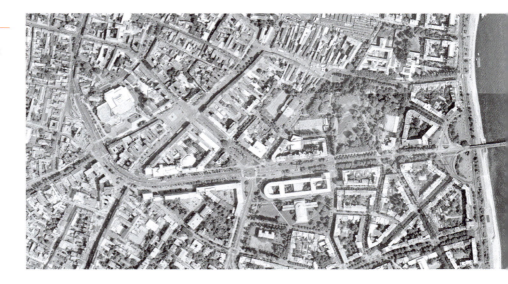

emerging democratic society. As a result, the stadium became less frequently used for handball alone. As of the 1990s, the stadium was gradually abandoned by the alternative music scene until it was finally closed, neglected, fenced off, and ultimately removed from the mental map of Novi Sad (Figure 13.3). Due to post-socialist property disputes, the handball stadium remains locked by the city until further notice.

The damaging decade of nationalism and crisis in Serbia during the 1990s resulted in the total neglect of both official and unofficial institutions for the youth. State priorities were obviously elsewhere: as Branka Ćurčić writes, the presumption is that largely Serbian war refugees from Croatia and Bosnia found their asylum in the city and influenced its urban development by also instigating the "clericalization" of Novi Sad. Namely, over twenty Serbian Orthodox Christian churches were planned and constructed in a so-called "spiritual ring" around the city (Ćurčić 2007). Most of these churches are located in the urban territories left incomplete by modernist planners and, as Vladimir Mitrović suggests, "do not deserve any serious architectural or artistic analysis" (Mitrović 2007).

For NAO, architecture with the added dimension of activism played a key role in the process of designing the new Center for Recreation and New Media. NAO's challenge as designers was thus twofold: First, we were about to design the first public facility dedicated to public recreation in more than two decades and, by doing so, to symbolize its complex program in the context of high social and cultural uncertainty; and second, we needed to figure out how to mobilize uncertain civic and social forces in order to seize the public space of the handball stadium before it was sold to a private investor and turned, as have many other public buildings in Serbia, into a shopping center. In 2007, School of Missing Studies' participants reviewed the ongoing action to preserve, renovate, and adapt the handball stadium into the new Center for Recreation and New Media. The idea was to amalgamate the new stadium as a vital space for recreation,

◀ **Figure 13.3**

Existing state of the Handball Stadium in Novi Sad. Even though gates are locked, local residents still play soccer there © NAO.

complimented with spaces for electronic creativity reaching out to local, regional, and international exchange. Instead of waiting for the state and municipal authorities to administer the process, NAO and kuda.org stepped in and proposed a hybrid program for the dilapidated handball stadium based on the two central agents for youth activity: recreation and electronic social media. The two activities in post-socialism define loose ends of the political spectrum in today's emerging democratic societies (Ryan 2006).

The new Center for Recreation and New Media was meant to become a new public space bringing young people together virtually as well as in face-to-face situations, to participate in recreation, play, and collaboration, and to explore the social and political impact of new technologies (Figures 13.4 and 13.5). The architecture of the new center took clues from a flow of political alliances that kuda.org has created in order to pursue this project toward realization. The emerging identity politics and ontology of electronic media that kuda.org practices are increasingly giving way for new urban ideologies based on collective actions. At the same time the handball stadium is surrounded by government buildings that are in modern style built both before World War II and after. Thus, the new stadium is designed to learn from socialist aesthetics and initiate identities that engage positive aspects of the socialist past while defining urban future on new terms; it does so by materializing the city's situation of being in a complex transitional space lingering at the outer edge of the European Union while being geographically so close to it. In that sense, the new stadium is meant to become a dialogic public space whose importance is both pragmatic and ideological. The pragmatic aspect is the urgency of preserving open spaces for urban recreation and play, adding new infrastructure for social interaction and architecture that supports youth activities in the multiethnic, multicultural, and multireligious city (Figure 13.6). The ideological aspect leans on the necessity to forge new cultural strategy for youth in emerging regional capitals like Novi Sad.

▲ Figure 13.4

Exploded axonometric view of the proposal © NAO.

▲ Figure 13.5

Perspective elevation of the proposed Center for Recreation and New Media viewed from the court © NAO.

▲ Figure 13.6

Perspective elevation of the proposed Center for Recreation and New Media viewed from the street © NAO.

CHAPTER 13 Center for Recreation and New Media

Privatization of public resources has already taken a toll on post-socialist Novi Sad. Elected to power throughout the 1990s, the ultra-right-wing Serbian Radical Party had renationalized all public spaces including the Danube Park where the handball stadium stands as the property of the Republic of Serbia. Through an illegal system of lobbying and bribing public officials, the privatized public spaces were then leased to small, often semilegal commercial ventures and entrepreneurs. The handball stadium was no exception: in fact, a group of suspect investors intended to buy the stadium and turn it into a commercial locus for bars and commercial kiosks. Working together, NAO and kuda.org developed the proposal for the redesign of the stadium and officially filed the project with the city of Novi Sad. We succeeded in preserving the recreational character of the stadium, added the cultural and social programs, and have managed to save the stadium from immanent privatization and potentially from demolition (Figure 13.7).

The theoretical aspect of the new Center for Recreation and New Media is related to the search for an architecture toward positive aspects of balkanization. This effort supports exceptionality and particularity in the emerging public realm. By that I mean that there is the possibility for conceptual architecture to be at the source of the production of urban space. There are multiple conditions caused by abrupt political transitions coloring what would usually be a straightforward process in a stable economy. It is the reality of political and economical conditions that make this effort to upgrade the handball stadium in Novi Sad a step concurrent with the concept of "projective theory" (Somol and Whiting 2002). According to Sarah Whiting and Robert Somol, the basic premise of projective theory is that architectural practice ought to contain a political direction.

◀ Figure 13.7

Perspective elevation of the proposed Center for Recreation and New Media viewed from the court © NAO.

Furthermore, the projective architecture can add urgency of political and ideological navigations in order to create new and innovative cultural strategies for civic places. In the case of the Center for Recreation and New Media this ideological navigation has driven design efforts to raise awareness of the neglected youth in Novi Sad. Thus the agitation to preserve and upgrade the abandoned handball stadium is both architectural and political. If this was not done, the free spaces of the handball stadium would vanish. In this way, projective theory as proposed by Whiting and Somol is in fact a practice of agitation of the public that has been left out of their role in building their own city.

NAO and kuda.org collaborators have been engaged not only in the design process, but also in the messy process of political lobbying. This mix of mutual competencies is due to the recent crisis in the Balkans brought about by wars and the ravaged economy during the 1990s. Building of cities such as Novi Sad, along with civic institutions and public spaces, vanished. At the same time illegal construction gradually went out of control. For the war refugees as well as migrants from rural areas the speed of illegal construction was more efficient than waiting for the failing socialist system to act on their behalf. Everyone acted on their own driven by urgency to be evasive both about illegal construction and about political corruption. Gradually this practice of hybrid competence of building the city solidified in Turbo Architecture that has changed the space and face of the Balkan city (Weiss 2006). The aspect of projective architecture in the proposition to preserve and upgrade the handball stadium is meant to meet a social urgency with the accelerated speed of architecture.

The projective idea for preserving the handball stadium is to combine physical recreation and digital media (Figures 13.8—13.10). The common rationale

▶ Figure 13.8

Interior view, with technological proposals for sun harvesting developed by Anna Dyson of Rensselaer Technological Institute, Troy, New York © NAO.

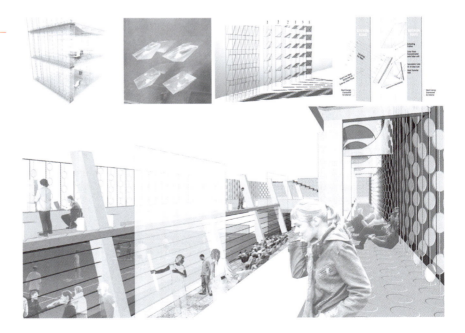

▶ **Figure 13.9**

View of the bookstore and social gathering space below street level © NAO.

▼ **Figure 13.10**

Perspective view of the proposed Center during a public event with an elevation © NAO.

has been that youth immersed in new media platforms often also needs active recreation to stay healthy, and that athletic youth usually finds new media enriching by the creative use of social media. By combining these two activities, the proposition is an amalgamated program for the new Center based on the roles that recreation and electronic media play in the emerging democratic society. The design of the Center for Recreation and New Media in Novi Sad, the *un-national* capital in the Western Balkan urban network, is meant to by-pass dominant ethnic aspirations of the Serbian state in a creative way by providing regulatory as well as institutional space for new programs for the general public, including its youth and minorities.

As a centrifugal force, balkanization has produced multiple national capitals in the space of the former Yugoslavia, each trying to self-style itself in order to achieve clear distinction from the others (Weiss 2010). The aftermath of balkanization also allowed for the emergence of *un-national* capitals in the region, such as Novi Sad in Serbia. The realm of spatial design, architecture and urbanism can play a much bigger role to balance the heightened economic ambitions of *un-national* capitals. This is urgent to protect former socialist open spaces, a particularity of modern urbanism, from neoliberal and corrupt takeover for private capital. Small victories of activism in Novi Sad such as the opening of CK13 Youth Center in 2007 and the protection of the handball stadium from commercial development can serve as reminders. Other creative cities such as Rotterdam, Basel, Maribor or Graz, have employed design and architecture to play a key role in crafting their new identities and teach us how the development of an *un-national* capital can also benefit the national capital. In that respect, activism aimed at protecting open spaces, parks and playgrounds, is what connects national and *un-national* capitals, such as Belgrade and Novi Sad. This connection is then not based on political opposition, but on the gradient of active participation of citizens in keeping open urban and recreational spaces for everyone, no matter which political option prevails in the future.

The project for the Center for Recreation and New Media was met with attention from the changing city governments in Novi Sad, oscillating between right-wing and liberal-democratic political parties. Both have shown interest in the project, however no political will has prevailed to date. The current municipal administration is looking at our proposal as a model of transition from top-down socialist planning to more interactive and participatory planning models (Weiss 2010) that include a range of participants gathered around a collaborative design process. The ongoing battle for the new Center for Recreation and New Media exemplifies the challenge of defining and forging the role of architecture and design vis-a-vis these political processes in the immediate future and beyond.

Notes

1. NAO is a collaborative office for architecture, curating and urbanism.
2. Design team: Srdjan Jovanović Weiss (chief architect), Ivana Sovilj, Tom Zoli; Models: Jason Harrell, Kevin Keller, Holly Landela, Ally Unha Hyun, Shuni Feng; Renderings: Thomas Julliard Zoli; curatorial concept: Katherine Carl & kuda.org—New Media Center Novi Sad; interns: Emir Hadziahmetović, Andreja Mirić, Dejan Mrdja, Joseph R. Roumeliotis, Dubravka Sekulić, Mallory Malkasian, Gwen Prinsen; structural advice: Jane Wernick Engineers, London; urbanism: Arch. Ružica Jovanović, public relations: Jovana Navalusić, kuda.org, social and political research: Zoran Pantelić, Branka Ćurčić, Kristijan Lukić, Orfeas Skutelis, kuda.org.
3. This is particularly the case in the context of European integration: according to the Serbian government, European integration is the political priority. See the government's

web-site at: www.seio.gov.rs/home.50.html. See also: Normal Architecture Office (NAO). "Stadium Culture Novi Sad." For reference see: www.thenao.net/NAOsk.htm. (Last accessed on February 15, 2015).
4. *Balkanization* is a geopolitical term originally used to describe the process of fragmentation or division of a region or state into smaller regions or states that are often hostile or non-cooperative with each other. The term has arisen from the conflicts in the 20th century Balkans. The first balkanization was embodied in the Balkan Wars 1912–13. The term was reaffirmed in the Yugoslav wars of the 1990s. Balkanization is also used to describe other forms of disintegration including the subdivision of the Internet being divided into separate enclaves and the breakdown of cooperative arrangements due to the rise of independent competitive entities. The term has been used in American urban planning to describe the process of creating gated communities. There are contemporary attempts to use the term Balkanization in positive ways equating it's meaning to the need for sustenance of a group, society, or distinct voices vis-a-vis the rise of global hegemony and capitalism.
5. Another city that doubled during the 1990s crisis is Prishtina, the capital of Kosovo.
6. The five states were Slovenia, Croatia, Bosnia and Herzegovina, Montenegro, Serbia and Macedonia.
7. "Collective property" in the Yugoslav juridical system meant everyone's elusive ownership of land as well as infrastructure.

Bibliography

Ćurčić, B. (2007) "The Critique of Clericalization of Novi Sad: Analysis of Socio-Political and Aesthetic Discourse of New Orthodox and Church Strategies." *The Critique of Clericalization of Novi Sad*, Anti-dogma ed. Samizdat, pp. 54–56.

Mitrović, V. (2007) "Contemporary Serbian Church Buildings: From Tradition to Political Correctness." *The Critique of Clericalization of Novi Sad*. Anti-dogma ed. Samizdat, pp. 61–62.

Ryan, Z. (2006) "Stadium Culture." Ryan, Z. (Ed.) *The Good Life: New Public Spaces for Recreation*. Princeton Architectural Press, p. 25.

Somol, R. and Whiting S. (2002) "Notes around the Doppler Effect and Other Moods of Modernism." In: *Perspecta* 33, The Yale Architectural Journal, MIT Press, pp. 72–77.

Weiss, S. J. (2006) *Almost Architecture*. Akademie Schloss Solitude.

Weiss, S. J. (2010) "The Ninth City." Milovi, L. (Ed.) *Ideologije i Ideali: Prilozi Istraživanju Arhitekture 20. Veka u Vojvodini*. Muzej Savremene Umetnosti Vojvodine, pp. 171–181.

Weiss, S. J. (June 29, 2012) "On Spatial Distinction as a Positive Aspect of Balkanization." Goldsmiths University of London. Available online at: http://roundtable.kein.org/node/792 (Last accessed on February 15, 2015).

Chapter 14

Concurrent Urbanities: Design, Civil Society, and Infrastructures of Inclusion[1]

Miodrag Mitrašinović

The patterns, flows, and volumes of mobility that have transformed the expansive geography of New York City since the early 1990s—discussed in Chapter 1—are not unique: Analogous processes and figures characterize the unprecedented degrees and modes of mobility of individuals and groups (and the influx of immigrants) across the megalopolitan regions of the United States and the world. These largest and most dramatic global migrations in history have been caused by wars, uneven geographic development, economic inequalities, environmental degradation, lack of access to natural resources (particularly to water) and the commons, and natural disasters of historic proportions. Such are the predicaments and degrees of global mobility in today's "urban age" and such are the growing concentrations of human settlements that more than half of all humans today live in over 400 city-regions (UN-DESA 2014). Even though the concept of "urban age" has been contested,[2] few would disagree that as the process of rapid and largely uncontrolled urbanization unfolds, pressures on existing human settlements, infrastructure, food and water sources, housing provisions and public services exponentially escalate. In parallel, the process of urbanization has acquired a "planetary" scale through the integration and consolidation of world financial markets, regulation of transnational economic flows, and the deregulation of national economies.[3] In the process, the role of nation states has been reduced to facilitating debt-financed urbanization (Harvey 2007, 2008) as well as regulating the social consequences of market failures and uneven urban-geographical development (Harvey 2006; Smith 2008) evident in unprecedented concentrations of both wealth and poverty. As Neil Smith argued, "today's world map is more one of environmental and religious difference, migration patterns and economic flows, local irruptions and postcolonial wars than a stable mosaic of national states" (Smith 2008: 260–261). Along with the idea that state institutions are "a necessary evil" and have by and large abandoned much of their responsibility for social reproduction to become the "midwives of globalism" (Smith 2008), one recognizes that states still have the capacity to influence relations between the market and civil society, and thus to varying extents limit the power of capital to commodify all spheres of public and private life (Young 2000: 173).

Even though the World Bank and the United Nations claim that over the past thirty years the extent of global poverty has rapidly declined[4] and that it could be "completely eradicated" by 2030,[5] the lines demarcating socio-spatial exclusion, abuse of human and citizen rights, and aggressive privatization of the public sector and the commons continue to push growing numbers of people into poverty. This emerging global context of urbanization has produced a fiscal crisis at the municipal level, influencing the privatization of municipal assets and public and social services alike via the implementation of pressures on public spending and investment. It has also forced regions, cities, and municipalities towards interurban rivalries and the adoption of entrepreneurial strategies and methods of competitive urbanity in order to vie for direct (often foreign) investment (Brenner and Theodore 2002; Mitrašinović 2006: 49, 272). It is indeed the global financial and development organizations such as the World Bank, the Organization for Economic Co-operation and Development (OECD), and the International Monetary Fund (IMF), among others, who have supported deregulation and forced policies of macroeconomic restructuring at all levels of government, transfer of responsibility for the civil society to private corporations and the market, and encouraged direct private investments in developing economies (Martin 2001; Harvey 2008).

The unprecedented population growth and increased modes of mobility have also placed incredible strain on urban infrastructures. As a result, industrial cities of the 19th and 20th centuries are experiencing a serious and systematic breakdown of most of their material, social, and ecological infrastructures (Hall 1988; Hall and Ulrich 2000). Among the seven major obstacles to "urban prosperity" identified by UN-HABITAT, poor governance and the lack of appropriate infrastructure are most prevalent and most critical across the world (HABITAT 2013).[6] It is no surprise that of particular significance today are the social struggles around urban services and infrastructures, and—in the context of "collective consumption" (Castells 1984)—that these two areas have seen the highest volumes of transnational investment and most intense privatizations since the 1980s. Privatization—as a systematic policy of public sector reforms and macroeconomic structural adjustment measures—has been the solution of choice for neoliberal ideologues. In the mid-1980s, in what many consider to be the impetus of global neoliberalization, it was Margaret Thatcher's and Ronald Reagan's administrations in the United Kingdom and the United States respectively that organized the first mass deregulations and privatizations of public resources, state assets, and the commons.[7]

As cities across the world continue to cut capital projects and operating budgets, and as private investors experience a shortage of available capital or economic incentives to engage in public–private partnerships in urban territories that lack immediate commercial potential, a fissure between public needs and aspirations on the one hand, and available municipal and government resources on the other, has turned into an abyss. Many municipal governments across the United States and the world have failed disadvantaged citizens in providing basic public services and provisions, be it disaster preparedness, waste collection, water supply, energy, education, public safety, architectural or civil engineering services, or managing public parks. The government's response to the disaster caused by Hurricane Sandy gave the NYC councilman Carlos Menchaca "a whole new way of thinking about how important government was" and framed his political race in the media with headlines such as "Menchaca Looks to Areas Forgotten by Government."[8] The struggle of the Brooklyn councilman to create a legal platform for community participation in the redevelopment of residents' own neighborhoods is emblematic of global attempts to find ways of reimaging and redesigning connectivities between the interests of civil society, the government, and the private sector.

Just like public infrastructure, since the early 1990s public and municipal services have been subject to encroaching privatizations. Under such conditions, numerous municipalities across the world have opted to privatize public services in order to bridge the gap between needs and resources. Privatization has also been popularized as a way of shifting the provision of public and social services from governments to private companies or other nongovernmental organizations (the "third sector"). Its appeal is based in the belief that the private sector can provide higher quality services at lower costs. Promoters often cite accountability, effectiveness, and equity as the main qualities that distinguish private over public management of public resources (Parks Council and Central Park Conservancy 1993: 27). As I have suggested in Chapter 1 when discussing "The Bloomberg Way," what these advocates do not emphasize is the repositioning of urban citizens as customers in what Zukin calls "a vision of civility bounded by consumption" (Zukin 1995: 55). Major methods for privatization of public services and provisions vary in degree from outsourcing, to public–private partnerships, to competitive contract bidding, all the way to complete privatization.[9] In 2012, the National Council of Public-Private Partnerships estimated that on average American cities have privatized around thirty percent of public service provisions (Meyer 2012). Another growing form of privatization of public sector services is government-to-government services (G2G)[10] through which municipal governments enlist external government agencies in order to more efficiently deliver public goods and services. The argument for this practice is that "urbanization is peaking in the developing world at a time when the capacity to govern is still in short supply"[11] and that given the population growth rates and the decrease in public funding, there is little indication that regional and local governments will be able to manage the complexities in areas as diverse as healthcare and public health, conflict and dispute resolution, and environmental protection (Fuller and Romer 2014). Alarmingly, given that solutions such as privatization are imposed in a top-down manner and, more often than not, by global financial and political organizations, the capacity to devise alternative strategies in order to face local challenges has been systematically undermined (Martin 2001: 35). As Robles-Duran rightfully asked,

> if state and municipal governments can barely meet the social support exigencies of [. . .] capitalist organizations, and the new profit-oriented partnerships that direct contemporary urban growth refuse to intervene in urban areas where little or no profit can be readily extracted, then who is addressing the growing conditions of urban poverty and its socio-spatial consequences?

(Robles-Durán 2014)[12]

Within the context of deregulation of public and social services, precarious employment patterns, crumbling material infrastructures, growing urban poverty, and increasingly difficult access to resources, a range of innovative community- and self-organization practices have emerged through individual and solidarity-based collective actions, mobilizations of communal resources, and participatory processes in which the capacities and capabilities of local stakeholders are amplified. Among the most prominent of such mobilizations have been practices of insurgent and urban citizenship, informal human and material infrastructuring, new urban movements for socio-spatial justice and "the right to the city," forms of localized governance and management, urban coalitions, as well as social cooperatives and communal micro-economies. In addition, moving to ameliorate the damage done by processes of neoliberalization, local states, governments, and municipalities have attempted to strengthen the work of civil society and the third sector organizations by urgently building new forms of alliances and coalitions. In order to begin to lay the groundwork for my arguments to follow, I will distinguish here five fairly distinct domains in which the above listed urban practices unfold. I will call the first "insurgent," where most of the activity is of ad hoc type and often does not translate into more complex forms of socio-spatial praxis. The second is the domain AbdouMaliq Simone calls "people as infrastructure" (Simone 2004) where modalities of self-organization begin to emerge as patterns of fairly regular tactical activity in the domain of "everyday urbanism." Unlike the first domain, I will frame this one as "emergent." The third is the domain where forms of socio-spatial activity are deliberately configured to produce value propositions (exchange values) for specific urban communities of practice which often translate into forms of alternative economic exchange with links to the market place. The fourth is the domain of organized social and political activity commonly synonymous with the notion of civil society, the third sector, which to me inscribes the "infrastructural" dimension to processes, practices, and spatial extensions of civil society. The fifth is the "institutional" domain that intentionally links the above with institutions and agencies of the state and also that of the market.

Significantly for this book, also emergent have been innovative forms and modalities of design activism and design praxis. From a component of radical urban activist practices, to a vehicle by which governments and disenfranchised urban communities connect via third sector organizations, design has emerged as an instrumental medium. On the one hand, design functions as a medium through which the self-organizing associational activities in the social space of civil society acquire the capacity to transform the environment through which the political is produced by enabling the emergence of new political subjectivities, shared meanings, and new civic and political imaginations. On the other hand, it operates as a means for urban coalitions and communities as well as the third sector organizations to define and represent their needs, desires, expectations, and demands to others in the public realm, and by which they contest and negotiate desired outcomes in their interactions with institutions and systems of power. Indeed, it is in the interstitial spaces between the old forms of governing that have become increasingly obsolete, and emergent forms of organizational and communal self-management and civil governance, that designers and design-led urban activists labor to introduce or boost democratic processes by codesigning broad participatory processes, middle-out organizational approaches, networking strategies, and innovative edifice ideas.

The argument *Concurrent Urbanities* puts forward is that the modalities of design praxis represented in this book are ultimately aimed at reframing and strengthening both conceptions and practices of civil society—understood as process-based and activity-defined social space of voluntary participation (Young 2000)—by producing the spaces of concurrency where bottom-up and top-down forces collide. According to Chantal Mouffe, this is where "the political" resides (Mouffe 2000). In short, design is instrumental as an enticement to action in the process of envisioning "transformative possibilities" through middle-out approaches.

It is commonly understood that urban citizens as well as communities of practice with which authors in this volume work (across the five domains listed above) are firmly embedded in sites of production of urban knowledge and experience. However, what often gets overlooked is that these urban actors tend to conceive of their everyday practices primarily as a function of *time*; they indeed develop time-based imaginaries and tactics of occupying and producing urban space. As self-motivated urban tacticians, they are driven by self-interest (a desire to endure in the city that has no resources available to them), but also by a shared purpose to transform the often-predatory urban space. In that sense, *Concurrent Urbanities* explores how design can be employed to strengthen their daily practice, spatialize their time-based imagination, scale-up their localized initiatives, and scrutinize their concurrencies, ways through which they resonate with each other, where and how they intersect, and what kind of emerging urban conditions they create in the process of coexistence and of continuous juxtapositions. In addition, *Concurrent Urbanities* argues that the role of design is to create places, vectors, and spaces[13] of concurrency ("the forest of gestures," De Certeau 1984: 102) to enunciate opportunities for co-producing new visions of urban space, propose new tools for social conviviality, and search for innovative configurations of social, cultural, economic as well as political affinities, alliances, and coalitions.

Michel De Certeau reminds us that tactical dimensions of the practice of everyday life are commonly inscribed *in time* by means of manipulating everyday events into opportunities. Since tactics cannot count on the "proper"—that is spatial and institutional localizations—they are a calculus of force relationships held by the "weak." The "strong" on the other hand—what Michel Foucault called "institutions of knowledge and power"—control the strategic domain and, by way of constructing the "proper," count on the "victory of space over time" (De Certeau 1984). For De Certeau, producing a proper means producing a "configuration of positions" which "implies an indication of stability" (De Certeau 1984: 117). The task of design is to encourage and support the discourse and practice of the social production of places of "cooperation" (proper) by organizing conditions of co-existence (Mouffe 2005: 8, 9) and coproduction, and by enabling "action in conjunction." The work featured in *Concurrent Urbanities* represents manifestations of operationalized notions of "concurrency," through three essential aspects of concurrent practice: (1) *synchronization* (aligning, coordinating, and creating synergies; articulating processes of self-organization); (2) *configuration* (building capacities and capabilities of social groups and organizations in order to propose new and tangible expressions and articulations of civil society); and (3) *communication* (coproducing differentiated public realms by coordinating vectors and points of concurrency). Synchronization, configuration, and communication are not here understood as isolated activities that occur in a particular methodological sequence, but as meta-categories of urbanist praxis.

Building on Iris Marion Young's work on civil society (Young 2000: 10, 163–180),[14] I propose that design here acts as a normative link between the notion of civil society and the "democratic impulse" of urban citizens (Young 2000: 5) aimed towards radical democratization of the society. Young defines the "ontology of civil society" via three associational levels: private, civic, and public (political).[15] In framing ways in which these levels of associational activity affect social and political transformations, Young distinguishes between two fundamental aspects of associational activity defined by their intentionalities: *self-organization* and *public sphere*. *Self-organization* is the way in which associations of urban citizens and urban social movements develop forms of solidarity, articulate social voices and identities, and envision possibilities for political participation and social transformation. Associational activities, institutions, and organizations created in the process are imbued with the capacity to encourage "social innovation" (alternative social practices whose dissemination in the public sphere often triggers larger-scale social change), as well as to provide "goods and services" (such as social care, homeless services, or those typically provided by social cooperatives) outside of the strategic and instrumental realms of the state and the market. *Public sphere*[16] refers to the ways in which the associational activity of the "differentiated social sectors" (Young 2000: 155) is vectored towards envisioning transformative possibilities for policies, procedures, institutions, and terms of public discourse in order to create openness towards plurality, inclusion, and socio-spatial justice, and to reconfigure the terms of political debate and democratic practice. The juxtaposition and concurrencies of differentiated public spheres are not only the discursive spaces formed through communicative interaction but also "arenas for the formation and enactment of social identities" (Fraser 1991: 68) and spaces of social differentiation and political power formation. Moreover, they are also vibrant "agonistic" public spheres of contestation "where different hegemonic political projects can be confronted" (Mouffe 2005: 3).[17] More than mere spaces of "free discussion," public spheres are, for Chantal Mouffe, also locations of conflict, antagonism, and critical decision-making (Mouffe 2005: 11).

Within the framework established above, I will distinguish between the following basic modalities of design praxis that emerge out of the preceding chapters: (A) *designing as tactical practice*, where (1) design acts as a catalyst for building dispositions and capacities for self-organization in urban communities and among urban citizens where such capacities are not present and (2) designers work towards disambiguation, mobilization, or conceptualization of new and emerging forms of urban practice and knowledge; and (B) *designing as strategic practice*, where (1) design is employed as a vehicle for building capabilities for critical urban action by aggregating, synergizing, and coordinating existing urban initiatives and scaling them up, (2) design and designers empower the capabilities of the third sector organizations, and (3) design adds strategic capabilities to state and government agencies by enabling new connectivities and coalitions with the organizations of civil society and with community-based organizations alike. The above are neither restricted fields of practice nor suggested areas of specialization, but domains of urbanist praxis across which nearly all of the authors in this book have worked.

Catalyzing Capacity Building by Design

In this modality of work, designers operate as urban activists, working tactically in urban locations and communities with groups of individual urban citizens in acute need of self-organizing capacities. In such places, urban citizenship is suppressed often through simultaneous workings of top-down state policies and predatory market practices. More often than not, clusters of immigrants and disenfranchised citizen groups are in need of creating alliances as well as building affiliative and organizational capacities. Designers as well as non-designers who employ modalities of design reasoning often catalyze processes of self-organization by first identifying opportunities and then developing dispositions and capacities for self-organization.

For 20 years now, the Stalker group has employed walking across "actual territories" as one of its methods for catalyzing the self-organizing process. Walking became a means of access, a practice of stitching together spaces that have been disconnected by the aggressive onslaught of what Romito names "the contemporary," a force that disables diversity, inclusion, and the spontaneous encounter of differences. As Romito asserts, in this sense walking is an "aesthetic practice" aimed at reorienting perceptual space and thereby upsetting socio-culturally predetermined modalities of producing and inhabiting the everyday. This definition is akin to Markussen's notion of design activism as a "disruptive aesthetic practice" (Markussen 2013) whose goal in this particular case is to construct the political through confrontation with "the contemporary" by "taking actions to catalyze, encourage or bring about change" in order to "disrupt existing paradigms of shared meaning, values and purpose to replace them with new ones" (Fuad–Luke 2009: 6, 10). In their work in Campo Boario in Rome, Stalker created Ararat, a Kurd-refugee community center that also gathered diverse groups of urban citizens. The camp-like material and cultural enclosure of Campo Boario enabled Stalker to comprehend the complexity of transformations taking place in Rome and to employ design "subversively" in order to create an autonomous living space and a creative circularity that attempts to "reconcile seemingly irresolvable conflicts": a "theater of the commons to invent and inhabit." The devices Stalker designed in the process—the relays—are collective games that address various aspects of associational practice in the "magic circle" of this experimental social theater. In this work Stalker is not motivated by a preconceived end result, particularly not a material effect, but by the goal of creating conditions for the formation of relationships, affinities, and interests while negotiating complex sets of incommensurabilities in a situation of general uncertainty.

For both Cohabitation Strategies (COHSTRA) and STEALTH.unlimited a modality of this work has been the establishment and institutionalization of social cooperatives. COHSTRA employs a range of innovative methods in order to stimulate self-organization as an activity aimed at generating authentic participation in the processes of urban research, design, and action/transformation. For their project in Tarwewijk, in Rotterdam, The Netherlands, their work catalyzed self-organization of local residents, citizen groups, community leaders, and activists into a social cooperative. As Rendon suggests, the process first involved the creation of a neighborhood-based research, community, and learning hub, to be followed by the Urban Union, the Strategic Research Unit, and the Action Research Unit. All these operations were designed to recognize local issues and concerns, identify available resources, and eventually propose and coordinate actions to be taken and the types of socio-spatial transformation to be attained. Local residents remained self-organized long after COHSTRA completed its involvement, and managed to halt the proposal put together by a public–private partnership meant to redevelop the neighborhood in order to resolve social challenges with material means. By designing strategies and devices that established innovative relationships between community members and leaders, local groups and associations, as well as the non-profit organizations, COHSTRA managed to create an autonomous civic structure and simultaneously pursue the strategy of political intervention in institutional politics (Mayer 2011: 57).

In Chapter 4, Dzokic and Neelen describe their ongoing work on conceptualizing the first social housing cooperative in Serbia. In the process, they are creating new forms and expressions of the emerging Serbian civil society, inventing a new civil economy for social and relational goods based on reciprocity and civic values, and proposing new roles that the government ought to assume in order to negotiate a new social contract (Restakis 2010: 109).

In the context of urban citizenship, design also acts as a method of scrutinizing the generalized notions of "citizenship" and "participation" in the search for greater degrees of specificity and belonging, new modes of accessibility and sociability, renewed rights and responsibilities, and innovative models of political representation and participation. Baxi and Cheng examine the forms, modalities, and conditions of citizenship in the context of fluid and antagonistic national borders, processes of globalization, and "flexible" multiple belongings. First, they investigate the national passport as a material and symbolic signifier and question its relations to the increasing asymmetries in the freedom of movement. Second, Baxi and Cheng relate their experience of working with the non-profit organization Asian Americans for Equality (AAFE) and organizing a workshop during the Chinatown Summer Street Festival in New York City. They recount that the workshop examined ideas of belonging as well as aspirations of "polymorphous citizens" and attempted to frame parameters for the design of a hypothetical passport that reflects heterogeneous national affiliations, virtual identities, global aspirations, and emerging political subjectivities that increasingly direct their claims for rights as well as responsibilities elsewhere.

Baxi's and Cheng's exploration is akin to Holston's and Appadurai's differentiation between what they call "formal" and "substantive" citizenship. While the formal refers to membership in the nation-state, the substantive citizenship refers to an ensemble of civil, political, socio-spatial, economic, and cultural rights. Although it seems that access to rights historically depended on formal membership, that's no longer either necessary or sufficient (Holston and Appadurai 1996: 190) for new forms and modalities of substantive urban citizenship (Crawford 2008). This development has rendered contemporary cities sites of struggle for "new kinds of citizen power and social justice" (Holston 2008: 34) that destabilizes the dominant regime of citizenship for the purposes of rendering it vulnerable (Holston 2008: 23) and creating conditions for the emergence of "insurgent citizenship" (Holston 2008).[18] For it is in the space of the everyday practice (Holston and Appadurai 1998) where frequently marginalized, tactically minded "urban citizens" interact and often collide with the institutions of state and corporate power. Conducive to counterpolitical action, "insurgent public spaces" (Hou 2010: 2)—reclaimed sites, reappropriated spaces, informal gathering places—present opportunities for reconfiguring the archetypal categories of urban space and urban practice, and for reconstituting citizenship (Appadurai 2001: 25). As Holston and Appadurai have suggested, under the conditions of transnational urbanization (Appadurai 2002), and in the context of rights to the city and rights to political participation, rights are increasingly conceived as a function of social relatedness (Appadurai and Holston 1996) and based on social demands that are not constitutionally defined but that people increasingly perceive as "entitlements of citizenship" (Crawford 2008: 279): "Urban citizens" thus no longer direct their claims for rights and their aspiration to belonging to nation states but understand the city as a "primary community of reference" (Holston 2008: 23).

Designers as Theorists of Urban Transformation

An important area of work for designers has been the sustained engagement with the insurgent, emergent, and organizational domains of associational urban activity in instances of observed practices of social innovation. This work has been mostly threefold. First, designers have set out to unearth, codify, translate, and map patterns of urban practice of individuals and communities that exhibit varied degrees of socio-spatial innovation in their attempts to create new modalities of sustainable urban cohabitation and governance. Second, designers committed to the production of transferable forms of urban knowledge are committed to strengthening and scaling up practices of such innovative urban communities, and also to mobilizing its principles to other urban communities in need. Finally, an important aspect of this line of work is to transform the work of urban social *heroes* into *concepts* of urban innovation.

In the ongoing attempt to recognize "creative acts of citizenship" in the spaces of everyday life, Teddy Cruz identified the cooperative practice of a group of San Diego teenagers who established Washington Street SkatePark, a skateboard park in the underpass of the interstate highway I–5. Employing the "tactics of translation," Cruz produced the procedural knowledge of that act of urban commoning by visualizing practices, procedures, and protocols and subsequently translating and interpreting them into what he calls "a chronology of invasion." The key question that drove Cruz's inquiry was "how had an act of insurgent citizenship scaled-up into an organized activist practice capable of modifying state policy?"

The Genetics of Uncontrolled Urban Processes project by the Stealth group[19] studied processes of self-organization—the informal, semi-legal, tactical practices of urban dwellers in Belgrade during the 1990s—and, as a result, has generated a lexicon of innovative urban practices. Initially sporadic and ad hoc, they incrementally scaled up to the level of emergent and then organizational practice, with all of the characteristics of *Systeme D* (Neuwirth 2011a), creating in the process a large-scale gray economy that blossomed under the conditions created by the international economic embargo. As Kucina writes, this work has generated algorithmic alternative concepts for post-socialist futures and provided insights into the relationship between the receding power of the state and the increasing power of self-organized urban citizenry.

In their work on identifying creative communities in New York City, Parsons DESIS Lab searched for communities that have (1) exhibited innovative ways of using scarce resources, (2) been deeply rooted in specific places and promoted new modalities of social exchange and cooperation, and (3) have successfully aligned individual interests with shared communal and social agendas and goals. Once they identified community gardens as loci of social innovation, they studied the social, relational, and affiliative activities in an attempt to map, codify, translate, and provide spatial logic for the collaborative modalities discovered. Just as in Cruz's study of the teenage skaters, DESIS Lab discovered that what was originally an act of dissent by radical urban activists in the 1960s also scaled-up and acquired social and spatial intelligence and political power to change top-down policy.

Tobias Armborst identifies three roles that Interboro Partners assume as urbanists, one of which is that of the "ghostwriter." The role of ghostwriting is precisely to discover the genetic code of the city, and map out, describe, draw, and name often hidden and obscured practices of self-interested urban tacticians. Their work in Detroit attempts to render visible and legible the practice of "blotting" and to write a retroactive blotting manifesto in order to aggregate and retrospectively render individual blotters into a community of practice.

Some of the above work is aimed solely at abductive reconstruction, that is, at disambiguation. Some, however, employs the interpretation of innovative practices into heuretic insights and premises: the procedure for generating new work (Ulmer 2002: 42). In that sense, the work of San Diego skaters is not solely a "model" of urban commoning, but a heuretic "relay" whose goal is "to extend the abductive reconstruction of the poetics of discovery produced after the fact into a generator for making further discoveries of a different sort." This is a heuretic procedure, the logic of invention (Ulmer 2002: 307) by way of which the logic of original practice is not abandoned but employed to produce different dimensions of urban experience and praxis (Ulmer 2002: 47). This procedure works conductively by channeling the "raw" power of organizing and intelligence found in the work of the skaters into a reliable generalized practice of innovation and, often, invention (Ulmer 2002: 114). Cruz calls it "the transference of procedural knowledge." By means of conduction, designers move beyond the abstractions of "cases," "rules," and "models" to produce the premises for the logic of invention. In conduction, the inference path moves not between "things" and "ideas" (concepts), but between "things" and "things." The process of storytelling is not as much the building of a body of knowledge or a theory—by way of a model—as it is a representation of an urgency "in the way of a relay that may not keep its charge," and thus must be passed on (Ulmer 1989: 89). In many ways, conduction as a "logic of passage" involves "the flow of energy through a circuit" (Ulmer 1989: 63), a circuit that now mobilizes the claims as well as the effects into the public realm where it can be further syncretized as well as contested.

As Penin suggests, such mobilizations render designing "an activity that aims to make social innovation practical and desirable" (Jégou and Manzini 2008: 23) to larger audiences by representing the authentic work of urban and social innovators. On the other hand, such a situated understanding opens up opportunities for the reconceptualization of design as social praxis that moves beyond traditional interventions manifested through physical objects and public amenities to the design of new capacities, capabilities, social protocols, processes, and infrastructures for radically rethinking the workings of democracy "on the ground." In addition, through this process designers also develop critical insights into potential domains of contribution and the reconfiguration of the boundaries of professional design practice.

Transforming the work of urban social heroes—notable innovators who brought about significant urban transformation in their cities—into concepts of urban innovation (Havelock 1988; Ulmer 2002: 30; Manzini 2015: 62) is an important modality of this line of work. What it aims to accomplish is transference of anecdotal forms of knowing from an essentially context-dependent, oral culture to literate forms of knowledge that are formalizable and transferable. Concepts produced thereby *de facto* prototype new category formations and new systems for organizing urban praxis (neologisms, order, logic, method), but even more importantly they suggest institutional practices for learning and applying new categories of thinking. In short, they offer a syncretic apparatus that brings technology, institutions, and identity formations into innovative configurations. More often than not, this engagement discovers conflict and struggle at the root of urban innovation, and reveals deeply antagonistic dimensions of urban social life. Working abductively and then also conductively, designers have the capacity to invent "passages" by way of which the rationale of "the political" is channeled towards practices of agonistic engagement, where "politics" as spatial praxis can be imagined and conceptualized. As Cruz argues, urban conflict is *de facto* operationalized in this way. Cruz has attempted to "stitch" together anecdotal references, community narratives, and government strategies into a meta-narrative of the democratization of urban development across Latin America since the 1970's by analyzing the work of, and interviewing, the protagonists in Curitiba, Brazil (Jamie Lerner), Bogota (Antanas Mockus) and Medellin, Colombia (Sergio Fajardo Valderrama and Alejandro Echeverri), and many others. The resulting "complex palimpsest of institutional relationships and dialogical processes with communities" presents a lineage of institutional transformations that can be instrumentalized—by way of a relay—toward the production of the new civic and political imagination across geographical boundaries.

Designing New Capabilities

As a strategic practice, design is employed as a vehicle for building capabilities for critical urban action by aggregating, synergizing, and coordinating existing urban initiatives. Design here also channels the transfer of associational activity from introvert (self-organization) to outward oriented (public realms) and determines the modalities of agonistic engagement in politics via propositional and normative praxis. This level of associational activity occurs at what is often called the "micro level" of civil society, or the domain of "civic engagement." Beyond what Putnam called "interest articulation and interest aggregation" (Putnam 1993: 90), design is employed here to synchronize, communicate, and configure normative propositions by building capacities and capabilities for politicizing struggles of everyday life in order to formulate and raise questions as well as to determine courses of action to be taken. Design acts as a conduit through which the intangible dimensions of social life—such as confidence, relationships, trust, symbolic and cultural values, social capital[20]—are embedded in the processes and connectivities that stand at the core of the idea and conception of civil society (Kaldor 2003).

In 2009, Ivan Kucina and his team decided to engage in the struggle of a self-organized group of citizens in Belgrade, Serbia to resist the destruction of Peti Park, a local public park slated for commercial development. Typical of many urban movements as well as of instances of insurgent citizenship, once the defensive dimension of self-organizing succeeded, and the now destroyed park was returned to public use, the coalition of citizens found itself faced with new challenges. First, the Parks Department had no resources to return the liberated park to its previous state, leaving a pile of rubbish on its grounds. Second, and more importantly, the coalition lacked the capabilities to produce alternative visions and scenarios. The design team engaged members of the citizen coalition and other residents in a ten-week period of visioning and codesigning sessions in order to build the configurative and spatial capabilities of the group and to enable them to envision the political implication of their ideas. This engagement with issues through the process of codesigning moved the attitude of the coalition from one based in *positionality*, necessary to win the battle with the developer, toward one of *propositionality*. Not only did the coalition then begin to understand self-organizational capacity differently, they also clearly understood the spatial dimensions of the political and of the public realm.

An important aspect of this urban work is the development of "the design attitude" (Boland and Collopy 2004; Bason 2014). The most fundamental aspect of the development of design attitude is to cultivate the recognition that designing is neither necessarily a problem-solving procedure, nor a protocol for choosing the best option available; rather, design signifies a process of producing new and possibly unforeseen alternatives. Even more importantly, such alternatives are produced collectively and validated through group critique, iteration, and prototyping in group settings. This process enables the anecdotal dimension of urban experience to acquire scale and significance beyond the original context-dependency as well as to build social capital and articulate voices propositionally and publicly. In that sense, the process and activity of designing are reframed as "diffused design" (Manzini 2015: 37), an activity aimed at building the design capabilities of the social group (citizen coalition) rather than remaining exclusively a domain of practice and knowledge associated with professional designers. In the final stage of work, Kucina's team and the citizen coalition took another step: in an attempt to spatialize the implications of the proposal for the new park, they marked all areas of intervention on the actual territory in life-size scale. That act of projection enabled the community to embody, enact, perform, and experientially grasp the proposal. It also rendered the proposition normative, visible, and therefore tangible, and thus offered the coalition opportunities and resources to take the process of contestation further.

The work of Gans Studio in Sheepshead Bay, New York also unpacks what Deborah Gans has termed "the missing scales of design action." Namely, by engaging with a citizen coalition in Sheepshead Bay post-Hurricane Sandy, Gans and her Pratt Institute colleagues managed to provide spatial and economic coherence for the work of an organized and proactive group of citizens. By codesigning a sequence of new spatial configurations that link the individual property, the urban block, the community, and the city, and by providing tangible and actionable links between available federal funding streams and the socio-spatial organization of the citizen coalition, they managed to bridge the gap between large-scale environmental actions, individual actions, and community needs, and thus, to enable the long-term residents of this community to coproduce a resilient plan that supports complex regional ecologies.

A part of the process of developing capacities for self-organization and capabilities for enacting political propositions in the public realm is also the work of designers in scaling-up emergent communal practices by designing new modalities of microeconomic productivity. Design advances emergent forms of self-organization into strategic urban operating systems driven to produce both symbolic and exchange values: These are characterized by spatial intelligence, resilience, self-organization, group solidarity, and organized improvisation that follows well-defined rules of engagement (Neuwirth 2011b). Through what they call "urban agronomadism," Stalker has attempted to boost urban social movements focused on issues of social justice and immigrant rights by (1) developing their self-organizing capacity, (2) creating alternative sources of income, and (3) enabling the projections of their voices in the public realm. In an organized urban commoning scheme, Stalker mapped out public land in and around Rome covered with orange trees. With their partners, collaborators, and hundreds of citizens they collected oranges and produced orange jam that was then sold through their solidarity network. The project Oranges Don't Fall from the Sky (Le Arance Non Cadono Dal Cielo) was done to raise awareness of the devastating living and working conditions of undocumented

African orange-pickers in the south of Italy. The funds made through this process of reappropriation of the commons were used to construct a social center for African workers in the town where immigrant workers were beaten with iron bars just a year prior. Such new socio-economic practices reappropriate and restructure urban space (Crawford 2008: 280) in ways that suggest possibilities for larger-scale urban transformations. Cruz's work along the San Diego–Tijuana border similarly identifies opportunities for scaling-up the emergent work of economically impoverished, yet innovative, immigrant communities. The necessary purpose of this work is to create spaces of confrontation and provide opportunities and resources for people to take part in the processes of political, economic, and spatial contestation (DiSalvo 2012).

Design as Strategic Asset of Third Sector Organizations

Since "the third sector" (not-for-profit, voluntary sector) was first theoretically formulated in 1973 by Amitai Etzioni as the balancing factor between the state (the public sector) and the market (the private sector), it has been characterized by value-based motivations for voluntary participation and by independence from the institutionalized power structures of the government and free-market entrepreneurship alike (Etzioni 1973: 316; Corry 2010). This is a domain of organized social, cultural, and political activity commonly synonymous with the notion of civil society, and in many ways inscribes the "infrastructural" dimension to processes, practices, and spatial extensions of the civil society. Even though organizations that comprise the third sector are all voluntary, community-based, and not-for-profit, the sector is extremely diverse and often conceptually, ideologically, and politically fragmented. As Mayer suggests, the success of the "the non-profit industrial complex" (NPIC) since the mid-1990s has enabled the retreat of government- and state-provided services and has served as an invitation for the neoliberalization of local political life (Mayer 2011: 49–51). Indeed, in the United States, policies of Presidents William J. Clinton, George W. Bush, and Barack Obama have initiated and promoted volunteerism, civic engagement, and the third sector organizations (be they of religious or secular orientation) in order to ameliorate the devastation brought to local communities by the processes of neoliberal urbanization in the United States and abroad. In that sense, the growth of the third sector has been a function of the restructuring of the welfare state and has been essential to the expansion of neoliberal urban policies because of its emphasis on the entrepreneurialism of local actors and community organizations through public–private partnerships and through competitive funding mechanisms. Through this process, municipal and city governments have ceased to be the objects of urban struggle and antagonists of urban social movements, and have reframed themselves as partners and collaborators of the third sector organizations by creating political alliances, contracting and funding community organizations, and also building local coalitions to attract funding for community projects from the state as well as from private foundations (Mayer 2006: 205).

Although some argue that the role of NPIC has been to control social justice movements, divert public funds to private parties through foundations, manage dissent, and derail political movements (INCITE! 2007), the third sector has also emerged as an answer to the increased differentiation in the spaces and practices of civil society. As NPIC organizations seek to regulate relationships between the state and public funding, private not-for-profit foundations, and the free market and for-profit sector, they also organize new connectivities and facilitate processes of negotiation as well as contestation. In this respect, they are also "power technologies" that attempt to re-organize processes of urban governance (Corry 2010: 15–16). The ultimate contribution of the third sector organizations may be in their latent ability to generate political visions and imaginaries, strengthen the culture of political participation in democratic processes, and produce dispositions and possibilities for urban social action (Åkerstøm 2008).[21]

In this "intermediary sphere" of civil society (the "meso-level" of voluntary associational activity of citizens), design catalyzes the production of institutional and regulatory frameworks, human and organizational capital, systems and resources as well as networks and associations. This is a type of associational work that develops primarily at the level of multiple concurrent public realms. In many ways, the work of design here is to strengthen the capabilities and capacities of what Fraser called "weak publics" in the process of social differentiation and political power formation. In this domain, design is employed in a variety of ways: from professional designers providing services to third sector organizations, to designers "diffusing" (Manzini 2015) design attitudes, knowledge, and skills, and thus configuring additional capabilities at the very core of these organizations.

The Center for Urban Pedagogy (CUP), itself a non-profit organization, translates complex urban and public policy and planning documents into visual explanations with the aim of laying down the foundation for more effective practices of civic engagement and democratic participation, particularly around issues of social justice. CUP's model revolves around working with community organizers (and not with urban communities directly) with the objective of employing organizers as conduits for the didactic aspect of this work. For this process to work, CUP builds a knowledge base that renders state policies "imageable" and thus opens them up for contestation. Identified social justice issues are each represented by a kit of parts designed to enable organizers to engage their constituencies in hands-on, interactive, and participatory workshops. The kit may be composed of posters, booklets, pamphlets, video documentaries, interactive online computer platforms, and maps. CUP employs the design process and design reasoning in a twofold manner: first, to arrive at a set of easily reconfigurable devices (kits) that community organizers use in order to shape their own agendas for engagement; and second, to configure the interaction between organizers and their constituencies through what is essentially a practice of coproduction of urban knowledge, political attitudes, and actionable insights that may lead to forms of self-organization. Ultimately, as Christine Gaspar argues, CUP's work is based on the idea that rendering public policy "imageable" leads to social change. The application of design-led models of urban education and urban pedagogy has led to capacity building through design, reexamination of the modes of engagement with public institutions, as well as scrutiny surrounding the political protocols of inclusion of urban citizens in the processes of urbanization.

Srdjan Jovanovic Weiss and Normal Architecture Office (NAO) worked with kuda.org, a non-profit, third sector organization in Novi Sad, Serbia to create a Center for New Media. The proposed new facility is supposed to save a dilapidated youth facility (handball stadium) from demolition and privatization by reappropriating the commons and the collective property (a juridical remnant of the socialist past). In a situation of high political, social, economic, and cultural uncertainty surrounding this emerging democracy, the proposal for the Center for New Media attempts to mobilize civic and social forces via the design of the new stadium. In this respect, the NAO-designed stadium is a vector of the democratic impulse and enables civic actors and third-sector organizations led by kuda.org to materialize and concretize ideas, beliefs, desires, and discourses of the emerging civil society. As a communicative tool, the design enables embodied claims and arguments to enter the public realm and make the demands for democracy and participation tangible, experiential, and known, thus enabling contestation and the formation of new political subjectivities. Additionally, the proposal builds capacities for further self-organization and in that sense signifies a call to political action.

In the aftermath of Hurricane Katrina, Gans Studio worked in New Orleans with the Association of Community Organizations for Reform Now (ACORN) to empower their constituency through design approaches, attitudes, and processes. The work consisted of codesigning "tactical game changers" on what Deborah Gans calls "the middle scale," where catalyzing community scale of governance and action was urgently needed in order to counteract the city's top-down policies. The social cooperation catalyzed by design also contributed to the success of the middle-scale (the meso-level) alignment of individual and communal needs with larger environmental agendas and with municipal and regional objectives alike.

For Weiss, Gans, and others, design conceived also as a material practice has the capacity to articulate political arguments through transformative processes of engagement with the material environment that differ radically from the cognitive and discursive processes of deliberation necessary for the articulation of political messages (Traganou 2016). Materially-driven social action by designers, urbanists, and architects also redefines their professional roles in strengthening the third sector organizations and rebuilding urban communities.

Designing New Modalities of Governance

Conceived as a strategic activity, design is often employed to create new coalitions and cross-sector connectivities in socio-spatial contexts where design expertise is distributed among multiple stakeholders and where context-dependent relations and interactions constitute the main focus. Particularly in complex and necessarily collaborative situations, design often enables capacities and capabilities for invention by way of conceiving innovative connections between social actors, civil associations, state institutions, funding streams, and market organizations. The task here is not to attempt to create a totalizing ecology where everything is connected to everything else, but to figure out which existing connections are relevant and in need of preserving and, more importantly, what connectivities must be codesigned anew. As Levi Bryant argues, central socio-political challenges seem to revolve not around the question of *how* people and organizations are related, but the fact that they are *not* related (Bryant 2014). The question for designers thus becomes how to configure existing—and design new—artifacts that have the capacity to bring people and organizations together in innovative socio-spatial ensembles. In this context of work, design operates in the realm habitually defined as that of social innovation.

Among new alliances and partnerships between organizations of civil society and the state one recognizes three models in which design has played a significant role. First, design and designers work in non-profit, non-governmental as well as community-based design-driven organizations to conceptualize, organize, and provide public and community services that governments either no longer provide or have never provided. This kind of work occurs at the level of self-organization, but also often in coordination with governmental agencies which provide human and material resources. In Chapter 5, Anne Frederick describes how Hester Street Collaborative (HSC) transitioned from a client-based practice (linked to its founders, Leroy Street Studio) to an activist mode of practice, and then to a practice of "infrastructuring" (Manzini 2015: 151). As a social justice-driven non-profit organization dedicated to bringing the design process to the practices of community development, HSC's first step was to work closely with grassroots and community-based organizations and build associational activities and social capital in communities on the Lower East Side (LES) in New York City. As Frederick notes, it was only later that HSC realized its actual potential through the practice of "infrastructuring." In this respect, a particularly illuminating project is Sara D. Roosevelt Park, where HSC and Partnership for Parks (PFP) created People Make Parks (PMP), a collaborative initiative designed to facilitate direct community participation in the design of local parks. PFP itself is a joint program of City Parks Foundation and NYC Parks founded in 1995 as a public–private partnership to support civic and community leaders and park advocates as they "network" with the city government, and to provide "the skills and tools" necessary to turn green areas into community parks. In addition, City Parks Foundation is a non-profit organization whose mission is to create inclusive cultural programming in public parks across New York City. The role of Hester Street Collaborative—as a Lower East Side organization with substantial social network capacity and co-design capabilities—in the PMP project was to build a coalition with numerous local organizations in order to create community-driven proposals for Sarah D. Roosevelt Park. This in many ways epitomizes the practice of infrastructuring, an effort to produce complex platforms that bring together social actors, agencies, and organizations into a creative ensemble in order to connect and sustain many autonomous but related initiatives (Manzini 2015: 152). When regional governance is combined with community-based participatory organizations based on group affinities, Young calls this a practice of "differentiated solidarity" through which design configures the platform for the "relationally constituted structural differentiation [. . .] of socially situated interests, claims and proposals" (Young 2000: 7).

Second, designers and design consultancies are nowadays often employed by the government as third-party service providers, particularly in areas where governments no longer have the capacity, resources, or the know-how to successfully imagine public services in areas of emerging need. For example, Teddy Cruz consults for municipal and regional governments, such as the City of San Diego (as special advisor on Urban and Public Initiatives for the City of San Diego, and previously as a member of the board of directors of San Diego's Center City Development Corporation), while members of Cohabitation Strategies consults for the government of Ecuador on a comprehensive new plan for national territorial development (National Strategy Center for the Right to the Territory, CENEDET) as part of President Rafael Correa Delgado's National Plan for Good Living.[22] Parsons DESIS Lab regularly advises different public agencies of the City of New York, while the design consultancy IDEO offers lessons in the human-centered approach to innovation to the United States government in areas of public services provided by the Social Security Administration.[23]

Third, numerous governments across the world have recognized the impact the application of design reasoning, knowledge, and processes (often under the umbrella of "design thinking") can have in the area of public services, and have consequently initiated design-driven agencies within governments in order to redesign existing public services and invent new ones, as well as to foster a culture of innovation within government. For instance, MindLab is an innovation agency within the ministries of Business and Growth, Employment, and Taxation of the national administration of Denmark whose task is to involve the public in co-creating new public services and policies.[24] In the same vein, Lab for the City is a design-innovation platform initiated by the government of Mexico City to bridge the growing gap between city agencies and citizens.[25] Another design-led innovation office was initiated in 2010 by Thomas Menino, the legendary Mayor of Boston, as the Mayor's Office of New Urban Mechanics (MONUM) in order to blend digital technology, community participation, and enhanced citizen responsiveness into an innovation model of urban governance. Today, New Urban Mechanics is a network of civic innovation offices across the United States. In all of these examples, design has emerged as an instrumental medium through which individuals, social groups, and organizations (public and private) engage in coproducing alternative systems and modalities of governance. In this sense designing has become both a core capability and a strategic asset in the socio-spatial practices of urban citizen groups, communities, and organizations alike.[26]

Another way of producing new connectivities is through a practice Tobias Armborst has dubbed "matchmaking" wherein Interboro identifies constituents, initiatives, funding streams, and material sources, and then finds innovative ways of relating and synergizing them. In their Holding Pattern project, done in collaboration with MOMA PS1 in Long Island City, Queens, Interboro Partners turned a short-term funding stream into a long-term benefit for the participating communities. Namely, they identified over fifty local community organizations and citizen coalitions and worked with them to understand and document their needs and aspirations. They were then categorized and classified (from trees and books to game and sports equipment), and used in the courtyard during the Warm Up music summer festival. After the festival was over, MOMA distributed the goods to the communities who had previously identified them as priorities.

À *propos* design and the political

Design has the capacity to frame and operationalize urban conflict and vectorize two fundamental dimensions of democratic practice: the production of *the political*, and the reconfiguration of the conditions necessary for engagement in *politics* (Mouffe 2000). Design praxis in the domain of politics intends to support and improve the nexus of processes, practices, and discourses of governance as well as the institutions that attempt to produce social order by organizing conditions of coexistence (Mouffe 2005: 8, 9) and cohabitation. On the other hand, design praxis in the domain of the political aims at engaging directly with the antagonistic nature of urban conflict and struggle. For Mouffe, the political refers to the dimension of antagonism that is intrinsic to social relations. Through the different modalities of engagement at the level of self-organization as well as the level of public spheres, design delineates the necessary from the contingent because, in principle, design is "concerned not with the necessary but with the contingent" (Simon 1969)—not with how things are, but with how they ought to be. If, as Mouffe argues, the goal of democratic politics is "to transform antagonism into agonism," the work featured in *Concurrent Urbanities* attempts to show that design can channel "collective passions" over issues of urban conflict so that they can be identified and articulated in ways which render political opponents not as enemies to be destroyed but as adversaries, "somebody whose ideas we combat but whose right to defend those ideas we do not put into question" (Mouffe 2000: 101–102).[27] From the vantage point of "agonistic pluralism," the objective is to enable new collective subjectivities to self-organize and, simultaneously, to produce new public realms in order to "democratically battle each other." The political workings of design in this context are also marked by the articulation and configuration of infra-structures of socio-spatial inclusion that would enable countless urban citizens to acquire "the right to have rights." Namely, as Arendt claimed, "something much more fundamental than freedom and justice, is the deprivation of the right to opinion, action, and to belonging to an organized community" (Arendt 1951: 177).

The reader will certainly detect differences in political approaches among the contributors to this anthology. The objective of this book is not to create a totalizing narrative intended to frame and describe contested processes of the production of urban space from a singular perspective; it is to expose ways of changing them from reformist and radical perspectives alike. While it could be argued that the work in the realm of self-organizing transforms relations within the existing system of power relations, at the same time the work on the political attempts to configure and prototype parameters, fragments, and relations of a new system, and makes the *possible* tangible, visible, and actionable. My own editorial idea is not to claim that the work featured in this book manages to make a difference without challenging the principal values and practices of neoliberal urbanization. To the contrary, my belief is that the work featured in *Concurrent Urbanities*, in aggregate, goes beyond challenging the framework of existing capitalist relations to provide clear insights and offer unparalleled ways of discovering configurative possibilities while proposing new ways of being urban (Dilnot 2006). As AbdouMaliq Simone suggests, "What it is possible for people to do with each other is largely a question of what it is that exists between them, and how this 'between' can be shaped as active points of reference, connection and anchorage." (Simone 2013: 243) Configuring the "between" is the work of designing, the critical work of coproducing new propositions for resilient civic infrastructures of socio-spatial inclusion and justice. For it is my belief that at stake in strengthening the processes and practices of civil society are questions central to our time: that of the political, that of the very future of democracy, and that of the emerging "urban society" (Lefebvre 2003). In all of them, design and designing could play a central role.

Notes

1. This chapter is a reworking of the intro speeches at the three Concurrent Urbanities conferences that took place in 2009, 2011, and 2013. Fragments of this chapter were previously published and presented in public settings as a way of promoting the book (Mitrašinović 2014).
2. Brenner and Schmid note that "urban age" has become the "framing device or reference point for nearly anyone concerned to justify the importance of cities as sites of research, policy intervention, planning/design practice, investment or community activism." (Brenner and Schmid 2014) They argue that the "urban age" thesis has been empirically untenable and theoretically incoherent because it is empirically impossible to consistently and verifiably determine the urban–rural divide across the world. For an illuminating critique of the measurement techniques and standards for demarcating the "urban/rural boundary" used by United Nations agencies, see Brenner and Schmid (2014).
3. Neil Brenner's work on planetary urbanization puts forward the argument that urban theory should no longer be premised on the assumption that cities are bounded and distinctive types of human settlement to be clearly and readily differentiated from the "non-urban" territories such as the countryside, the rural, and the natural. Drawing on the work of Henri Lefebvre, Brenner's epistemology of planetary urbanization proposes an emergent worldwide urban fabric to which there no longer is any "outside" (Brenner 2013).
4. The World Bank 2013 Annual report claims that "the percentage of people living in extreme poverty in 2013 is less than half of what it was in 1990." For reference see: http://siteresources.worldbank.org/EXTANNREP2013/Resources/9304887-1377201212378/9305896-1377544753431/1_AnnualReport2013_EN.pdf (Last accessed on February 15, 2015).
5. *A New Global Partnership: Eradicate Poverty and Transform Economies Through Sustainable Development*. United Nations Report, 2013. At: www.post2015hlp.org/wp-content/uploads/2013/05/UN-Report.pdf (Last accessed on February 15, 2015).
6. Seven main impediments to urban prosperity are the following: poor governance and weak institutions; lack of appropriate infrastructure; high incidence of slums and poverty;

high costs of doing business; low levels of human capital; high crime rates; and corruption (HABITAT 2013: XVII).
7. As David Harvey argues, it was the Pinochet military dictatorship in Chile in the 1970s that had been responsible for the first comprehensive national experiment in privatization of state property and the commons, followed by the 1978 neoliberal economic reforms of Deng Xiaoping in China. Both preceded Reagan and Thatcher restructuring in the mid-1980s (Harvey 2007).
8. For reference see: www.dnainfo.com/new-york/20130314/red-hook/carlos-menchaca-looks-areas-forgotten-by-government-city-council-race (Last accessed on February 15, 2015).
9. In 2010, the Center for Research and Innovation at the National League of Cities published its *Municipal Action Guide* where it identified major methods for privatization of public services. Interestingly, through the so-called "managed competition" privatization also includes competitive contract bidding between private and public service providers. In this scenario, an internal unit of the Department of Sanitation is expected to bid against a private company bidding for waste collection service in its municipality.
10. For reference see: "Unbundling the nation state: countries have started to outsource public services to each other." *The Economist*, February 8, 2014 At: www.economist.com/news/international/21595928-countries-have-started-outsource-public-services-each-other-unbundling-nation (Last accessed on February 15, 2015).
11. See Richard Florida's endorsement of this line of argumentation: "The Developing World's Urban Population Could Triple by 2210: Can we possibly prepare?" City Lab, The Atlantic Monthly, February 20, 2014. At: www.citylab.com/housing/2014/02/developing-worlds-urban-population-could-triple-2210/8431/ (Last accessed on February 15, 2015).
12. As Robles-Durán further suggests,

> It is indeed alarming that there is an immense lack of operative strategies that focus on the urban spaces where the majority of the world's population lives—that vast gray space in cities where there is little crime, no large-scale development commissions, and no glamorous urban design or architectural competitions.
>
> (Robles-Durán 2014)

13. In geometry, a set of waves, lines, or curves are said to be concurrent if they all intersect at the same point, the "point of concurrency." In a triangle, the three medians, three perpendicular bisectors, three angle bisectors, and three altitudes are each "concurrent." In computer science and programming discourses, as DeBakker and Zucker write (1982), three distinct notions are fundamental in the study of concurrency: parallel composition, synchronization, and communication. For reference see DeBakker and Zucker (1982).
14. In theorizing civil society, Young builds on the work of Jürgen Habermas (1989, 1992, 1996), Cohen and Arato (1992), Nancy Fraser (1991), and Laclau and Mouffe (1985).
15. Private level defines activities whose claims cannot be universalized and are mostly need-based and inward looking. Civic level delineates activities that are outward looking, open to all, and principally inclusive. Political (public) level outlines activities that politicize social and economic issues and allow conflict to surface so that it can be contested (Young 2000: 161–162).
16. For Young, the public sphere is the instrumental "social space" produced via associational activities through which people demand connections with institutions and organizations of political and economic power (Young 2000: 170–173): in that sense, "the public sphere is the primary connector between people and power." Where I depart from Young's view of the public sphere is in relation to her argument for the singularity of the public sphere (Young 2000: 171). Instead, I employ the argument initially formed by Nancy Fraser (1991) who argued that "subaltern counterpublics"

produce concurrent discursive arenas "where members of subordinated social groups invent and circulate counter discourses, which in turn permits them to formulate oppositional interpretations of their identities, interests, and needs." (Fraser 1991: 67)

17. Laclau and Mouffe argued that social objectivity is constituted through acts of power, or that power is constitutive of social identities as such; the convergence of power and objectivity is what Laclau and Mouffe refer to as "hegemony" (Laclau and Mouffe 1985).

18. Holston writes:

    The sense of "insurgent" I use to investigate this entanglement is not normative. It has no inherent moral or political value. Insurgent citizenships are not necessarily democratic or just, socialist or populist [. . .] Rather, insurgence describes a process that is an acting counter, a counterpolitics, that destabilizes the present and renders it fragile, defamiliarizing the coherence with which it usually presents itself. Insurgence is not a top-down imposition of an already scripted future. It bubbles up from the past in places where present circumstances seem propitious for an irruption. In this view, the present is like a bog: leaky, full of holes, gaps, contradictions, and misunderstandings.

    (Holston 2008: 34)

19. Members of the Stealth group were: Ana Džokić, Milica Topalović, Marc Neelen and Ivan Kucina.

20. For Bourdieu, "social capital is the sum of the resources, actual or virtual, that accrue to an individual or a group by virtue of possessing a durable network of more or less institutionalized relationships of mutual acquaintance and recognition." (Bourdieu and Wacquant 1992: 119)

21. As cited in Corry (2010: 16).

22. For reference see: www.unosd.org/content/documents/96National Plan for Good Living Ecuador.pdf (Last accessed on February 15, 2015).

23. For reference see: "IDEO takes over the government." In: *Metropolis*, June 2011. At: www.ideo.com/images/uploads/news/pdfs/Metropolis_IDEO_govt_June2011_1.pdf (Last accessed on February 15, 2015).

24. For reference see: http://mind-lab.dk/en/ (Last accessed on February 15, 2015).

25. For reference see: http://labplc.mx/labforthecity/ (Last accessed on February 15, 2015).

26. For an excellent overview of the above listed initiatives, see: Staszowski, E. (Ed.) (2015) (New) Public Goods. *Journal of Design Strategies*, Vol. 8, Fall 2015. For reference see: http://sds.parsons.edu/designdialogues/ (Last accessed on February 15, 2015).

27. As Mouffe writes,

    I consider that it is only when we acknowledge the dimension of "the political" and understand that "politics" consists in domesticating hostility and in trying to defuse the potential antagonism that exists in human relations, that we can pose what I take to be the central question for democratic politics. This question, pace the rationalists, is not how to arrive at a consensus without exclusion, since this would imply the eradication of the political. Politics aims at the creation of unity in a context of conflict and diversity; it is always concerned with the creation of an "us" by the determination of a "them." The novelty of democratic politics is not the overcoming of this us/them opposition—which is an impossibility–but the different way in which it is established. The crucial issue is to establish this us/them discrimination in a way that is compatible with pluralist democracy. Envisaged from the point of view of "agonistic pluralism," the aim of democratic politics is to construct the "them" in such a way that it is no longer perceived as an enemy to be destroyed but as an "adversary," that is, somebody whose ideas we combat but whose right to defend those ideas we do not put into question.

    (Mouffe 2000: 101–102)

Bibliography

Åkerstøm, N. (2008) *Partnerships: Machines of Possibility*. The Policy Press.

Appadurai, A. (2001) "Deep Democracy: Urban Governmentality and the Horizon of Politics." In: *Environment and Urbanization*, Vol. 13, No. 1, pp. 23–43.

Appadurai, A. (2002) The Right to Participate in the Work of Imagination. Brouwer, J., Mulder, A. and Martz, L. (Eds.) *Transurbanism*. NAi Publishers, pp. 33–48.

Appadurai, A. and Holston, J. (1996) "Cities and Citizenship." In: *Public Culture*, Vol. 8, No. 2, pp. 187–204.

Arendt, H. (1951) *The Origins of Totalitarianism*. Schocken Books.

Bason, C. (Ed.) (2014) *Design for Policy*. Gower Publishing Company.

Boland, R. J. and Collopy, F. (2004) *Managing as Designing*. Stanford University Press.

Böttger, M. and Fitz, A. (Eds.) (2014) Cities and Citizenship. *Weltstadt*, No. 5.

Bourdieu, P. and Wacquant, L. J. D. (1992) *An Invitation to Reflexive Sociology*. University of Chicago Press.

Brenner, N. (2013) Urban Theory Without an Outside. Brenner, N. (Ed.) *Implosions/Explosions: Towards a Study of Planetary Urbanization*. Jovis, pp. 14–35.

Brenner, N. and Schmid, C. (2014) "The 'Urban Age' in Question." In: *International Journal of Urban and Regional Research*, Vol. 38, No. 3, pp. 731–755.

Brenner, N. and Theodore, N. (Eds.) (2002) *Spaces of Neoliberalism: Urban Restructuring in North America and Western Europe*. Blackwell.

Bryant, L. R. (2014) Black Ecology. Cohen, J. J. (Ed.) *Prismatic Ecology: Ecotheory Beyond Green*. University of Minnesota Press, pp. 290–310.

Castells, M. (1984) *The City and the Grassroots*. University of California Press.

Cohen, J. L. and Arato, A. (1994) *Civil Society and Political Theory*. MIT Press.

Corry, O. (2010) Defining and Theorizing the Third Sector. Taylor, R. (Ed.) *Third Sector Research*. Springer, pp. 11–20.

Crawford, M. (2008a) Contesting the Public Realm: Struggles Over Public Space in Los Angeles. Kelbaugh, D. and McCullough, K. (Eds.) *Writing Urbanism: A Design Reader*. Routledge, pp. 271–280.

Crawford, M. (2008b) Introduction. Chase, J., Crawford, M. and Kaliski, J. (Eds.) *Everyday Urbanism*. Monacelli Press.

DeBaker, J. W. and Zucker, J. I. (1982) "Processes of the Denotational Semantics of Concurrency." DeBaker, J. W. and Rutten, J. J. (Eds.) *Ten Years of Concurrency Semantics*. World Scientific Publishing, pp. 28–80.

De Certeau, M. (1984) *The Practice of Everyday Life*. University of California Press.

Dilnot, C. (Fall 2006) "What are Architects For?" In: *Scapes*, Vol. 4, pp. 11–12.

DiSalvo, C. (2012) *Adversarial Design*. MIT Press.

Etzioni, A. (1973) "The Third Sector and Domestic Missions." In: *Public Administration Review*, Vol. 33, No. 4, pp. 314–323.

Foucault, M. (1980) [1972] *Power/Knowledge: Selected Interviews and Other Writings, 1972–1977*. Pantheon Books.

Fraser, N. (1990) "Rethinking the Public Sphere: A Contribution to the Critique of Actually Existing Democracy." In: *Social Text*, No. 25/26, pp. 56–80.

Fraser, N. (1991) "Rethinking the Public Sphere: A Contribution to the Critique of Actually Existing Democracy." In: *Social Text*, No. 25/26, pp. 56–80.

Fuad–Luke, A. (2009) *Design Activism: Beautiful Strangeness for a Sustainable World*. Routledge.

Fuller, B. and Romer, P. (2014) Urbanization as Opportunity. Glaeser, E. and Joshi-Ghani, A. (Eds.) *Rethinking Cities: A Roadmap Towards Better Urbanization for Development*. World Bank.

Habermas, J. (1989) *The Structural Transformation of the Public Sphere: An Inquiry into a Category of Bourgeois Society*. Polity (originally published in German in 1962 as Strukturwandel der Öffentlichkeit: Untersuchungen zu einer Kategorie der Bürgerlichen Gesellschaft).

Habermas, J. (April 1992) "Citizenship and National Identity: Some Reflections on the Future of Europe." In: *Praxis International*, Vol. 12, No. 1, pp. 1–19.

Habermas, J. (1996) *Between Facts and Norms: Contributions to a Discourse Theory of Law and Democracy*. The MIT Press.

Hall, P. (1988) *Cities of Tomorrow: An Intellectual History of Urban Planning and Design in the Twentieth Century*. Blackwell Publishers.

Hall, P. and Ulrich, P. (2000) *Urban Future 21: A Global Agenda for Twenty–First Century Cities*. Routledge.

Harvey, D. (2006) *Spaces of Global Capitalism: A Theory of Uneven Geographical Development*. Verso.

Harvey, D. (2007) *A Brief History of Neoliberalism*. Oxford University Press.

Harvey, D. (2008) "The Right to the City." In: *New Left Review*, No. 53, pp. 23–40.

Havelock, E. A. (1988) *The Muse Learns to Write: Reflections on Orality and Literacy from Antiquity to the Present*. Yale University Press.

Holston, J. (2008) *Insurgent Citizenship: Disjunctions of Democracy and Modernity in Brazil*. Princeton University Press.

Holston, J. and Appadurai, A. (1996) "Cities and Citizenship." In: *Public Culture*, No. 8, pp. 187–204.

Holston, J. and Appadurai, A. (1998) *Cities and Citizenship*. Duke University Press.

Hou, J. (2010) *Insurgent Public Space: Guerrilla Urbanism and the Remaking of Contemporary Cities*. Routledge.

Kaldor, M. (2003) *Global Civil Society: An Answer to War*. Polity Press.

Laclau, E. and Mouffe, C. (1985) *Hegemony and Socialist Strategy: Towards a Radical Democratic Politics*. Verso.

Lefebvre, H. (2003) *The Urban Revolution*. University of Minnesota Press (First published in French in 1970 by Gallimard as La Révolution Urbaine)

Manzini, E. (2015) *Design, When Everybody Designs: An Introduction to Design for Social Innovation*. The MIT Press.

Markussen, T. (Winter 2013) "The Disruptive Aesthetics of Design Activism: Enacting Design Between Art and Politics." In: *Design Issues*, Vol. 29, No. 1, pp. 38–50.

Martin, B. (2001) *Privatization of Municipal Services: Potential, Limitations and Challenges for the Social Partners*. International Labour Office, Geneva. Working Paper. Available online at: www.publicworld.org/files/ilomunicipal.pdf (Last Accessed on February 15, 2015).

Mayer, M. (March 2006) "Manuel Castells' the City and the Grassroots." In: *International Journal of Urban and Regional Research*, Vol. 30, No. 1, pp. 202–206.

Mayer, M. (2010) *Civic City Cahier 1: Social Movements in the (Post–) Neoliberal City*. Bedford Press.

Mayer, M. (2011) Neoliberal Urbanization and the Politics of Contestation. Kaminer, T., Robles-Durán, M. and Sohn, H. (Eds.) *Urban Asymmetries: Studies and Projects on Neoliberal Urbanization*. 010 Publishers, pp. 46–61.

Mayer, M. (2013) "First World Urban Activism: Beyond Austerity Urbanism and Creative City Politics." In: *City*, Vol. 17, No. 1, pp. 5–19.

Meyer, K. S. (2012) *Testing Tradition: Assessing the Added Value of Public–Private Partnerships*. The National Council for Public–Private Partnerships.

Mitrašinović, M. (2006) *Total Landscape, Theme Parks, Public Space*. Ashgate.

Mitrašinović, M. (2014) "Concurrent Urbanities: Designing Infrastructures of Inclusion". In: Böttger, M. and Fitz, A. (Eds.) (2014) Cities and Citizenship, *Weltstadt*, No. 5.

Mouffe, C. (2000) *The Democratic Paradox*. Verso.

Mouffe, C. (2005) *On the Political*. Routledge.

Mouffe, C. (Summer 2007) "Artistic Activism and Agonistic Spaces." In: *Art & Research*, Vol. 1, No. 2. Available online at: www.artandresearch.org.uk/v1n2/pdfs/mouffe.pdf (last accessed 15 September 2015).

Neuwirth, R. (2011a) *Stealth of Nations: The Global Rise of the Informal Economy*. Pantheon.

Neuwirth, R. (October 28, 2011b) "The Shadow Superpower: Forget China, the $10 Trillion Global Black Market Is the World's Fastest Growing Economy—and Its Future." *Foreign Policy*. Available online at: http://foreignpolicy.com/2011/10/28/the–shadow–super power/ (Last accessed on February 15, 2015).

Parks Council and Central Park Conservancy (1993) *Public Space for Public Life: A Plan for the Twenty–First Century*. New York Parks Council and Central Park Conservancy.

Putnam, R. D. (1993) *Making Democracy Work: Civic Traditions in Modern Italy*. Princeton University Press.

Restakis, J. (2010) *Humanizing the Economy: Co–operatives in the Age of Capital*. New Society Publishers.

Robles–Durán, M. (Winter 2014) "The Haunting Presence of Urban Vampires." In: Urbanism's Core? *Harvard Design Magazine*, No. 37. Available online at: www.harvarddesign magazine.org/issues/37/the–haunting–presence–of–urban–vampires (Last accessed on February 15, 2015).

Simon, H. A. (1969) *The Sciences of the Artificial*. MIT Press.

Simone, A. M. (Fall 2004) "People as Infrastructure: Intersecting Fragments in Johannesburg." In: *Public Culture*, Vol. 16, No. 3, pp. 407–429.

Simone, A. M. (2013) "Cities of Uncertainty: Jakarta, the Urban Majority, and Inventive Political Technologies." In: *Theory Culture Society*, No. 30, pp. 243–263.

Smith, N. (2008) *Uneven Development: Nature, Capital, and the Production of Space*. University of Georgia Press.

Staszowski, E. (Ed.) (Fall 2015) "(New) Public Goods." *Journal of Design Strategies*, Vol. 8. Available online at: http://sds.parsons.edu/designdialogues/ (Last accessed on February 15, 2015).

Tang, E. (2007) Non Profits and the Autonomous Grassroots. INCITE! Women of Color Against Violence (Eds.) *The Revolution Will Not Be Funded: Beyond the Non Profit Industrial Complex*. South End Press, pp. 215–257.

Traganou, J. (2016) *Designing the Olympics*. Routledge.

Ulmer, G. L. (1989) *Teletheory: Grammatology in the Age of Video*. Routledge.

Ulmer, G. L. (1994) *Heuretics: The Logic of Invention*. The John Hopkins University Press.

Ulmer, G. L. (2002) *Internet Invention: From Literacy to Electracy*. Longman.

United Nations Department of Economic and Social Affairs, Population Division (UN–DESA). (2014) *World Urbanization Prospects, the 2014 revision*. United Nations Publications.

United Nations Human Settlements Programme (HABITAT). (2013) *State of the World's Cities Report: Prosperity of Cities*. United Nations Human Settlements Programme and Routledge.

Young, I. M. (2000) *Inclusion and Democracy*. Oxford University Press.

Zukin, S. (1995) *The Cultures of Cities*. Blackwell Publishers.

Index

Activism 8, 36, 59, 166, 169, 171, 177, 182, 185, 198, 201–202
Africa 29, 32, 35, 86, 118, 140, 192
agriculture 40, 145–147
agonism 184, 197; agonistic engagement 189, 190; agonistic pluralism 197, 200; agonistic public spheres of contestation 184
Allen and Pike Street Pedestrian Mall 64
Americans with Disabilities Act (ADA) 157, 166
Appadurai, Arjun 187, 201–202
architecture 1, 3–4, 6–7, 23, 25–26, 29, 37, 44, 51, 57, 60–61, 76, 87, 120, 124, 129, 155–156, 166, 168, 172–175, 177; architect x, 35, 85, 87, 169, 177; architecture competition 23, 44, 46, 60; architecture firm 61; architecture school 51; Dept. of Architecture, University of Belgrade 87–88, 91–93, 95–98
Arendt, Hannah 197, 201
Armborst, Tobias 124, 126, 128, 130, 132–134, 136, 138–139, 188
art 4, 7, 17, 25–26, 50, 61, 72–73, 76, 83, 86, 100–102, 106, 112, 120, 124, 128–129, 133, 152, 202; art-based project 101–102; art education 51; Art for an Urban Re-Evolution 106; art history 50; art institution 128; art-making 83; art organizations 102; art production 100; art with political content 76; artist 35, 60, 77, 108; artistic analysis 171; artistic practices 10, 106; public art 4, 7, 72, 124
Asian Americans for Equality (AAFE) 121, 186
Aycock, Alice 3

Balkans 40, 48, 98, 170, 175, 177–178; balkanized 169, 170; balkanization 174, 177–178
Barretto Point Park in the South Bronx (SoBro) 156
Bartlett, William 43, 48, 98
Baxi, Kadambari 114, 116–122, 186–187
Baxi and Cheng 116–122; American Icon 116; Citizenship by Design 114–115, 117, 120–122; Henley Visa Restriction Index 117; Polymorphous Citizens 117, 186; Summer Street Festival 121–122, 186; World Passport 116; World Service Authority 116
Belaćević, Branko 91, 98
Belgrade 37–40, 42–44, 48, 56–60, 87–88, 90–93, 95–98, 169–170, 177, 188, 190
Beogradski Sindikat (The Belgrade Union) 91
Betsky, Aaron 35, 155
Bloomberg, Michael (Mayor) 1–8, 86, 148, 181
blot 125–127; blotters 126–127, 138, 188; blotting 126, 136, 138–139, 188; *see also* Interboro Partners
Bogota 12, 20, 189
Bordeaux 106–109
border 9–11, 13, 16, 21, 29, 35, 114, 115, 121, 186, 192; border territories 10; border urbanism 10–11, 16; cross-border urbanization 13; United States-Mexico border 9, 16, 192
Botsman, Rachel 141, 154
Bourdieu, Pierre 200–201
Brady, Timothy F. 85–86
Brash, Julian 3, 8
Brazil 9, 18, 20, 119, 140, 189, 202
Brenner, Neil 180, 198, 201
Bronx 77, 156

Brooklyn vii, 1, 3–4, 7, 61, 142, 148, 151, 161, 181
Brown, Cynthia Strokes 85
brownfields 13, 156
Bryant, Levi 195, 201
Buckles, Daniel J. 94, 98
building 3, 13, 19, 29, 31, 38, 40–41, 43, 52, 56–57, 59–63, 76–76, 90–91, 102, 109, 134–136, 138, 144, 147, 155, 166, 170, 175, 182, 184–185, 189–193; abandoned public buildings 31, Building Codes 76; illegal or semi-legal buildings 38
Bush, George W. (President) 155, 192

California 10, 13, 23, 139, 201
Caltrans 13, 23
Careri, Francesco (Stalker) 25
Castells, Manuel 180, 201–202
Center for Recreation and New Media (in Novi Sad) (NAO) 168–177, 194
Center for Urban Pedagogy (CUP) x, 50, 52, 76–78, 80–86, 154, 193; Community Education programs 77, 83, 86; Envisioning Development Toolkit (series) 77, 83, 154; Urban Homesteading Assistance Board 85; What is Affordable Housing? 77–78, 80–84; What is Zoning? 78, 85
Cheng, Irene 114–122, 186–187
China 1, 9, 121, 140, 199, 202
Chinatown 62, 121–122, 142, 186
cities 1–2, 4–5, 9–10, 12, 18–19, 37, 43, 48, 53, 56–57, 85, 87, 99, 106, 125, 133–134, 137, 139, 141, 166, 168–169, 175, 177, 180–181, 187, 189, 198–199
citizen 3, 52, 60, 62, 87, 98, 111, 115, 119, 166, 180, 185–187, 190–191, 196; citizenry 188; Citizen's Coalition 91; citizenship 4, 12, 20, 54, 114–115, 117–121, 123, 182, 185–188, 190
civic 1, 5–6, 9–10, 15, 18–21, 29, 31, 38–40, 42, 51, 62, 64, 76, 83, 90 91, 108, 110, 112, 155, 166, 171, 175, 182, 184, 186, 190, 192–196, 198; civic architecture 1, 6; civic associations 5, 9, 29, 38–39, 42, 62, 108, 110, 112, 175; civic education 51; civic engagement 76, 83, 155, 166, 190, 193; civic groups 5, 29; civic imagination 9, 20, 190; civic space 15
civil 4, 37, 41, 42, 59, 85–86, 117, 168, 179–187, 190, 192–195, 198–199, 201–202; civility 4, 181; civil rights 85–86; civil society 179–186, 190, 192–195, 198–199, 201–202
Clark, Septima Poinsette 85–86
Clinton, William J. (President) 143, 192
cohabitation 29, 187, 197; see also Cohabitation Strategies
Cohabitation Strategies (COHSTRA) 99–113, 186, 196; The *Bordeaux Report* 106, 108–109; City of Guelph, 109; Consortium for Useful Knowledge 102; Craft-Work 102; *Grand Parc* 106, 109; The Guelph-Wellington Rural-Urban Program 109, 110; Musagetes Foundation 109; The Other City: Exposing Tarwewijk, 102–105; Rotterdam 99, 102, 106, 133, 177, 186; Saint-Michel 106, 108; Tarwewijk 102–105, 186
collaborative processes 54, 148
collective 5, 16–17, 25, 27, 30, 34–35, 38, 41,43, 46, 60, 62, 76, 87, 90, 91, 94, 96, 102, 111, 134, 140, 147–148, 154, 159, 163, 165–166, 169–170, 172, 178, 180, 182, 185, 191, 194, 197; collective action 32, 41, 46, 163, 172, 185; collective consciousness 34–35; collective consumption 180; collective contribution 25; collective designing 43, 94; collective experience 27; collective games 30, 185; collective good 134; collective imagination 94; collective housing 38, 60; collective passions 197; collective processes 60; collective property 169–170, 178, 194; collective struggle 91; collective subjects 25, 197; collectivization 3; *see also* design
Colombia 9, 18, 20, 199
commodity 1, 16; commodification 31; commodified 3; commodify 179
Common Ground Community 157
Common Interest Development 134, 138
commons 7, 25–26, 29, 31, 34, 87, 91, 93, 179–180, 185, 192, 194, 199; (urban) commoning 5, 31, 46, 188, 191
Committee Against Anti-Asian Violence (CAAAV) 66, 75, 138
community 3, 5, 9, 10, 13, 15, 16, 17, 18, 20–23, 29–30, 34–35, 41–44, 49–50, 53–55, 57–59, 61–64, 66, 68–70, 72–77, 81–86, 90, 94, 99–102, 106, 110, 112, 114, 126, 128, 129, 132–134, 136, 140–142, 144–148, 151–154, 156–159,

161, 163–167, 170, 178, 181–198; community action 13, 101, 198; community-based organization 5, 63, 74, 83, 101, 110, 112, 128, 132, 166, 185, 192, 195–196; community-based social economy 15; community-based social innovation 140; community-based social organization 17, 41, 50, 51, 77; community-based urban development 20, 62; community-designed 69; community education 77, 83, 86; community engagement 50, 61, 62, 64; community garden 129, 144–148, 151, 188; community-led change 51, 61, 62; community-led design 61, 62, 69; community organizer 5, 76–77, 81, 83–84, 86, 193; community of practice 15, 16, 126, 182, 188; community participation 63, 75, 181, 196; community of reference 187; community services 90; creative community 59, 140–141, 144, 148, 154; immigrant communities 17, 29, 136; gated communities 178; self-contained community 44

construction 3, 6–7, 12–13, 20, 22, 24, 39–42, 44, 46, 59–60, 73, 87, 90–91, 112, 118, 162, 175; construction taxes 46; illegal construction 38, 60, 175

cooperative 31, 44, 46, 99–102, 106, 112, 136, 155, 178, 182, 184, 186–187; cooperative housing settlement 44; cooperative organization 44; housing cooperatives 41, 44, 46, 155

Correa Delgado, Rafael (President) 196

Corry, Olaf 192–193, 200–201

Cruz, Teddy x, 9–10, 12, 14–16, 18–19, 21–23, 187–189, 192, 196; Border urbanism 10–11, 16; *Estudio Teddy Cruz* vii, 10–12, 14–16, 18–19, 21; institutional transformations across Latin America 19; Medellin interviews 18; Tijuana/San Diego Border 9; Washington Street Skatepark 14, 187

Curitiba, 9, 18, 20, 189

De Blasio, Bill [Mayor] 1, 6

De Certeau, Michael 138–139, 183, 201

Debord, Guy 25, 36

democratization of urban development 17, 189; see also urban development

design 3–7, 10–11, 15, 20–21, 27, 29, 31–32, 34–35, 44, 48–57, 60–64, 66, 68–69, 72–74, 76–77, 83–85, 87–88, 93–94, 96, 98–102, 112, 114–116, 121, 124–125, 128–129, 133, 135–138, 140–142, 147–148, 151, 153, 155–158, 164–166, 169, 171, 175, 177, 182–186, 189–191, 193–199; co-design 30, 62–63, 94, 183, 190–191, 194; design 191; design action 155, 166, 191; design activism 87, 182, 185, 201–202; design attitude 190, 193; design competition 44; design devices 31; design-driven 5, 195–196; design education 62, 112; design initiatives 54; design installations 72–73; design knowledge 48–50; design practice 11, 49, 54, 61, 140, 142, 148, 154, 189, 198; design praxis 182–184, 197; design processes 53, 74, 87, 101, 156; design project 61, 136; design professionals 15; design recommendations 68–69; "design revolution" 49; design as a socio-spatial praxis 5; design studio 88, 98; design team 84, 93; design theories 5; design thinking 196; design workshops 61; designer 5, 13, 21, 48–50, 53, 55–56, 73–74, 77, 83–86, 106, 108–109, 113, 116, 135, 137, 142, 147–148, 171, 183–185, 187, 189, 191, 193–196; designing 5, 15–16, 29, 31, 40, 43, 50, 56, 61, 136, 151, 171, 184, 186, 189–191, 196, 198; designing geographies 29; diffused community-led design 61–62; graphic design 76; human-centered design 196; product design 54, 156–157; redesign 34, 62, 64, 114–116, 174, 181, 196; user centered research 94; vernacular design 49

DESIS Lab 140–141, 143–148, 150, 152–153, 188, 196; Abrons Art Center 147–148, 150; Amplifying Creative Communities 140–143, 147–148, 151, 153; Domino Sugar factory 151; Emerging User Demands for Sustainable Solutions (EMUDE) 140–141, 153–154; Green Map System 141; Green Thumb program 145; Henry Street Settlement 147; In your Own Backyards (ioby) 142; Lower East Side Ecology Center 141–142; Lower East Side exhibition 147

democracy 4, 24–25, 42, 189, 194, 198, 200

Detroit 125, 127, 137, 139, 188
Deutsche, Rosalind 4–5, 7–8
development [urban] 1, 3–7, 10, 16–17, 20, 24, 39, 42, 50, 54, 57, 62, 66, 69, 72, 75, 77, 79, 83, 87–90, 99–101, 106–107, 109, 112, 124, 126–127, 141, 147, 153, 155, 166–167, 171, 177, 179–180, 187, 189–190, 195–196, 199; developers 7, 15, 17, 42, 57, 87–88, 91, 98, 102, 133–134; *see also* Common Interest Developments; urban development
diagram 103; diagramming 117
dialectical (urban pedagogies) 56, 100–101, 113; dialogical processes 20, 190
DiSalvo, Carl 148, 153–154, 192, 201
displacement 1, 6, 10, 106, 123
Djilas, Dragan (Mayor) 93
dlandstudio 72
D'Orca, Daniel (Interboro Partners) 124
Džokić, Ana 37, 48, 57, 58–59, 88, 98, 186, 200

Echeverri, Alejandro 189
ecology 1, 16, 62, 75, 128, 135, 138, 141, 161, 180, 195, 201; ecotheory 201; urban ecology 135, 161
economy 1–6, 9–10, 14–20, 23–25, 27, 29, 31–32, 34, 37–38, 40, 42–43, 48, 58–60, 75, 79, 87–88, 90, 98–100, 102, 104, 107, 109, 112, 118–119, 123–124, 141–142, 144, 151, 159, 163, 166, 170, 174–175, 177, 179–180, 182–183, 186–188, 191–192, 194, 198–199, 202–203; economic crisis 27; economics 48; economies 18, 31, 102, 104, 112, 163, 179–180, 182; economies of scale 163; informal economy 17, 18, 202; grey economy 88, 188; micro-economies 31, 182
Ecuador 116, 196, 200
education 6, 20, 40, 51–53, 62, 76, 85, 112, 180, 193; Community Education 77, 83, 86; popular education 76, 85
emergent 10, 17, 34, 38–39, 88, 136, 182, 187–188, 191–192, 198
entrepreneurship 17, 192; entrepreneurs 20, 169, 174
environment 1, 10, 12, 16, 25, 31, 39, 53, 72, 88, 93, 100, 113, 125, 138, 140–142, 153, 156–159, 161, 166, 179, 181–182, 191, 194, 201

Etzioni, Amitai 192, 201
European Union 58, 60, 116–117, 119, 172

Fajardo Valderrama, Sergio 18, 189
Fals-Borda, Orlando 101
Favela-Bairro (Rio de Janeiro) 20
Foucault, Michel 4, 8, 183
Fraser, Nancy 184, 193, 199–201
Frederick, Anne x, 49, 53, 61, 195

Gans, Deborah x, 49, 51–53, 155, 191, 194
Gans Studio 156–165, 191, 194; Association for Community Organization Now (ACORN) 158, 161, 166, 194; Dwyer pumping station 161; Dwyer Road 161; Environmental Protection Agency (EPA) 159; First Step housing prototype 157; Floating Pool Lady 155; Plum Orchard 161; Sheepshead Bay 161–167, 191The Workbox-Next Generation School Desk 156
Gaspar, Christine x, 76, 78, 84, 86, 193
Gehl, Jan 3, 7
gentrification 1, 6, 20, 66, 106, 138, 146, 148, 151; mass displacement 1
global 3, 9, 10, 22, 29, 34–36, 42, 52–53, 86–87 117, 123, 155, 178–179, 181, 186, 198, 202; global city 3, 9, 86; globalism 179; globalization 36, 87, 186
governance 3, 9, 16–17, 19, 77, 101–102, 159, 180, 182, 187, 193–198; civic governing 40; collateral democratization 39; democracy 42; governing apparatus 24; government 3, 9, 14, 19–21, 38, 41, 76–77, 85–86, 90–91, 115–116, 118–119, 159, 172, 177, 180–181, 185–186, 189, 192, 195–196, 199–200; governmentality 215; Housing Relations Law of 1990 43; political and civic processes 18; political project 18; The Residence Law 43

Habermas, Jürgen 199, 201–202
Hardt, Michael 5, 8
Harvey, David 3–8, 87, 98, 179–180, 199, 202
Havelock, Eric 189, 202
healthcare 181
Heathcott, Joseph xi, 48
Hester Street Collaborative (HSC) 64–65, 67–74, 195; Allan and Pike Street Malls

64; Alliance 72; Avenue of the Immigrants 64; Community Board 3 64, 69; Dr. Sun Yat Sen Middle School (M.S. 131) 62; East New York Urban Youth Corps (ENYUYC) 61; East River Waterfront 64; Hester Street Playground (in Sara D. Roosevelt Park) 64; Leroy Street Studio 61, 72, 195; Luther Gulick Park 64; Partnership for Parks 64; People Make Parks 64; People's Plan 68; Pier 42 68, 69, 72

Holston, James 187, 200–202

home 43, 118, 121, 123, 125, 134, 156, 166–167, 178; homebuyers 42; homeless 2, 29, 133,157, 166,184; homelessness 6; homeowner 126; homesteading 85

Hou, Jeffrey 187, 202

housing 16–17, 23, 31–32, 38, 40, 42–44, 46, 57–58, 60–61, 66, 77, 79, 82–83, 85–86, 88, 90, 101–102, 106, 108, 112, 128, 134, 139, 146–147, 155, 157–158, 166, 179, 186, 199; affordable housing 61; housing authorities 17; housing loan 42; housing shortage 40; housing stock 43; informal housing provision 38; (subsidized) public housing 16, 23, 43; Section 8 82; social housing 57; the right to housing 40

Hurricane Katrina 158, 194

Hurricane Sandy 5, 128, 156, 167, 181; post-Hurricane Sandy 191

IDEO 142, 147, 196, 200

illegal 32, 38, 40, 42

Illich, Ivan 153–154

immigrant 1, 3, 5–6, 17, 29, 32, 63–64, 67, 109–110, 112, 114, 117, 121, 136, 142, 144, 179, 185, 191–192; immigrant communities 17, 29, 64, 136, 192

INCITE! 193, 203

inclusion 5, 15–17, 19–20, 42, 63, 109, 133–135, 138–139, 179, 184–185, 194, 197–198, 202, 203; inclusionary 82, 135; inclusive 5, 9, 63, 66, 147, 156, 195, 199

India 140

industry 3, 4, 7; industry city 3, 4, 7; industrial 3, 66, 125, 148, 151, 153–154, 180, 192, 203

informal 9, 12, 14, 16–17, 18, 38, 40–42, 49, 56, 60, 66, 77, 87, 88, 93, 145, 182, 187–188, 202; informality 9; informal settlements 40–43, 49; informal urbanization 41

infrastructure 16, 18, 20, 27, 40, 52, 87, 141, 151, 161, 162–163, 164, 166, 172, 178–182, 189, 198, 203; ecological infrastructures 180; infrastructures of inclusion 179, 198; infrastructure spaces 27; people as infrastructure 182, 203; public infrastructure 18; public infrastructural projects 9; public schools 40; roads 40; sewage 40; shared infrastructure 40; water 40

innovation 24, 39, 106, 137, 140–142, 144–146, 148, 151, 153, 155, 175, 182–183, 184, 186, 187–189, 192, 194, 195–196; design innovation 196; cultural innovation 153; social innovation 140–148, 151, 153–154, 181, 184, 187–189, 195, 202; urban innovation 39, 187, 189

institution 9, 10, 12, 16–17, 19, 20, 22, 23, 29, 32, 34, 38, 41–42, 48, 50, 52, 58–61, 88, 98–100, 102, 106, 109, 112, 125, 128–129, 133, 138, 140, 164, 166, 168, 170–171, 175, 177, 182–184, 186–187, 189–190, 192–195, 197–200; institutional transformation 9, 15, 19, 20, 190; institutions of exclusion 10; civic institution 38, 175; institutional architecture 170; institutions of knowledge and power 183; public institution 29, 38, 60, 112

insurgent 182, 187–188, 190, 200, 202; insurgent citizenship 182, 187–188, 190, 200, 202; insurgent public space 187, 202

Interboro Partners 124–129, 131–132, 134, 188, 196; The Arsenal of Inclusion and Exclusion 133; Fair Houses Act of 1968 133; Holding Pattern 128; Rest Stop 128; urban blots see blots

interdisciplinary 52; see also multi- and transdisciplinary

International Architecture Biennale Rotterdam (IABR) 102, 133

International Monetary Fund (IMF) 180

Internet 178, 203

Italy 32, 35, 59, 140, 192, 203

Jégou, François 140–141, 154, 189

Jonathan Kirschenfeld Architects 156

Jovanovic Weiss, Srdjan 168, 175, 177, 178, 181, 194

Kaldor, Mary 190, 202
Kelly, Kevin 39, 48
Koolhaas, Rem 36
Kucina, Ivan 48, 57–60, 87–88, 90, 92, 94, 96, 98, 138, 188, 190–191, 200
kuda.org [Center for New Media] 168, 169–170, 172, 174–175, 177, 194
Kurd 29–30, 35, 185; Azad 29; Kurdish 29–30, 35, 185; Kurdistan 29–30; Kurds 30

Lab for the City 196
land [urban] 1, 3, 7, 13–14, 27, 29, 31–32, 40, 46, 66, 77, 86–87, 90–91, 93, 114, 137, 169, 178, 191; land value 3, 40, 46; land expropriation 90; land use 13–14, 29, 66, 77, 86; public land see public; wetlands 156, 158, 159, 166
landscape 8, 22, 40, 52, 72, 139, 202; total landscape 8, 202
Latin America 9–10, 18–20, 142, 189
Latour, Bruno 53
Laurel, Brenda 94, 98
Lefebvre, Henri 135–136, 198, 202
Lehrer, Brian 2
Lerner, Jamie 20, 189
Levy, Aaron x, 35, 155
Library Parks 20
Liu, John C. [NYC Comptroller] 2, 6
Lower East Side (LES) 61–62, 64, 66, 72, 75, 128, 137–139, 141–142, 147–148, 154, 195
local 3–5, 13, 16, 19, 22, 25, 34–35, 41–43, 52, 62–64, 66, 69–70, 72, 74, 77, 79, 83, 86, 90–91, 93–94, 99–102, 104, 106–110, 112, 136–137, 140, 142, 144, 146–147, 151, 153, 159, 161, 166, 169–170, 172, 179, 181–182, 186, 190, 192, 195–196; localized 9, 110, 182–183
Long Island City 129
Los Angeles Urban Rangers 135
Lower East Side Waterfront Alliance 66, 75

Magalhães, Sèrgio 20
Manzini, Ezio 140–141, 153–154, 189, 191, 193, 195, 202
marginal 40; marginalization 9–10, 99; marginalized 112, 187
market 38, 42–43, 46, 79, 82, 86–87, 108, 151, 179–180, 182, 184–185, 192–193, 195; black market 202; free market 42, 192–193; grey market 38; market and civil society 179; state controlled market 38
management 3, 16, 18, 20, 98, 109, 129, 134, 161, 163, 181–182; public management 18, 20, 181; self-management 98, 182; water management 161, 163
Medellin 9, 18–21, 189
Menchaca, Carlos (NYC Councilman) 4, 5, 181
Menino, Thomas (Mayor) 196
Menking, Bill x, 155
Mexico City 196
MindLab 196
Mockus, Antanas 12, 20, 189
MoMA PS1 129
Mouffe, Chantal 4, 8, 183–184, 197, 199–200, 202
movements 24, 39, 48, 52, 86, 99, 115, 117, 182, 184, 186, 190–193, 202; citizen movements 48, 93; cultural movements 24; social movements 52, 184, 191–193; political movements 193; urban movements see urban
multidisciplinary collaborations 76; see also inter- and transdisciplinary

National Strategy Center for the Right to the Territory (CENEDET) 196
Neelen, Marc 37, 48, 59, 98, 186, 200
neoliberal 1, 3–6, 17, 25, 42, 87, 98–99, 102, 177, 180, 192, 198–199, 202; capitalist spatial politics 5; neoliberal economists 87; neoliberal governance 3; neoliberal land-zoning policies 1; neoliberal policies 1, 42, 102, 192; neoliberal propaganda 25; neoliberal regimes 98; neoliberal urban developments 3; neoliberal urbanization 5–6, 99, 192, 198, 202; neoliberalism 8–9, 24, 26, 98, 201, 202; neoliberalization 180, 182, 192; privatization 43
neighborhood 2–3, 13, 17, 61–62, 66, 68, 79, 82, 90, 101–102, 108–109, 112, 132, 141, 144–146, 148, 151, 158–159, 161, 166, 186
New Orleans 52
New York City: New York City Department of Parks and Recreation (NYC Parks) 8, 20, 62–66, 68, 70, 72, 90, 96, 128, 145, 156, 190, 195, 202–203; New York City School

Construction Authority (NYCSCA) 156; New York Restoration Project (NYRP) 128; NYC Department of Planning 1; NYC Economic Development Corporation (EDC) 4

non-governmental organization (NGO) 13, 60, 169

nonhierarchical 17, 100, 112

non-profit organization 20, 100, 138, 186, 192–195, 203; the non-profit industrial complex (NPIC) 192, 203; not-for-profit organization 142, 151, 192–193

Normal Architecture Office (NAO) 168–178, 194

Novi Sad 168–172, 174–175, 177–178, 194

Obama, Barack (President) 192

organization 4, 7, 16–17, 22, 29, 31, 35, 41–42, 44, 56, 59, 61, 76–77, 90, 93, 101, 109, 116, 126, 141, 142, 144, 151, 161, 166, 182, 184–186, 188, 190–191, 193–195, 197; capitalist organization 4, 181; community organization *see* community; cooperative organization *see* 'cooperative'; grassroots (organization) 62, 66, 74, 76–77, 86, 99–101, 110, 112, 195; human organization 88; informal organization 38, 93; market organization 195; non-governmental organization *see* non-governmental organization (NGO); self organization *see* self organization; social organization 16–17, 35, 50; urban organization 94

Organization for Economic Co-operation and Development (OECD) 180

Paley, Albert 3

participatory 5, 7, 18, 20, 54, 61, 63, 66, 69, 93–94, 98, 100–102, 106, 109, 112, 153, 165, 177, 182–183, 193, 195; participatory action research 94, 100, 102, 109; participatory budgeting 5, 7, 18, 20; participatory planning 101, 177

PassivHaus standards 44, 60

Penin, Lara 136, 140, 189

Peti Park (The Fifth Park) 91–93, 95–98, 190

place 1, 9–10, 13, 19–20, 29, 37, 42, 50–51, 56–57, 66, 70, 83, 93, 106, 108, 114, 116, 119, 121, 125, 129, 137, 142, 156, 182, 185, 198; displacement 1, 6, 10, 106, 123; non-place 27

policy 13–14, 20, 53, 63, 76–77, 79, 83–84, 86, 99, 102, 107–108, 112, 133, 165, 180, 188, 193, 198; housing policy 83; planning policy 13, public policy 76; urban policy 20, 107, 108

Porto Alegre 18, 20

Pruitt Igoe 23

public 1, 3–7, 9–10, 14–18, 20, 23, 25, 29–32, 34, 38–41, 43, 51, 59–64, 66, 72, 74–77, 85, 87–88, 90–91, 93, 96, 98–102, 106, 108, 110, 112, 114, 117–118, 120–122, 124, 128–129, 133, 135–136, 141, 145–148, 153, 156, 162, 164, 166, 168–169, 171–172, 174–177, 179–182, 184, 186–187, 189–199; public access 3, 5, 77, 83; public agencies 62–63, 88, 90, 91, 98, 156, 196, 201; public art 4, 7, 72, 124; public housing *see* housing; public institutions 29; public investment 20, 193; public land 14, 31, 169; public-private partnership 3, 87, 106, 180, 181, 186, 192, 195, 202; public realm 5, 7, 174, 182, 184, 189–194, 197, 201; public sector 19, 43, 87, 90, 180, 181, 192; public services 1, 59, 77, 101, 108, 110, 141, 147, 148, 153, 179, 180, 181, 182, 192, 195, 196, 199; public space 8, 15, 16, 17, 20, 34, 63, 64, 75, 88, 90, 91, 96, 101, 129, 136, 162, 168–175, 178, 184, 187, 201, 202, 203; public sphere 117, 118, 179, 184, 197, 199, 201; *see also* space

Queens 1, 3–4, 133, 196

Queensboro Bridge 3

Ranciere, Jacques 54

Rao, Vyjayanthi x, xi, 51, 53, 57, 135, 137

Reagan, Ronald (President) 180

real-estate 1, 3, 4, 7, 10, 43, 86, 87, 133, 134, 139, 148

Rendon, Gabriela 99, 113, 136, 186; *see also* COHSTRA

Robles-Durán, Miguel 113, 181, 199, 202–203; *see also* COHSTRA

Roma 29, 58; Roma community 58; Roma Decade 58; Roma people 59; Roma settlements 59

Rome 21, 22, 25–32, 35, 58, 185, 191

Romito, Lorenzo xi, 21–22, 24–25, 35–36, 185

San Diego 9–10, 12–13, 17, 21, 118, 187–188, 192, 196
School of Missing Studies 171
segregation 100, 102, 109, 112, 133–134
self-organization 17, 25, 29, 31, 35, 43, 56, 59, 88, 90, 91, 93, 96, 101, 141, 142, 144, 156, 166, 182, 184, 185, 186, 188, 190, 191, 193, 194, 195, 197;
settlement 38, 40–41, 44, 46, 161, 198
Simone, AbdouMaliq 182, 198, 203
site 7, 13–14, 17, 29–31, 44, 58, 64, 68–70, 72, 91, 93, 109, 133, 161, 178; metropolitan site 40; non-site 27
slum 9, 20, 56–57,138, 198; slum development 57
social 1, 4–5, 10, 12, 14–20, 22–26, 29, 31–32, 34–35, 38, 43–45, 48, 50, 52–53, 57–61, 63, 76–77, 83, 85–86, 88, 93–94, 96, 99–100, 102, 106–110, 112–113, 118–119, 124, 135, 140–142, 144–146, 148, 151, 153–156, 161, 163, 166, 168–172, 174–177, 179–197, 199–200; social inequality 24; social justice 18, 22, 50, 63, 76, 77, 85, 86, 102, 112, 166, 187, 191, 193, 195; social transformation 35, 106, 184; social innovation *see* innovation; socio-spatial justice 5, 135, 182, 184
society 22, 25, 31, 35, 38, 40, 43, 58–59, 153–154, 156, 171, 177–186, 190, 192–195, 198–199; the society of the spectacle 25
sociogram 94, 110
smart growth 15
space 1, 3–5, 12–15, 17, 20–22, 25, 27–31, 34–35 ,39, 42, 44, 46, 57, 61–64, 66, 88, 90–91, 93, 96, 98, 100, 129, 133, 136, 138, 151–152, 156–157, 168–172, 174–177, 182–183, 185, 187, 192, 197, 199; abstract space 13; agonistic space 8, 202; civic space *see* civic; communal space 46, 47, 61–62, 93; convivial space 153; event space 151; governmental space 22; infrastructure space 27; institutional space 61, 177; loose space 36; perceptual space 185; public space *see* public; shared space 30, 61–62; transitional space 172; urban space *see* urban
squatting 31, 139
state 6, 13, 23, 31, 38, 39, 40, 43, 58, 77, 87, 90, 114–121, 155, 163, 169–172, 177–182, 184–185, 187, 188, 192, 193, 195, 199; local state 182; nation state 115–116, 179, 187, 199; state institutions 195
Stalker 25–36, 185, 191; (urban) agronomadism 31, 191; Ararat 29–31, 185; Campo Boario 29, 30, 35–36, 185; Oranges Don't Fall from the Sky (Le Arance Non Cadono Dal Cielo) 32–33, 191; Ortoboario (a public garden) 30; Stalker-ing 31
STEALTH.unlimited 37–39, 41, 44–47, 56–57, 59–60, 186; Kaludjerica 38–42, 48, 60; Smart Building project 43, 46; Who Builds the City 43
stop-and-frisk 1, 6
Storefront for Art and Architecture 76
sustainability 5, 10, 15–16, 22, 35, 43, 59, 96, 140–142, 151, 153, 154; economic and social sustainability 16; pragmatic sustainability 15; socioeconomic sustainability 10

tax credits 82
temporary use 14, 58, 64, 72, 128–129, 138
territory 1, 10, 13, 15, 22, 25, 30–31, 90, 94, 111, 135, 170, 171, 180, 185, 191, 196, 198
Thatcher, Margaret (Prime Minister) 180
The New York Times 1, 3, 6, 166–167
Theodore, Georgeen (Interboro Partners) 124
third sector 181, 182, 192–194, 201; organizations 181, 182, 192–194
transdisciplinary 99–100, 106, 112, 136; *see also* interdisc and multidisc
Turkel, Marc x, 50

Ulmer, Gregory 188–189, 203
UN-HABITAT 180, 199, 203
urban 1, 3–7, 9–21, 25–27, 29, 31, 34, 37–42, 46, 48, 53–54, 57, 59–60, 66, 75–77, 86–88, 90, 94, 96, 98–102, 106–110, 112–113, 124–127, 133, 135–137, 140–142, 144–146, 148, 151, 153, 155, 157, 161, 163, 166, 168–172, 174, 177–194, 196–199, 203; abandonment 25, 106, 125; conflict between top-down and bottom-up urbanization 12; emerging urban practices 10; exclusionary urban growth 10; impoverishment 25; inclusion 15; marginal metropolitan

sites 40; rezoning 1, 2, 5–7; urban activism 134 16; urban beautification 3, 10, 15; urban design 3, 7, 60, 85, 124, 139, 199; urban development *see* development; urban inequality 1; urban movements 39, 48, 52, 184, 190, 191, 192; urban plan 42, 90, 108, 166; urban planning 4, 41, 42, 54, 60, 76, 87, 124, 137, 157, 161, 178, 202; urban practice 9–11, 16, 101–102, 112, 113, 124, 137, 182, 184, 187–188; urban praxis 113, 189; urban space 1, 4–5, 12, 26–27, 39, 98, 133, 151, 174, 183, 185, 187, 192, 197, 199; urbanization of social production 16; Urban Union 102, 105, 186; urban uprising 88, 99; urban zoning *see* zoning; urbanism 5, 8, 10–11, 15–16, 48, 57, 60, 98, 124–125, 135, 139, 140, 168–169, 177, 182, 201–203; urbanist 46, 59, 87, 98, 124, 125, 135, 136, 184–185, 188, 194; urbanization 5, 6, 9, 12–13, 15–18, 20, 22, 27, 39, 41, 42, 99, 179–181, 187, 192, 194, 198, 200–203; urbanizing (society) 40

U.S. Department of Housing and Urban Development (HUD) 79, 82, 85, 163, 166

Van Heeswijk, Jeanne 108
Venice Architecture Biennial x, 35, 155

welfare state 23, 38, 192
Wild City 37, 39, 48, 58–59, 88; wild settlement 40; wild urbanization 39
WNYC/NPR The Brian Lehrer Show 2
Woo, Rosten 50–52, 85
World Bank 180, 198, 201

Young, Iris Marion 179, 183–184, 195–'96, 199, 203

zoning [urban] 1–3, 5–7, 14, 77–78, 82, 85, 133, 135, 148; downzoning 3; inclusionary zoning 82, 135; rezoning 5–7, 148; upzoning 3; zoning law 77
Zukin, Sharon 4, 8, 98, 181, 203